ENGLISH EDUCATION IN THE POST-WAR YEARS:
A SOCIAL HISTORY

EDUCATION IN THE POST-WAR YEARS:
A Social History

ROY LOWE

ROUTLEDGE
London and New York

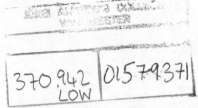

First published in 1988 by
Routledge
11 New Fetter Lane, London EC4P 4EE

Published in the USA by
Routledge
in association with Routledge, Chapman and Hall, Inc.
29 West 35th Street, New York NY 10001

© 1988 Roy Lowe

Printed in Great Britain

British Library Cataloguing in Publication Data

Lowe, Roy
    English education in the post-war years:
    a social history.
    Vol. I: 1945–1965: Accessible to all?
    1. Education — English — History —
    20th century
    I. Title
    370′.942   LA631.82

    ISBN 0-415-00592-2
    ISBN 0-415-00801-8 Pbk

Library of Congress Cataloging in Publication Data

ISBN 0-415-00592-2
ISBN 0-415-00801-8 Pbk

**Printed and bound in Great Britain
by Billing & Sons Limited, Worcester.**

Contents

To Kathy,
Jane, Ruth and Susan

Acknowledgements

I have to acknowledge a number of debts incurred in the writing of this book. The library staff of the University of Birmingham have been unfailingly helpful and courteous, and in particular Dr Peter Platt and his colleagues in the Faculty of Education Library have given willingly of their advice and expertise. Without them it would have been quite impossible to finish the task. I have been helped too by many professional colleagues, through discussion, comment and insights offered. They are far too many to mention by name, and, while it is invidious to select individuals, I must acknowledge publicly a special debt to Richard Szreter, Hywel Thomas and Peter Cunningham who each read parts of the manuscript at an early stage and who spared me some errors. Those which remain are entirely my own responsibilty. I thank too the many postgraduate and higher degree students in the Faculty of Education at Birmingham who, both informally and in class, have listened patiently to the exposition of ideas which became central to the theme of this book. They told me in the gentlest terms when they thought I was wrong and, above all, encouraged me to complete this work. One of them I name in particular, Peter Underwood, whose thesis I refer to in Chapter 9, made a number of important finds at the Public Record office while working under my supervision for a doctoral degree. I am grateful to him for directing me to them. During the time that I have been working on this book, I have twice had the privilege of working at the Centre for Studies in Higher Education at the University of California, Berkeley as a Visiting Associate. The opportunity to reflect at leisure on what I was about was very valuable, and I benefited greatly too from the comments of colleagues there on papers which presented some of my ideas: Sheldon Rothblatt, in particular, was unfailingly generous of his time and percipient in his comments. A period of study-leave from the University of Birmingham gave me time to complete the writing, and I thank those colleagues who made this possible, especially David Rolf and John Hurt, who covered my classes. Cathy Baker gave invaluable secretarial help and was largely responsible for getting the typescript into good order. Finally, and above all, I thank my family, in particular my wife, Kathy and my daughters Jane, Ruth and Susan, for their forebearance and unfailing encouragement. It is to them that this book is dedicated. I hope that it goes some way towards justifying the help I have received from all of these people. I have enjoyed writing it and I hope they get some pleasure from the reading of it.

Abbreviations

AEC	Association of Education Committees
ATCDE	Association of Teachers in Colleges and Departments of Education
ATTI	Association of Teachers in Technical Institutions
AUT	Association of University Teachers
BBC	British Broadcasting Corporation
CAC	Central Advisory Council for Education (England)
CCCS	Centre for Contemporary Cultural Studies
CEO	Chief Education Officer
CLASP	Consortium of Local Authorities Special Programme
CNAA	Council for National Academic Awards
CSE	Certificate of Secondary Education
EPA	Educational Priority Area
FBI	Federation of British Industry
FET	Further Education and Training Scheme
GCE	General Certificate of Education
HMI	Her Majesty's Inspectorate (or Inspector)
HMSO	Her Majesty's Stationery Office
HORSA	Hutting Operation for Raising the School Leaving Age
IAHM	Incorporated Association of Head Masters
IAPS	Incorporated Association of Preparatory Schools
LCC	London County Council
LEA	Local Education Authority
NACEIC	National Advisory Council on Education for Industry and Commerce
NACTST	National Advisory Council on the Training and Supply of Teachers
NAHT	National Association of Head Teachers
NALT	National Association of Labour Teachers
NCTA	National Council for Technological Awards (also known as the Hives Council)
NFER	National Foundation for Educational Research
NUT	National Union of Teachers
PRO	Public Record Office
RIBA	Royal Institute of British Architects
ROSLA	Raising of the School Leaving Age
RSA	Royal Society of Arts

Abbreviations

SSEC   Secondary Schools Examination Council
TEC   Technical Examinations Council
TES   Times Educational Supplement
UGC   University Grants Committee
WEA   Workers Educational Association

Introduction

The period after the Second World War was one of traumatic economic and social change in England. The economy underwent a major transformation as the old industries which had been central to the economic developments of the nineteenth century struggled to adapt to changing terms of trade and to the new demands of the post-war period. At the same time new growth points became evident, with a marked shift towards the tertiary sector of the economy, as service industries, distributive trades and administrative occupations assumed a growing importance.

The social implications were vast: one result was the reinforcement of the professions, a process which was central to post-war redefinitions of social class. Another concomitant, both fuelled by and stimulating the growth of the transport industry, was the rise of suburban commuting on a scale which was quite unprecedented. This meant the transformation of English towns and cities and caused deep adjustments in patterns of family life. The 'extended family' gave way increasingly to nuclear groupings which enjoyed greatly enhanced leisure opportunities. These adjustments were influenced too by the fact of an ageing population and by changes in gender roles. The growing recognition of the contribution made by women, and of their rights, involved some limited erosion of that male dominance which had been a striking characteristic of earlier periods. Against this background there began a major shift in the ethnic composition of the English people. As Britain abandoned her imperial role, and partly in response to the labour shortage engendered by economic change, earlier waves of immigrants from mainland Europe were succeeded by newcomers from the Caribbean and from the Indian sub-continent. Equally significant were the changes in popular culture which stemmed from the transformation of the mass media. Popular literature, journals and newspapers, together with television and radio, purveyed a new 'democratised' culture with messages radically different from those available to the working classes during the nineteenth and early twentieth centuries. The Second World War itself marked a decisive step towards collectivism, towards the corporate state; and the extension of state planning into the post-war years served only to emphasise the permanence of this process. In brief, it is arguable that the Second World War initiated a social transformation which, in its scale and significance, far exceeded the changes experienced in England during any earlier comparable period.

These developments offer a challenge and an enigma to the historian of education. The challenge lies in the attempt to unravel some of the intimate connections between these sweeping changes and the development of formal education in England. Throughout this book, therefore, the attempt will be made to locate the educational provision in its economic and social context to enable what must, at this historical remove, be no more than provisional judgements on the social functions of the English education system. This emphasis, and the breadth of the task undertaken, will inevitably lead to omissions and distortions, but it is hoped that the insights gained and the establishment of connections which might otherwise go unnoticed will vindicate this treatment.

The enigma to which I refer is central to this approach. It may perhaps be best summarised thus: the English education system, as it developed down to 1945, had clearly identifiable hierarchical characteristics. It succeeded in confirming or even bestowing advantages on males, on the upper and middle classes and (through the medium of the British Empire) on Anglo-Saxons. The extent to which these social functions were intended or planned is irrelevant alongside the observation that this was in fact the case. The period since the Second World War has seen (via the social transformation outlined above) some limited increase in the opportunities available for the participation of women, of the working classes and of ethnic minorities in economic and social life, and these opportunities began to expand during the years covered by this book. Yet the part played by formal education in this transformation is debatable. Did it, as apologists would claim, act as a catalyst, smoothing and clearing the route for the underprivileged, actively fostering a society in which opportunities were more widely shared? Or is the nature of the English education system, making only partial adjustments to changed social circumstances, one key reason why elite groups have been able to retain most of their characteristics and many of the accompanying privileges? This problem, it seems to me, is central to the book. Stated briefly, it becomes the question whether the objective which R.A. Butler proclaimed while introducing the 1944 Act to the House of Commons, that the English education system should become 'accessible to all', was realised during the following twenty years, and if so in precisely what ways. While it would be pretentious to claim that a sufficient answer is possible by a single individual or in one book, it is hoped that some of the material gathered here may help to contribute in a small way towards our definition of these problems and to their eventual resolution.

In the chapters that follow the central focus is on the formal provision of education in schools, colleges and universities. While this has the advantage of giving shape and coherence to the book and its central arguments, it is an emphasis which necessarily carries dangers with it. Among the most important of these are the risk that it may seem to suggest far too narrow a definition of 'education', and the fact that, first, it leads to the neglect of those ventures were were 'on the fringe' of the formal system of schooling and, secondly, it overlooks a range of influences which were educational in their nature. The history of children's literature during this period, for example, is clearly related to the issues under consideration, but I have relatively little to say about it in these pages. It is for this reason that I have prefaced each of the two substantive sections of the book by chapters which explore the broad social context and which attempt to speculate a little on these wider themes. I have decided to postpone discussion of the development of facilities for pupils with special needs until a later volume, which will deal with a period when that issue moved much closer to the centre of the political and educational agenda. What I have attempted to write is a social history of education in the sense that it attempts to keep in view the relationships between the developing education system and the changes that were taking place more generally in society. I have only a limited amount of material on what it meant and felt like to be educated during these years, and an account which is centred on that problem must await another author.

The methodological problem raised by trying to deal with such a recent period are considerable, and some might say so great as to make the whole venture problematic. The first difficulty is that the work is in some sense necessarily autobiographical, since it covers almost exactly the years between the author's own admission to an all-age elementary school which was about to become one of the new post-war primary schools and his graduation from one of the new universities whose foundation is described later in the book. The fact that I made my way from the first of these institutions to the second via a state grammar school, having won a place there in the 11 + examination, undoubtedly colours my own perceptions of formal schooling in England during this period in many ways of which I may be barely conscious. The historical immediacy of these events also raises difficulties of source material.

The thirty-year rule means that material deposited in the Public Record Office is available for only part of the period under review, so the sources are qualitatively different for the years before 1956 and those which follow. Partly because of this, I have decided to consider the educational press, and in particular the *Times Educational Supplement*, which is of course available for the whole period, as my major source. Since I have something to say later on about the political stance of that journal, it is clearly a strategy which is fraught with dangers and difficulties. But it has the advantage of bringing a colour and vividness to these issues which I have tried to capture in the material drawn from the *TES*, and the book also becomes a first stab at studying the development of educational opinion after the Second World War. While the problems inherent in any study of recent educational developments are clear, I believe that there can be no moratorium on the exploration of the immediate antecedents of our contemporary system of schooling. If this book does no more than encourage others who are better qualified to reconsider the issues it raises, it will have served a purpose.

Part One
Implementing the Act, 1945–1951

1
Reconstruction and Austerity: The Social Background

The difficulties experienced in returning to normal after the war served only to emphasise how traumatic had been the social upheavals involved and how permanent were some of its consequences. The late 1940s were, for those who lived through them, years of recurrent economic difficulty, with widely publicised balance of payments crises and widespread shortages of foodstuffs and raw materials for the war-weary industries. As one journalist wrote: 'The war is over, the conditions of war in some respects continue.'[1]

If rationing, fuel shortages (especially that of the bleak winter of 1947 which temporarily brought industry to a halt) and austerity provided one enduring memory of the period, there was also another, less immediately apparent reality. It is too easily forgotten that this was an era of full employment, in stark contrast with the pre-war years. The collectivism of the wartime years was redirected by Clement Attlee's government towards social reconstruction and the establishment of the welfare state. Investment in housing, health, national insurance, education and food subsidies meant that by 1951 a new and unprecedented personal economic security had been achieved for individual citizens at just the moment that national economic security was least sure. With the return of peace and the hope of a more certain future, there was a dramatic resurgence of popular leisure activities, most notably of the cinema and of professional soccer, while during the late 1940s, sound radio enjoyed its greatest golden age. It is appropriate to start, then, by looking in slightly greater detail at several aspects of the social background to this period, all of which impinged on 'educational reconstruction', before moving on to examine the schools themselves.

The Impact of War: Collectivism and Reconstruction

First and foremost was the impact of the war itself which led directly to a new readiness to tackle the reconstruction of society. The reasons are not far to seek. First, the unreal lull of the 'Phoney War' was rudely shattered by the reality of total war in 1940. The invasion of the Low Countries and the fall of France, the Battle of Britain and the sustained experience of the bombing raids on the major cities meant that by the end of 1940 England was suddenly plunged into her gravest national crisis. The sense of solidarity which this engendered was soon apparent. The new political leadership replaced the indolence of the appeasers with a directness and immediacy which appealed to all social classes. This immediacy was achieved in part by Churchill's use of the radio (a device used similarly by Stalin and Roosevelt), and one vestigial effect of this was that the power of broadcasting in general, and of the news bulletin in particular, was permanently enhanced. A sense of shared suffering was undoubtedly one of the mainsprings of this new solidarity. Although the Blitz was undoubtedly worst in those working-class suburbs close to munitions factories and ports, the fact that the Royal Family 'sat it out' in London was widely publicised and suggested the extent to which all social groups were threatened. Further, the entry of the USSR to the war in the summer of 1941 meant that, henceforth, a wide political spectrum was ranged against the Axis states, and this fact undoubtedly lessened the reservations which some members of the Left may have felt about participation in 'Churchill's war'. This sense of national solidarity, which was only heightened by the continuing experience of food shortages, was the first prerequisite for the acceptance of 'collectivism'.

Equally significant was the extent to which the government was forced into a direct control of national affairs which would have been unthinkable only a few years earlier. The war spawned a series of new ministries whose work meant a quite unprecedented exten-sion of central government power in England. The Ministry of Supply, quickly established at the outbreak of war, was soon comple-mented by Ministries of Aircraft Production, Economic Welfare, Food, Home Security, Information and Shipping. The ruthless denial of supplies to non-essential industries and the direction of manpower enabled the government to achieve a major redirection of the economy towards the war effort. During the war the engineer-ing and chemical industries almost doubled their labour force to

4

5.2 million, and the armed services increased tenfold to a figure of over 5 million in 1945. Utility standards, which were to persist into the post-war years, were introduced to cut out extravagance in clothing and furniture and in 1942 petrol disappeared from the private market. The extent of this sea-change is perhaps best illustrated by the provisions in 1941 which enabled the conscription of women to the armed forces.[2]

Another aspect of social change which was accelerated by the war and which continued into the post-war era was a social disruption which carried with it suggestions, perhaps illusory, of the collapse of social class-barriers. One historian estimated that during the war there were over 60 million changes of address (well beyond the total population); two out of every seven houses were affected by bomb damage, while the number of foreign troops garrisoned in England rose at one point to 1½ million.[3] The inter-war years had, of course, seen a growing readiness among the unemployed to move in search of work, most notably from South Wales to the industrial Midlands, but the scale of the wartime upheaval was unprecedented, and in this respect the war seems to have marked a permanent widening of the social horizons of the British people.

The most striking facet of this disruption from the educational point of view was evacuation. Over 750,000 children were evacuated from the urban centres in September 1939: within a few months a half had drifted back, to present a spectre of idle children (in many cases schools had been closed or requisitioned for other purposes) which galvanised those involved in the debate on educational reconstruction. There has been much interest in the extent to which evacuation led to a heightened sense of social distance between these town children and their hosts in the rural areas, but historians are beginning to realise that of at least equal significance may be the ways in which the process deepened the social rifts between evacuees. There is some evidence that working-class children may have had real difficulty in adjusting to the demands of evacuation, and in some cases may have suffered permanently from the experience, while children from more favoured social groups may have benefited in the long term from the wider range of experiences which evacuation entailed.[4]

These traumas led directly to wartime planning for the reconstruction of society, and it was clear from quite early in the war that education was to be assigned an important role in this process. As early as February 1940 the Archbishop of Canterbury told the House of Lords that far-reaching social changes must accrue from the war, and on 21 December 1941 a letter to *The Times* from an ecumenical grouping of church leaders nominated ten principles for the establishment of peace, one of which was 'equality of educational opportunity'.[5] A year later the Beveridge Report spelt out the programme necessary for the establishment of a comprehensive system of social security, and established education, together with health, housing and full employment, as the four major planks in the drive towards the permanent achievement of a fairer society.

There were, though, a series of deep-seated reasons for the fact that the educational settlement which emerged from the wartime disruption was essentially conservative in nature. First, the involvement of the Churches in the debate, added to the fact that the war seemed to take on increasingly the aspect of a religious crusade against Nazism, meant that in any settlement the dual system would be sustained and the Christian underpinning of English education would be confirmed. Although the 1944 Bill was presented in the Commons by its supporters as 'a revolutionary Bill, the answer to the secularism of the century',[6] it was, through its deference to the Established Church (Temple, the new Archbishop of Canterbury, a lifelong educationalist was particularly vociferous in the debate) in reality an assertion of the *status quo*.

Also, the educational settlement which was hammered out in a series of wartime policy documents and enshrined in the 1944 Act was in essence a vindication of Board of Education policy, and to this extent too it held out a limited vision of the prospect of educational reform. This arose partly from the fact that the politics of the 1930s were still awaiting implementation. The 1936 Education Act had been postponed on the outbreak of war, and the raising of the school-leaving age to 15 + remained a pressing need. Thanks to the influence of the psychometricians, who had concerned themselves increasingly with cognition and 'types of mind' during the pre-war years, the Board of Education was ready to take on board Labour's policy of universal secondary education, so long as it was closely linked to a differentiation of schooling. The 1938 Spens Report and 1943 Norwood Report both emanated from the Board's Consultative Committee, both emphasised the influence of educational psychologists, and both looked forward to a treble-track system of secondary education. In combination these two reports may be seen as one of the high points of the influence of psychologists upon the structure of the English educational system.

From November 1940 planning had been under way within the Board of Education on the needs of post-war reconstruction.

Growing frustration at the Board's inertia in response to the war-time dislocation of the education service and the shelving of the Spens Report was increasingly reflected in the press, and led to the distribution of the 1941 Green Book in 'a blaze of secrecy'.[7] This looked forward to the raising of the leaving age, the establishment of day continuation schools and 'the reform and expansion of the secondary school system so that a secondary education of a type suitable for every child over eleven would be available'.[8] Encouraged by FBI support, and spurred on by R.A. Butler, whose sights were set on educational legislation, the 1943 White Paper on *Educational Reconstruction* spelt out the principles on which reform would be based; the establishment of clearly defined 'stages' of education, and a version of universal secondary education which involved a diversity of pattern. It is now clear that the Board of Education officials who drafted these documents, and not R.A. Butler, were the true authors of the 1944 legislation. They had determined the scope of that legislation by May 1941, and fought off Butler's efforts to modify it. The policy which emerged triumphant in 1944 was that of the Board.[9]

Its widespread acceptability rested in part on the fact that this policy incorporated significant elements from the by now well-established ideas of the Labour Party, enunciated by R.H. Tawney as long ago as 1922,[10] but was also made more palatable by developments within the Party during the war. Although the Labour Party was 'in principle' committed to multilateral schools from 1939 (the National Association of Labour Teachers and London Labour Party had both been powerful influences at party conferences), the Party's planning for reconstruction fell back upon a gradualism which chimed with the mood of the Board of Education. Arthur Greenwood, within the Cabinet, and G.D.H. Cole at Nuffield College, were both involved in the Party's discussions, but it was the Norwood Report, published in 1943 which polarised the Party into a minority of out-and-out multilateralists and the dominant group, backed by Harold Clay, chairman of the Party's education committee. Clay and his supporters accepted the 'expert' advice that differing kinds of mind needed different environments, and fell back upon the establishment of parity of conditions and parity of esteem as the bases of party policy. So, for the Labour Party, educational reconstruction came to mean support of the 1944 legislation and for Board of Education policy.[11]

This inheritance from the war was to be critical for Clement Attlee's new administration in 1945. Educational reconstruction was widely interpreted as the wholehearted implementation of the 1944 Act. The Conservative Manifesto at the 1945 election sought to 'remodel our educational system according to the new law'. It referred to the supply of an adequate number of teachers and of school buildings, and called for the 'encouragement and improvement' of primary schools, adding that

> secondary education for all will have no meaning unless variety, practical training and, above all, quality of standards convince parents that the extra schooling for their children is worthwhile.[12]

The Labour Party Manifesto echoed this by claiming that 'Labour will put that Act not merely into legal force but into practical effect':[13] this convergence between the two major parties, which made educational reconstruction politically uncontroversial, was directly attributable to wartime developments.

There were other less immediately apparent consequences of the war which were to be of significance for education. The trade unions emerged from the war with a membership of over 8 million: this enabled them to play a more effective part in educational planning than had been possible during the inter-war years. Further, and more directly, this strengthened labour movement had, during the war, begun to play a fuller part in the government of education at a local level, and under Attlee this once-for-all shift in the composition of school governing bodies and local authorities was confirmed: a modern pattern of local political representation had emerged.[14]

The work during the war of the Army Education Corps may, as is often held, have influenced the result of the 1945 election, but certainly helped heighten the level of political consciousness among the working classes. Perhaps most significant was the sheer physical devastation of the war which meant that whichever party found itself in power after 1945 would be confronted by a major building crisis which was bound to threaten the efforts of the new Ministry of Education to bring school premises up to scratch.[15] It is clear from the outset that the events of the war not only precipitated demands for educational reconstruction but predetermined much of the pattern which that reconstruction was to take.

Demographic Changes

Since the war population change has been an increasingly important determinant of the educational provision, not only directly, but also as a factor of which educational planners were more aware than ever before, a consideration which stemmed in part from the increasing detail and sophistication of post-war censuses.

The Second World War had less impact on overall population trends than the First, although it probably precipitated a far greater degree of movement of population. It may be this population movement, and the dislocation of family life which followed from it, which helps explain the startling changes of the late 1940s which were critical for education. The birth rate stood at 16.2 per thousand in 1945, but increased suddenly, peaking at 20.7 in 1947 and falling only slowly back to 15.8 by 1951. The significance of this for educational planners was heightened by the fact that it was linked to a sharp decline in infant mortality, which between 1935 and 1938 had averaged over 43,000 deaths per year, but was only 24,800 in 1951 and less than 21,000 by 1954.[16]

The impact of this population bulge on the schools was made even more dramatic by the fact that it followed hard on the heels of a period of very low birth rates (the fear of a diminishing population had been widespread before the war, and in 1941 live births fell to 579,000, the lowest figure for decades). The impact of this upturn was not at first realised. The Royal Commission which reported on population in June 1949 anticipated that the fall in numbers would resume in the long term despite the effects of the post-war bulge. Further, this Commission foresaw that the increasing costs of education, impinging particularly on the middle and upper classes, would lead to differential fertility and so cause a fall in the general level of intelligence such as had been feared by eugenicists earlier in the century. These fears induced reservations about capital expenditure on education to meet the bulge, and help explain some of the difficulties of the late 1940s and early 1950s.

More immediately, the rise in the birth rate meant that in the short run the implementation of the 1944 Act fell upon the new primary sector and so, by diverting resources, postponed a major restructuring of secondary education. In this, the demographic imperative chimed precisely with the political will.

There were other population changes which impinged on the schools. Perhaps the most striking was a fall in family size, from 3.37 early in the twentieth century to 2.19 for those married between 1925 and 1929.[17] This involved a lessening of the contrasts between social classes and was, in the long run, to facilitate greater social mobility, greater investment in children and their education and the post-war redefinition of family life. Linked to this was a startling fall in the age of entry to marriage. In 1931 only a quarter of the women in the 20–24 age group were married: by 1951 this had risen to almost a half.[18] This change disguised the continuing social class contrasts in age of child-bearing, but it meant that, during the post-war period, school teachers found themselves dealing with the youngest cohort of parents of the twentieth century. Younger entry to marriage also contributed to the higher incidence of divorce, a long-term phenomenon which also impinged directly and often painfully upon the work of the schools.

There was also a steady and continuing rise in the proportion of the population which was of working age: this had stood at 59 per cent in 1871, 62 per cent in 1901, but by 1951 was an unprecedented 66 per cent.[19] Linked to the post-war pattern of full employment, this meant that English society was better able to bear the 'welfare burdens' of social security and investment on schooling. Equally significant was the fact that by 1951 England had become an urban country as never before. In this year 79 per cent of the total population of 41 million lived in an urban environment. During this post-war period the challenges to education became increasingly dominated by the towns. At a deeper level, these trends all contributed to the drift to the South, which was already under way but accelerated after the war. Between 1939 and 1954 there was a steady movement to the Midlands and South, with a 1 per cent fall in the population of London and the South-East standing in stark contrast to a 21 per cent increase in population in East Anglia, 20 per cent in the South generally and 12 per cent in the Midlands. Population grew much more slowly in the North: only a 3 per cent increase was recorded in the North-West and in Yorkshire during the same period.[20] The educational implications of this were that the professions became more dominant in the South, and this was clearly in the long run to lead to a reinforcement of the private sector. If educational investment during the post-war years was to suggest an end to 'the two nations', the demographic patterns suggested a deeper and more permeating reality.

Economic Development

In July 1936 unemployment stood at 12.7 per cent. The war ended this state of affairs and ushered in a lengthy period in which manpower, not jobs, was the scarce commodity. With the exception of the brief fuel and power crisis of February 1947 unemployment stood at below a half million (or less than 2 per cent) throughout the late 1940s. What little unemployment there was was in many cases caused by employees shifting between jobs. In December 1949 there were 346,000 unfilled jobs — the lowest figure recorded for the 1940s. Thus, after the war, the relationship between school-leavers and potential employers was transformed. The shift towards a more highly qualified society was made against this background of full employment.[21]

But this employment boom involved a redistribution of work which had major implications for the social structure. The late 1940s saw a swift rise in the numbers employed in manufacturing industry (this sector increased by over a million between 1948 and 1954) and a parallel upturn in the service and distributive sectors of the economy. Set against this there was a decline in the numbers employed in the primary sector: during the same period the workforce in agriculture, forestry and fishing fell by 13 per cent. It was the new manufacturing industries which saw the greatest upturn. The numbers employed in motor production rose by 26 per cent; there was a similar growth in both communications and aircraft industries, and the machine-tool, electronics and synthetic fibre industries all expanded quickly. In 1946 a total of 6000 television sets were manufactured: by 1953 annual production exceeded one million. The boom in these new industries ensured a steady growth in industrial production of 8 per cent per annum throughout the late 1940s.[22] For the first time in history it became possible for the schools to rely upon the availability of attractive employment outlets for large numbers of well-qualified leavers. For the young there was an added attraction to staying on at school as well as to moving on into further and higher education.

It is worth remarking the extent to which this transformed economic situation was triggered and sustained by governmental action. During the war government expenditure rose to almost three-quarters of gross national product. For the rest of the 1940s and into the early 1950s it never fell below 40 per cent — significantly above the 26 per cent of 1937. This sustained high level reflected an increasing commitment to social welfare as military expenditure tailed off: it was a commitment from which formal education was to benefit dramatically.[23]

Hardly surprisingly, the pattern of governmental investment in education reflected fairly accurately this economic transformation: it was those sectors of the education service able to contribute most directly to industrial growth which were the most favoured. Public expenditure on education was £107 million in 1940 and £272 million in 1950: allowing for inflation this meant a 70 per cent increase in real terms. The following figures[24] give some idea of how this greater amount was redistributed within the education service.

Table 1.1 Public expenditure on education by sector

	1940	1950
Primary	54.8	37.3
Secondary	19.1	27.4
Teacher training	0.6	2.0
Further and adult	4.9	7.5
Universities	6.7	8.0
Special schools	2.7	1.5
Meals	1.1	7.2
Health service	2.4	3.5
Administration and inspection	6.8	5.7
Total percentage	100	100

Despite this increased public investment, teaching salaries fell behind inflation during this period. The following figures[25] show that, while inflation ran at 36 per cent during Attlee's two post-war administrations, and the average weekly wage rose by 34 per cent, teachers' salaries improved by an average of between 20–25 per cent.

Table 1.2 Price and wage inflation

	Retail price index	Average weekly wage (£)	Qualified teachers' salaries (annual)			
			Male		Female	
			Min.	Max.	Min.	Max.
1945	100	6.27	300	525	270	420
1951	136	8.42	375	630	338	504
Percentage increase	36	34	25	20	25	20

It is significant that, against a background of full employment, the increased number of teachers required to cope with the raising of the school-leaving age was found despite a significant decline in the financial attractiveness of the profession. This fact may help explain the persistence of the view that teaching should be a vocation during the post-war era. These figures also suggest that the post-war emergency training scheme, which enabled many who would not otherwise have had the opportunity to enter teaching, may have had a harmful long-term effect on the status of the profession, and also that the large number of women teachers (an unprecedented number of whom were now contributing a second wage to a family budget) may have worked to retard salary increases.

Cultural Changes: Leisure and the Media

After the war shorter working hours and holidays with pay meant unprecedented leisure opportunities for the English people. By 1949 some 7 per cent of the population owned motor cars, and in 1951 almost half a million new passports were issued, more than twice the pre-war figure.[26] These are but two indices of permanently widened horizons. Yet despite this, there was a deep conservatism about leisure activities. The English seaside resorts remained a favourite destination for the family holiday, and traditional entertainments (most notably the cinema and professional soccer) enjoyed a golden age during the late 1940s. A large proportion of the 1½ million customers of the cinema in each year during the late 1940s were children. They were the harbingers of the new post-war situation in which children themselves became consumers of the leisure products of modern society. This process was not merely of economic significance, since through it children's attitudes to schooling and to adult society were modified as their expectations were raised.

The press enjoyed a renaissance too during and after the war, with daily sales rising from 10 million to 15 million between 1937 and 1947.[27] At just the moment that newspapers became popular among all social classes, the quality press made substantial gains in circulation, reflecting the subtle changes in social class which stemmed from contemporary economic developments. The *Daily Mirror* was the strongest supporter of Labour's reformism, both at and after the 1945 election. Increasingly during the late 1940s, the *Mirror* contributed to the uncritical

13

view that the key educational reforms were already achieved.

> The middle classes [wrote Cassandra] are the people who
> strive to give their children a better chance than they
> themselves ever had. But they are being wiped out by
> murderous taxation.[28]

By subscribing to the belief that popular education was a public
good and by eliding the debate on what form it might take, this
newly powerful popular press worked to minimise public and parental criticality of schooling, and thus played an important role in
the post-war era.

Equally significant was the contribution of the broadcasting services which offered an unashamedly elitist vision of society and of
culture during this period. The Director-General of the BBC, Sir
William Haley, was one of the architects of a three-tier division
of sound radio which would

> rest on the conception of the community as a broadly based
> cultural pyramid slowly aspiring upwards. This pyramid is
> served by three main programmes . . . the listener being
> induced through the years increasingly to discriminate in
> favour of the things that are more worth-while. . . . The
> listener must be fed from good to better by curiosity, liking
> and a growth of understanding. As the standards of the educa-
> tion and culture of the community rise so should the pro-
> gramme pyramid rise as a whole.[29]

This reflected a view of 'high culture' which pervaded attempts to
promote popular education in the post-war era. This readiness to
stand as the arbiter and interpreter of good taste ran through
the BBC's attempts to prepare the Forces for demobilisation
and to build up a broad programme of schools broadcasts. By
1947 two-fifths of the schools were registered for reception of schools'
broadcasts. Significantly, one writer in the *Times Educational
Supplement* saw links between the BBC's cultural hierarchy and
the hierarchy of schools, suggesting that 'a nightly rendez-vous
with the Third Programme is the best recipe for the cultural
education of sixth forms'.[30] Attitudes transmitted through the
popular media go some way to explain the power of the grammar
school model, with its links with this 'high culture' at the moment
when English society was confronting the problem of an appro-

priate form for universal secondary schooling.

The Educational Inheritance

These wholesale social and economic changes may be taken to suggest that English education was to undergo a transformation during the post-war years, and in some senses this proved to be the case. But it would be wrong to overlook at the outset the extent to which the education system itself was inoculated against revolutionary developments by its own characteristics. The historical development of English schooling, the social functions which it fulfilled and popular expectations of the educational system all worked to predetermine its responses to changed social conditions. This was never more true than at the start of the second great expansionary phase of English education immediately after the Second World War.

Several of these 'constraining characteristics' can be traced back to the first phase of expansion which extended from roughly the mid-nineteenth century to the outbreak of the First World War and which coincided with the second phase of industrialisation. The first and most basic point to be made about English education during these growth periods is that, at every level, it developed through a series of accretions which tended to confirm existing practice rather than through radical departures which would have been more likely to raise doubts about the very bases of earlier patterns of schooling. Thus, the voluntary societies of the early nineteenth century were content to extend the benefits offered by eighteenth-century charity schools more widely, and the School Boards of the 1870s were set up in order to 'fill the gaps' rather than to challenge existing concepts of elementary schooling. It is worth remarking that this, in retrospect, inexorable trend towards universality was marked by an increasing state surveillance, first through the Churches and later directly through new governmental departments, which reflected what one historian has called:

> an enormously ambitious attempt to determine, through the capture of educational means, the patterns of thought, sentiment and behaviour of the working class.[31]

A similar imperative of social control is discernible in the major debate of the 1860s on the curricula of the grammar schools which precipitated a similar extension of secondary schooling. Again, the drift towards universality (which was to be completed in the aftermath of the 1944 Act) involved a succession of accretions which served only to confirm the primacy of the grammar schools. The reformed grammar schools of the 1880s and 1890s, the early twentieth-century municipal and central schools, and the senior elementary schools of the inter-war years were frequently justified on the grounds that they would extend the variety of secondary schooling, in reality they helped achieve a surprising uniformity of curriculum. At times, as with the 1904 *Regulations on Secondary Schooling*, this uniformity was encouraged by central government, which, as had happened with elementary schooling, came to play an increasingly active role in the supervision of secondary education. One key social function of these secondary schools was to offer career advantages, through access to the universities or to the professions, for their pupils, who were drawn predominantly from the middle and upper classes. In periods of economic expansion, such as the late nineteenth century or the period after the Second World War, it proved possible to underpin this elitist function with an egalitarian rhetoric which emphasised the availability of this favoured education to a wider social catchment.[32] But this could only be done at the price of curricular uniformity. In this respect the experience of the post-war years was to prove almost a replication of developments fifty years before.

Similarly, in the field of higher education, new institutions, which were originally founded to compensate for the shortcomings of existing universities, soon found themselves imitating the style and ethos of the very colleges they had set out to challenge. This was true of the 'redbrick' universities at the turn of the century and was to influence the post-war new universities in much the same way. The civic university colleges, in every case, were founded with a view to providing a higher education which would relate to the developing local industries. But the grant of a charter marked the moment when a subtle change came over their aspirations, partly because of the colonisation of the most powerful posts in these colleges by alumni of Oxford and Cambridge. In 1918, Sir Charles Grant Robertson, the Dean of the Arts Faculty at the University of Birmingham, lamented the general impression that Birmingham was no more than a glorified school of applied science. He was but one of a number of leaders in the civic universities who worked to resuscitate the ideal of a humane education in the early twentieth century.[33] It will be argued later in this book that the attractiveness of existing elite models was felt particularly in the arena of higher education after the Second World War and influenced profoundly the pattern of expansion.

Other factors worked jointly to strengthen the resistance of the educational system to radical change. An increasing governmental control and direction, at every level, was exerted through bureaucracies which tended to increase with size over time. The establishment of the Board of Education in 1899 and the 1902 Education Act which set up new local education authorities gave these bureaucracies their modern form. Brian Simon has shown the extent to which the Board of Education was able to use its directives, circulars and policy statements during the period before the Second World War to restrict educational advance on several fronts.[34] With a growth in scale which was accelerated after the Second World War, this tendency towards inertia was enhanced. The growth in size of industrial corporations and professional organisations was mirrored by a corresponding growth in the size of schools, which required larger bureaucracies to administer them. The small village school became increasingly anomalous during the post-war years while the large urban school became the norm. In this changing situation radical departures in policy became increasingly difficult to accomplish.

Another element in the educational inheritance which exercised a profoundly conservative influence during the modern period was the power of the Churches. The secularisation of society began in the late nineteenth century and gathered pace during the twentieth, checked only by a brief resurgence of popular religion during each of the two world wars. It was natural that the Churches should seek to maintain some popular hold through schooling, especially since the Dual System enabled some direct control of the voluntary schools and some indirect influence upon the work of state schools. In a situation where church-going became increasingly confined to the middle and upper classes, even though a majority chose to observe the major religious ceremonies, such as marriage and baptism, it was possible for those in government to claim that they were voicing the highest unspoken aspirations of the people. Thus Viscountess Astor claimed in the parliamentary debate on the 1944 Act that Britain remained 'the most Christian country in the world'.[35] So, religious instruction and acts of worship became compulsory in English schools, and, equally important, one criterion for the selection of staff — especially head teachers — remained an ability to conduct Christian assemblies. The Churches retained some influence over the teaching profession too, through the maintenance of voluntary training colleges. If English schools were slow to respond to the coming of a multi-ethnic society during the 1960s and 1970s, the cause lay in part, at least, in the pervasive effects of this continuing Christian influence.

Commentators have tended to emphasise the permissive nature of the 1944 educational settlement. Asa Briggs reflected, for example, that the Act was

> nothing more than an outline . . . the new Ministry of Education became more of an executive in its relations with the Local Education Authorities. Continued educational progress and the implementation of the ideals of the Act depended to a large extent on its implementation on the spot.[36]

While it is true that a few local authorities were able to strike out in new directions — Leicestershire under Stuart Mason and the West Riding under Alec Clegg are the most notable examples — the extent to which this educational inheritance coincided with governmental policy and militated against innovation must not be overlooked.

Overriding all was a fairly generalised ethic which emphasised the benign influence of formal education. In 1949, a Ministry of Education pamphlet on citizenship captured neatly the mood of the moment, proclaiming that in a society such as ours, which has temporarily lost its bearings, the homes and schools are the guardians of our sense of standards.[37] The Minister, George Tomlinson, emphasised in his foreword to this document the growing recognition that we are members of a society that needs to rediscover its moral bearings and its sense of purpose.[38]

While the moral crisis was nowhere precisely defined, it was clear that this view encapsulated the belief that one central purpose of the schools was the moral regeneration of the nation. A similar self-confidence was apparent in the official ministry view of the raising of the school-leaving age in 1947:

> The main value of the lengthened school course lies in the fact that the schools will now be able to do more effectively in four years what they had previously to compress into three. . . . It is a mistake to suppose that, to be of value, the 'extra year' must include something new. . . . It gives a better chance of exercising a permanent influence for good.[39]

18

This widely held belief that formal education had leavened English society and should continue to do so underpinned the continuity between pre- and post-war education in England. This deep popular faith in schooling was arguably the strongest aspect of 'the educational inheritance' and helps explain why it would be wrong, as we move on to consider developments in more detail, to anticipate a deep-seated transformation of English education during the post-war era.

References

1. A. Marwick, *British society since 1945* (Penguin, Harmondsworth, 1982), 22.
2. A. Marwick, *Britain in the century of total war* (Pelican, London, 1970), 292; D. Thompson, *England in the twentieth century* (Penguin, London, 1965), 202.
3. Marwick, *Britain in the century of total war*, 263–4.
4. A. Preston 'The evacuation of schoolchildren from Newcastle on Tyne', 1939–42, M.Ed. diss (University of Birmingham, 1985).
5. N. Middleton and S. Weitzmann *A place for everyone: a history of state education from the eighteenth century to the 1970s* (Victor Gollancz, London, 1976), 204–8.
6. House of Commons Debates, vol. 397, col. 2252.
7. P.H.J.H. Gosden, *Education in the Second World War* (Methuen, London, 1976), 265–7; R.A. Butler, *The art of the possible* (Penguin, London, 1971), 93.
8. *The Times*, 13 May 1941, 2.
9. R.G. Wallace, 'The origins and authorship of the 1944 Education Act', *History of Education*, 10, 4 (1981), 283–90.
10. R.H. Tawney, *Secondary education for all: a policy for Labour* (Labour Party, London, 1922).
11. R. Barker, *Education and politics, 1900–1951* (Clarendon Press, Oxford, 1972), 65–80.
12. Conservative Party election manifesto, 1945, see also R.B. McCallum and A.V. Readman, *The British general election of 1945* (OUP, London, 1947).
13. Labour Party, *Let us face the future* (Labour Party, London, 1945).
14. E.P. Thompson, 'Mr. Attlee and the gadarene swine', *Guardian*, 3 March 1984, 9.
15. P.H.J.H. Gosden, *The education system since 1944* (Martin Robertson, Oxford, 1983), 1–7.
16. G.D.H. Cole, *The post-war condition of Britain* (Routledge and Kegan Paul, London, 1956), 6–9.
17. Ibid., 9.
18. A.H. Halsey (ed.), *Trends in British society since 1800* (Macmillan, London, 1956), 6–9.

19. Cole, *The post-war condition*, 9.
20. Ibid.
21. Ibid., 47.
22. G.D.N. Worsnick and P.H. Ady (eds), *The British economy, 1945-50* (Clarendon Press, Oxford, 1952), 10.
23. A.J. Youngson, *The British economy, 1920-1957* (George Allen & Unwin, London, 1960), 262.
24. Halsey (ed.), *Trends*, 169; see also J. Vaizey, *The costs of education* (George Allen & Unwin, London, 1958); and J. Vaisey and J. Sheehan, *Resources for education* (George Allen & Unwin, London, 1968).
25. Times Newspapers, *The British economy, key statistics, 1900-1970* (London, 1971); Ministry of Education, *Reports of the Burnham Committee on scales of salaries for teachers* (HMSO, London, 1945, 1948 and 1951).
26. Halsey (ed.), *Trends*, 550-1.
27. R. Williams, *The long revolution* (Penguin, London, 1961), 229.
28. A.H.C. Smith, *Paper voices: the popular press and social change, 1935-1965* (Thames & Hudson, London, 1975), 114.
29. A. Smith (ed.), *British Broadcasting* (David & Charles, Newton Abbot, 1974), 83-4, quoting from W. Haley, *The Lewis Fry Memorial Lectures* (London, 1948).
30. A. Briggs, *The history of broadcasting in the United Kingdom*; vol. 4, *Sound and vision* (OUP, Oxford, 1979), 828.
31. R. Johnson, 'Educational policy and social control in Early Victorian England', *Past and Present*, 49 (1970), 119.
32. O. Banks, *Parity and prestige in English secondary education* (Routledge & Kegan Paul, London, 1955); P. Gordon, *Selection for secondary education* (Woburn Press, London, 1980).
33. R. Lowe, 'The expansion of higher education in England', in K.H. Jarausch, *The transformation of higher learning, 1860-1930* (University Press, Chicago, 1983).
34. B. Simon, *The politics of educational reform* (Lawrence & Wishart, London, 1974).
35. House of Commons Debates, vol. 397, col. 2423. See also C. Cannon, 'The influence of religion on educational policy', *British Journal of Educational Studies*, 12, 2 (1964); M. Cruikshank, *Church and State in English education* (Macmillan, London, 1963); J. Murphy, *Church, State and schools in Britain, 1800-1970* (Routledge & Kegan Paul, London, 1971).
36. Worsnick and Ady, *The British economy*, 365.
37. Ministry of Education pamphlet no. 16, *Citizens growing up* (HMSO, London, 1949), 7.
38. Ibid.
39. Ministry of Education, *Education in 1947* (HMSO, London, 1948), 13.

2

Primary Concern: Educating
the Under Twelves

The 1944 Act demanded the recognition of a primary stage of education, through which all children should pass before moving on to
secondary schooling. Although no precise formula was laid down
in the legislation, it was widely assumed that 11 + would be the
age of transfer. Thus the old distinction between elementary and
secondary education, which had persisted for over two centuries,
was ended. The two systems, which had originally catered for
different social groups, had already drawn closer together in the
late nineteenth and early twentieth century. Scholarships had taken
increasing numbers of ex-elementary school pupils into the
secondary schools, while innovations in the elementary sector (most
notably the appearance of higher-grade, central and senior
elementary schools) had involved the establishment of 'quasi-
secondary' forms of education under the elementary code. Now
primary and secondary were viewed as stages in the education of
all pupils, in accord with the advocacy of the Labour Party during
the inter-war years, and with the 1926 Hadow Report on *The Education of the Adolescent*.

   The Act seemed to herald a new dawn for nursery education
too. Clause 8(2)(b) instructed the local education authorities to plan
for the needs of pupils under five either 'by the provision of nursery
schools or, where the authority consider the provision of such schools
to be inexpedient, by the provision of nursery classes in other
schools'. The nursery school lobby was ecstatic. Lillian de Lissa,
recently retired as Principal of Gipsy Hill Training College,
commented on behalf of the Nursery Schools Association that
'nursery schools have been given their proper place within the
national system of education'; while the Fabian Society noted that
the future of the nursery school 'is now assured . . . recognized

by the state as an integral stage in every scheme for universal education.'[1]

The prospect of reform was strengthened by the fact that each local education authority was now required to prepare a development plan. In many cases this strengthened the belief that the prophesied post-war reconstruction was becoming a reality. The LCC produced in 1947 a booklet on the replanning of London schools which explained that

> nearly half were built before 1904 and only one in nine since the first World War. . . All this has made preparing the London plan a big problem, but it has provided a great opportunity. It has removed the temptation to make do and mend. There is nothing for it but a root and branch reform.

As part of that reform it was noted that the nursery movement had been strengthened during the war through the establishment of many new schools. It was planned to make this a permanent gain by providing nursery places in London 'for about half the children between two and five'. A whole series of new primary schools was also envisaged, each for a maximum of 350 children and 'not too far apart.'[2] This optimism in the capital was reflected elsewhere in the country as authorities looked forward to the phasing out of all-age schools, to the reform of the primary sector and to the extension of the benefits of education to a growing number of under fives.

It was a revolution that never took place. In July 1950, the *Times Educational Supplement*, reporting a Parliamentary debate on education, reflected that 'so much of this Act is still on paper' that it risked being hung 'in the gallery of unrealized intentions.'[3] In April 1951, in an emergency Commons debate on overcrowding in primary schools, it emerged that there were still 1700 classes containing over 50 children, while 37,000 more contained over 40 and a further 106,000 catered for more than 30.[4] At the same time Ronald Gould, the General Secretary of the NUT, doubted whether the 1944 Act would ever be fully implemented and called for a Royal Commission to review post-war educational progress, a demand which was supported by the *Times Educational Supplement*.[5] This failure to accomplish educational reconstruction meant that the new primary education was unable to shake off many of the characteristics of the old elementary schooling, and some were even reinforced because of the greater emphasis upon streaming in preparation for selection at 11 + . This is all the more remarkable in view of the dominance of a progressive ideology during these years. R.J.W. Selleck has argued that by the time of the Second World War the 'progressives' had produced a fairly uniform set of ideas and procedures which were to modify classroom practice during the years after the war.[6] While it is certainly true that post-war thinking remained deeply influenced by this progressive lobby, there remain doubts about how widely a 'child-centred' education based on activity methods was practised during the late 1940s.

During the war several developments had strengthened the hand of the progressive lobby. In 1942 a research report was published by D.E.M. Gardner which compared the attainments of children in schools following traditional and experimental curricula. It was to be widely cited by the NUT after the war to give support to its advocacy of progressive methods.[7] In 1944 the Board of Education arranged for the reprinting of its *Suggestions for teachers in elementary schools* to coincide with the Education Act. Although it favoured streaming of children under 11, much of this work was broadly in tune with contemporary progressivism. It reasserted the central tenet of the 1931 Hadow Report on *The Primary School* that 'the curriculum is to be thought of in terms of activity and experience rather than of knowledge to be acquired and facts to be stored.'[8]

This 1931 Report became almost an article of faith for supporters of the progressive movement after the war, who saw it as a statement of unrealised aspirations. In 1947 an HMI, C. Schiller, reminded an audience of Hertfordshire primary teachers that the 1931 Report 'stressed the importance of activity in education, pointing out that its recommendations were still well short of realization.'[9] The 1931 Report clearly influenced the Scottish Advisory Council's *Primary Education*, which appeared in 1946 and was warmly welcomed in England as further evidence of the viability of progressive education.[10]

Among the leading protagonists of the progressive cause during these years were Mary Atkinson, W.K. Richmond and Lillian de Lissa. Mary Atkinson, a tutor in the University Education Department at Newcastle upon Tyne, used the North-Eastern Junior Schools Association to promote teachers' meetings and the dissemination of ideas. In 1949 this resulted in primary school teachers from the region cooperating to produce their own book *Basic Requirements of the Junior School*, which ran to two editions.[11] Mary Atkinson used the educational press to advocate child-centred approaches in the primary school, and, in 1949 too, her own book identified the traditional conception of the purpose of the junior school as the greatest stumbling block to reform. For too long many junior school teachers have acted as if they thought that by concentrating on the requirements of the grading examination in English and arithmetic they were not only giving children the most adequate preparation for the examination but were also doing their utmost for the children's welfare.'[12]

W.K. Richmond was also involved in teacher-training, and used his book, *Purpose in the junior school*, to argue similarly that schools were settling into a pattern similar to that of the past, that the 1931 Report and the Scottish Advisory Council Report should be heeded and implemented, and that the process of selection for secondary education was threatening the response of the primary sector to the 1944 Act. He went on to make a powerful plea for activity methods in the junior school.[13] Lillian de Lissa was not only a leading member of the Nursery Schools Association (in which capacity she planned the involvement of English educationalists in international conferences to help disseminate new thinking: in April 1947, for example, Jean Piaget addressed the Nursery School Association at Geneva) but also she chaired the National Union of Teachers' Consultative Committee which, between 1946 and 1949, considered the question of nursery-infant education. Its report committed the Union to support of activity methods, and, in particular, picked out the issues of class size, ancillary help and refresher courses for teachers as prerequisites to the proper implementation of the 1944 Act.[14]

Beyond this, a host of books and pamphlets canvassed the new child-centred primary education. The Ministry of Education produced pamphlets for both parents and children.[15] M.V. Daniel,[16] Nancy Catty and J.C. Gagg were only three among numerous authors who produced books for primary school teachers, Nancy Catty proclaiming her aim to be

> to suggest ways in which the formal school of the well-known type can be converted into the democratic school where both teachers and children are free to think for themselves and work out their own salvation.[17]

Gagg, who had only recently retired as Adviser for Primary Education to the Shropshire Authority set out 'to suggest ways in which you can make some use of the progressive ideas which are abroad.'[18]

Another source of progressive ideas was the educational press, which was strongly in favour of new child-centred approaches, particularly in the primary sector. Several journals directed at teachers and administrators, shared the same ideology; *Education*, the *Journal of Education* and *New Era* were among the foremost. The *Times Educational Supplement* gave qualified support to this progressivism. On the one hand it ran articles on Montessorian methods, on the new primary education, and, in 1946, commented that 'the evolution of the nursery school illustrates a fundamental change in the social structure . . . Children, rather than adults have become the focus of new conceptions.'[19] But, on the other hand, this journal found room for views which, if not directly antagonistic, threatened, at least by implication, the spread of child-centred education. Most significantly, it promoted record-keeping in the junior school and gave some support to the idea of streaming.

It is in the pages of the *Times Educational Supplement* that we can discern the first antecedents of views which were to be more fully worked out twenty years later in the *Black Papers*. In 1950 G.H. Bantock used the *TES* to mount one of the very few contemporary attacks upon this progressive movement:

> Undoubtedly, something has been lost. In my experience today far too little attention is being paid to what is learnt and why it should be learnt . . . . The expectation is that children can somehow recreate from within themselves forms which it has taken many years to evolve, seems to me both dangerous and time wasting.[20]

An editorial gave qualified support to this view by deploying the argument that

> a big change in what happens in school could make a big change in the national character. That is why any new line of action, such as the methods in vogue today, should be constantly open to criticism and discussion.[21]

Bantock's was the minority view: there was overwhelming support for progressivism which was seen as being of particular significance for the new primary schools. What, then, were the practical constraints which limited the effectiveness of this movement?

First and foremost was the progress of the building programme. In fairness, many authorities faced an almost impossible task. In

1938 Middlesex had planned to spend £4 million on school buildings, most of it on elementary schools. This was frustrated by the war, while population movement and war damage only increased the urgency of the problem. As C.E. Gurr, the Chief Education Officer commented:

> the very conditions which created the need for new school buildings in fact proved one of the biggest obstacles to providing them, for it was often in the most densely developed and populous districts that suitable sites were most elusive.[22]

He singled out the old suburbs (Willesden, Hornsey, Edmonton, Enfield, Tottenham and Wood Green) as those whose solidly build elementary schools were least suited to modern educational methods and were also hardest to restructure: 'their very solidity precludes any extensive alteration . . . unhappily many still wait.'[23]

These problems were typical, and they coincided with a drive by the new Ministry of Education to raise standards in primary school building. The new building regulations issued in 1945 imposed statutory minima on the areas of school sites and on classroom size which were ahead of the practice of the inter-war years.

The local authority which responded most swiftly to the problems created by this initiative was Hertfordshire, whose Chief Education Officer, John Newsom, decided in 1946 to apply the wartime skills of prefabrication to the Cheshunt primary school, later described as 'one of the most important post-war British buildings.'[24] By 1948 the county had planned over thirty primary schools using standardised components: one of them, the Templewood school of Welwyn, won an RIBA award in 1951, the first prefabricated building to be thus recognised.[25]

The Ministry of Education was not slow to encourage wider application of these ideas. Several Hertfordshire designers were invited on to the architectural development group set up in 1948 which produced a series of influential building bulletins and encouraged the cooperation between neighbouring local authorities which was to lead, during the 1950s, to the adoption of the CLASP system of school design. These new buildings were not only cheap, but incorporated design features which favoured modern teaching methods, so that S.A.W.Johnson-Marshall, head of the architects' branch at the Ministry, could claim with some justice in 1951 that governmental influence on school design had become 'a positive instead of a negative one . . . We are concerned to do what we can to help authorities build as well as possible.'[26]

But it is important to emphasise that these developments, achieved against a background of economic crisis, impinged mostly on the new suburbs peopled by the socially mobile lower middle class. For those in the old suburbs, government cuts meant not cheaper school buildings, but no new buildings at all. As early as 1946, Ellen Wilkinson directed LEAs to concentrate their school building programmes on the raising of the leaving age, on training for industry, the training of teachers and on the new housing estates. The outcome was that, when George Tomlinson succeeded her as Minister, he came under growing pressure to do something about older school buildings. He conceded in the Commons in 1947 that

> the building programme up to 1951 can do little more than provide for the raising of the compulsory school leaving age to 15, the increase in the birth rate and new schools on housing estates.[27]

By 1950 he was forced to admit that the cutbacks introduced in 1948 had brought to an end the building of new nursery schools and that 636 of the 2827 school buildings blacklisted in 1925 were still in use.[28]

A letter from R.J. Unstead to the *Times Educational Supplement* in October 1951 offered a gloomy summary of the impact of post-war school building policy:

> As you point out, new schools are perforce being built only where new housing estates make them a bald necessity, but one wonders why the same energy and sense of urgency which provided HORSA huts for raising the school leaving age cannot furnish extra rooms for overcrowded and often derelict junior schools.[29]

The second major constraint which militated against the introduction of modern teaching methods was the problem of teacher supply. As happened with school building, the needs of the primary sector were subordinated to the demands of the secondary, where the raising of the school-leaving age was seen as the first priority. The problem was chronic: G.C.T. Giles of the NUT complained in 1946 that the Education Act might not be implemented before 1958 for lack of teachers. He warned too that the concentration upon raising the leaving age was making the reduction of class sizes (a long-term aspiration of the labour movement) an impossibility.[30] In this situation desperate remedies were canvassed: in 1946 the Ministry rebuked those LEAs which were reintroducing compulsory retirement at 60,[31] and the suggestion of James Fairgreave that the best way out of the crisis was to omit training entirely by offering immediate employment to new applicants was warmly supported in the educational press.[32]

The Ministry eschewed this extreme course, but committed itself to raising the teaching force from 126,000 to 197,000 in these years through an emergency training scheme, by which intending teachers were trained for one year rather than two.[33] The scheme lasted until 1951 and succeeded in training an extra 34,000 entrants to the profession. Of the 54 emergency colleges, 17 survived: the remainder were closed down in 1951, despite a continuing shortage of teachers. The emergency scheme catered mainly for demobilised ex-servicemen: in 1946, for example, ten recruiting panels were despatched to military bases overseas.[34] There was little difficulty in finding recruits. By the summer of 1946, 44,000 men and 12,000 women had come forward, and new applications were coming in at 1200 a week. It is hardly surprising that over 17,000 suitable applicants had to have their entry to training deferred for want of facilities. 'The numbers are impressive', commented the NUT, 'but the same cannot be said of the facilities.'[35]

This unprecedented pattern of recruitment had important implications for the teaching profession and for the primary schools. The vast majority of emergency-trained teachers found employment either in the new secondary moderns or in the primary sector: in the process they unwittingly strengthened the status hierarchies which were already evident in the teaching profession. Several authorities took the view that the swiftly expanding primary sector was best served by female staff who had themselves been educated in secondary modern schools; the *TES* came under attack for its view that 'in secondary modern schools there are not a few who possess the "essential quality" . . . a genuine interest in and liking for the care of young children.'[36] There is some evidence, too, that this stratification of the profession was in fact happening. One speaker at the 1947 conference of the National Association of Head Teachers complained bitterly that

'so long as heads of grammar schools and members of interviewing panels advise against service in infant and junior schools, so long will official exhortation from the centre to take it up be of little avail . . . The deep-rooted tradition of the inferiority of primary school work must at all costs be eradicated.[37]

The fact that teachers' salaries were eroded during this period reflects, too, the swift rise in the number of teachers and the fact that, but for the emergency scheme, many new entrants would never have aspired to a teaching career in the post-war situation of full employment. *The Times Educational Supplement* commented more blandly that 'the erosion of teachers' salaries is a concrete expression of the equalitarianism which many educationalists have been moved to preach.'[38] Further, the emergency training schemes were so rushed that it was impossible to give the new recruits more than the briefest introduction to the child-centred teaching methods so dear to the hearts of educationalists. The failure to recruit enough teachers to make any effective impact on the problem of class size gave a final blow to any hopes of a widespread adoption of progressivism in the primary school classrooms. Against this background it is hardly surprising that, in practice, the late 1940s proved a bitter disappointment to those who had hoped for an end to the traditions of the old elementary school.

One area where advances were anticipated, and were necessary if women were to stay in employment during peacetime, was nursery education. The Nursery Schools Association foresaw 'many new nursery schools after the war', and issued a booklet to help LEAs in the planning of nursery facilities.[39] But the new Labour administration was at first ambivalent towards nursery education and later restrictive. On the one hand, the Ministry's *Not Yet Five* was repeatedly reprinted during the 1940s, encouraging the establishment of nursery facilities, and in 1946 a two-year campaign was launched to relocate the large number of under fives in infant schools in separate nursery classes.[40] When, in the same year, Clement Attlee appealed to women to stay in industry after the war, the London Women's Parliament protested indignantly that this was impossible so long as nursery schools were being closed. They produced figures to show that the permissive nature of the 1944 Act had resulted in the closure of 220 nursery schools in the first twelve months after the war.[41] Nor did the situation improve: the economy measures introduced by George Tomlinson in December 1947 allowed for no new nursery schools or classes, except where they would help mothers enter industry. Within six months John

Edwards, Parliamentary Secretary to the Ministry of Health, announced that 'the government's opinion was that the proper place for a child under two was at home with his mother . . . Mothers of children under two ought to be positively discouraged from going out to work.'[42]

Lady Allen of Hurtwood ran a vigorous campaign on behalf of the Nursery Schools Association to show the damage being done by the government. Unregulated private nurseries were springing up in industrial areas to meet the pressing need: in south Lancashire alone over 100 had been established since 1945. At the beginning of 1948 only 19,000 children out of the two million aged between two and five had access to nursery education: waiting lists usually numbered between two and three hundred. Lady Allen pointed out: 'The present economy cuts follow the familiar pattern of favouring the older children at the expense of the youngest.'[43]

The plight of the nursery sector is illustrated by the fact that, in 1951, the Kent LEA announced the closure of all its nurseries in response to governmental indifference.[44] Against this background, the fact that English nursery schools were committed to activity methods and play, in contrast to the formal instruction given in many continental schools,[45] was of little account: they were for a lucky few.

Turning to the junior and infant schools, there is again a marked contrast between the sanguine tone of some contemporary official publications and the clear evidence of deprivation and neglect. The Manchester Education Committee's *Trends in Junior School Education*, published in 1947 claimed that junior schools were introducing discovery methods, topic and project work and a variety of practical activities, as well as experimenting with house systems, timetabling and record-keeping.[46] The *TES* thought that this document reflected 'the spirit of experiment and revaluation animating primary education throughout the country.'[47] The LCC was equally optimistic when, in 1950, it collated over thirty inspectors' reports for publication and concluded:

the most striking impression is that primary education is on the move . . . the emphasis is changing — away from a situation in which classes of children are being taught most of the day sitting still at desks or standing rigidly in lines, towards one in which individual children are actively learning through experiences that appeal to their natural interest.[48]

These comments were contradicted by the first CAC report which appeared in 1947 and gave a damning indictment of conditions in primary schools:

> They have had a particularly raw deal as a result of the partial application of the Hadow Report . . . districts vary tremendously. The new suburbs usually have good school buildings (with the additional advantages of good houses, books in the home and social family contacts) . . . . In congested urban areas children are usually at school in a poor building; and even if the schools have been 'reorganized', which is often not the case, children of primary age normally go on being taught in the same old building.[49]

At both infant and junior level there were sustained criticisms which focussed upon staffing, class size, buildings and the harmful effects of the 11 + examination.

Conditions in infant schools and departments were particularly difficult. The CAC concluded that 'in schools provided for infants there is often a complete contradiction between theory and practice'.[50] In some areas children had to defer entry to school or be taught on a part-time basis because of the shortage of infant teachers, which was estimated in 1949 at 2500 if classes were to be brought down to a maximum size of 40.[51] In some schools, as the full impact of the bulge hit the schools in the early 1950s, only a minority of infant staff were trained teachers: the remainder were mothers and untrained helpers. So pervasive were the effects of the 11 + examination that in some cases streaming extended down to the infant department, where euphemisms such as 'squirrels' and 'rabbits' were used to avoid the perjorative labels of A and B streams.[52]

Nor was the situation much better in junior schools. Old-fashioned sloping desks and, in extreme cases, stepped classrooms militated against progressive teaching. One delegate to the 1947 conference of the National Association of Head Teachers claimed that 'the buildings in which the juniors and infants are housed are notoriously among the most out-of-date, cramped and inconvenient in the country'.[53] A year later a correspondent to the *TES* argued:

> in most schools today classes are too large . . . . The intelligence level may vary from the mentally retarded to the highly intelligent. In classes of this kind the indulgence in free activity

makes teaching a nightmare . . . . We have not yet reached the point when most teachers either believe in or are competent to undertake activity methods in junior classes . . . . It is open to doubt whether, by ignoring the limitations imposed upon schools today, teachers are making a rod for their own backs.[54]

Against this background the universalising of school meals and free milk may be viewed as major gains. But it must not be overlooked that they brought their own problems by making extra demands on facilities: in one school in Southport, for example, meals had to be taken in the washplaces.[55] Similarly, although external examinations were often defended on the ground that they gave junior schools children targets at which to aim, the heavy reliance upon attainment tests in English and arithmetic which stemmed from the fact that most local authorities used variants of the Moray House tests worked to reinforce the tradition of the 3 Rs. A.G. Hughes, Chief Schools Inspector to the LCC, was right when he concluded in 1949:

> A visit to a typical junior school today reveals how little progress we have made . . . . Junior schools have not been able to shake themselves free of the elementary school tradition. Many teachers, who have painstakingly developed a skilful technique in 'the old familiar business of imparting knowledge' to large classes, have been reluctant to change. Natural conservation has been reinforced by the demands of the special-place examination.[56]

If there were contrasts between primary schools serving differing areas during this period, the contrasts between the state sector and the preparatory schools were even more stark. The post-war years were a boom period for private education, despite the fact that the 1944 Fleming Report advocated closer links between the public and private sectors. During these years the preparatory schools had full waiting-lists and the reasons were not far to seek. They had more spacious accommodation, smaller classes and a wider curriculum than most primary schools. Further, they continued to offer the best route into the public schools, and their continuing commitment to the teaching of Classics reflected the fact that they were very little deflected by the new 11 + arrangements, which impinged on those wishing to go to grammar school. Indeed, one questioner in the

Commons in 1946 suggested that the way to alleviate this contrast between the two systems was through a reform of the curriculum of the state schools. He pointed out:

> many boys leaving independent preparatory schools at an age of 13 + had a working knowledge of algebra, geometry, French and Latin and possibly Greek and trigonometry, whereas most boys of comparable age educated under the state system learned nothing of these subjects and were, therefore, at a disadvantage in their future careers. He asked . . . what steps the Minister proposed . . . to raise the standard for the cleverer boys [sic] in the schools for which she was responsible.[57]

Ellen Wilkinson's reply made it evident that she saw no major difficulties in this contrast, and George Tomlinson, too, suggested, by implication at least, that the Fleming Report was a dead letter, when he assured the 1950 Conference of the Incorporated Association of Preparatory Schools that 'it need fear no qualms about this government's intentions toward their schools.'[58]

The shortcomings of the primary sector were undoubtedly one reason for a quick growth in the number of private schools for younger pupils, many run in converted houses and mansions, during the late 1940s. This growth led to some difficulty in staffing these schools; one commentator complained that there were few interested graduates and 'retired men with pensions, who often made good preparatory school teachers before the war did not come forward today.'[59] Consequently, the IAPS felt obliged to set up, in 1951, its own variant of the emergency training scheme, an 18-month correspondence course for intending preparatory school teachers.[60] But problems such as this were as nothing compared to the difficulties of the state schools, and the *TES*, which remained sympathetic to private education, was able to comment with some justice in 1951 that there was little prospect to closer liaison with the state system:

> many are in spacious surroundings, have good academic records, a fair proportion of graduate staff, and classes whose sizes made them easier to cope with. Being for the few, and not for the million, they have a much better opportunity of excelling.[61]

The education of children under twelve during this period suggests that one underlying reality of the years of austerity was that long-standing inequalities were not eradicated overnight. If anything they were intensified by the fact that educational policy focussed on a desperate struggle to accommodate social changes by raising the leaving age (which drew resources away to the secondary sector), catering for the rise in the birthrate and providing schools for the pupils on new housing estates. Ironically, as Shena Simon pointed out in 1949, the outcome of the 1944 Act was that contrasts were heightened and that the vast majority received no benefit from it:

> What are the gains of the Act? The minority who go to grammar schools have no fees to pay. There are better maintenance allowances at the universities. The minority who are fortunate enough to move into a new house on a new housing estate are slowly getting new schools. But there is no likelihood of nurseries for them. In the town centres and old suburbs old buildings suffice and parity at secondary level is a mockery for want of new buildings. Thus competition to enter the grammar school becomes more intensive than ever.

She concluded that, unless something was done, the Act would simply mean for most children in primary schools an increase in class size.[62]

By 1951 there was much to cause concern in the primary sector. In the struggle to cope with these problems the cost of providing a new school place had fallen from £195 to £140.[63] There were still almost a million pupils in all-age schools.[64] Even worse, in some areas, such as Essex, it was still necessary to exclude children of statutory age from schooling for want of facilities.[65] In April the Minister conceded in the Commons that the number of over-size classes was increasing.[66] It was a bleak picture, made worse by the effect of a system which made the primary schools feeders for the new, differentiated secondary education. In 1950, Max Morris of the NUT warned at a Communist Party conference of the way in which intelligence tests were being used solely to sift children at 11 + ,[67] and the *TES* criticised the way in which some authorities (notably Derbyshire) were using record cards which could 'cling to a child like a shadow.'[68] The 1944 Act had seemed to promise a new deal to the primary schools: those who worked in them discovered to their dismay in the years after the war that many of them remained elementary schools in all but name.

References

1. N. Whitbread, *The evolution of the nursery-infant school* (Methuen, London, 1972), 110–11.
2. LCC, *Replanning London schools* (London, 1947), 11–14.
3. *TES*, 21 July 1950.
4. *TES*, 20 April 1951.
5. *TES*, 30 March 1951.
6. R.J.W. Selleck, *English primary education and the progressives, 1914–1939* (Routledge & Kegan Paul, London, 1972), 156.
7. D.E.M. Gardner, *Testing results in the infant school* (Methuen, London, 1942) and NUT, *Nursery-infant education* (London, 1949), 22.
8. Board of Education, *Handbook of suggestions for the consideration of teachers and others concerned in the work of public elementary schools*, 2nd edition (London, 1944), 111.
9. *TES*, 28 June 1947.
10. *TES*, 11 January 1947.
11. North Eastern Junior Schools Association, *Basic requirements of the junior school* (London, 1949).
12 .M. Atkinson, *Junior school community* (Longman, London, 1949), 54.
13. W.K. Richmond, *Purpose in the junior school* (Redman, London, 1949).
14. NUT, *Nursery-infant education*, 37, 58, and 89.
15. Ministry of Education Pamphlet no. 14, *Story of a School* (HMSO, London, 1949) and Pamphlet no, 15, *Seven to eleven* (HMSO, London, 1949).
16. M.V. Daniel, *Activity in the primary school* (Basil Blackwell, Oxford, 1947).
17. N. Catty, *Learning and teaching in the junior school* (Methuen, London, 1941), 115.
18. J.C. Gagg, *Common sense in the primary school* (Evans, London, 1951).
19. *TES*, 6 April 1946.
20. *TES*, 16 June 1950.
21. Ibid.
22. Middlesex Education Committee, *Primary and secondary education in Middlesex, 1900–1965* (London, 1965), 42–53.
23. Ibid. 45.
24. Ministry of Education Building Bulletin no. 19, *The Story of CLASP* (London, 1961). 6.
25. M. Seaborne and R. Lowe, *The English school: its architecture and organization, 1870–1970* (Routledge & Kegan Paul, London, 1977), 163.
26. Ibid., 166.
27. *TES*, 19 July 1947.
28. *TES*, 24 March 1950.
29. *TES*, 26 October 1951.
30. *TES*, 25 May 1946.
31. *TES*, 23 February 1946.

32. *TES*, 15 June 1946.
33. *TES*, 25 May 1946.
34. *TES*, 20 April 1946.
35. *TES*, 25 May 1946.
36. *TES*, 28 December 1951.
37. *TES*, 31 May 1947.
38. *TES*, 30 December 1949.
39. Nursery School Association of Great Britain, *Planning the new nursery schools* (London, 1945).
40. *TES*, 9 March 1946.
41. *TES*, 27 April 1946.
42. *TES*, 5 June 1948.
43. *TES*, 17 January 1948.
44. *TES*, 16 March 1951.
45. *TES*, 30 April 1949.
46. Manchester Education Committee, *Trends in junior school education* (Manchester, 1947).
47. *TES*, 2 August 1947.
48. LCC, *Trends in primary education* (London, 1950), 3.
49. CAC, *School and life* HMSO, London, 1947), 9–17.
50. Ibid., 12.
51. *TES*, 20 May 1949.
52. Whitbread, *Nursery-infant school*, 118.
53. *TES*, 31 May 1947.
54. *TES*, 24 July 1948.
55. *TES*, 31 May 1947.
56. Atkinson, *Junior school*, viii.
57. *TES*, 28 March 1946.
58. *TES*, 15 September 1950.
59. Ibid.
60. *TES*, 14 September 1951.
61. Ibid.
62. *TES*, 30 April 1949.
63. *TES*, 20 April 1951.
64. Ministry of Education, *Education 1900–1950* (HMSO, London, 1951), 144.
65. *TES*, 20 April 1951.
66. Ibid.
67. *TES*, 3 November 1950.
68. *TES*, 30 December 1949.

3

Parity of Esteem: The Coming of Universal Secondary Schooling

The 1943 Norwood Report had claimed that it was possible to identify three kinds of child, and the years from 1945 to 1951 may be seen as marking the high point of the 'Norwood philosophy', a period when a thoroughgoing attempt was made by the Ministry of Education and many local education authorities to establish a tripartite secondary system of grammar, technical and modern schools. It is all too easy to dismiss this as a convenient and cynical device which permitted the public and grammar schools to experience minimal changes, while the new secondary schools, for those social groups which had previously had access only to an elementary education, were involved in a major consideration of their curricula and objectives. It is clear in retrospect that those Labour politicians who were most closely identified with this policy — Ellen Wilkinson, George Tomlinson and D.R. Hardman — believed genuinely that a differentiated secondary system offered the best hope to disadvantaged social groups, and it was for this reason that Labour in power clung so tenaciously to a defence of policies which it inherited from the wartime coalition and which the Ministry of Education supported.

This is all the more surprising in view of the fact that much expert opinion was sceptical of the Norwood proposals. A group of educationalists at London University established themselves as the Council for Curriculum Reform and, in 1945, issued a publication which dismissed the Norwood Report as 'pernicious' because of its failure to consider the functional relationship between a society and its schools.[1] There were reservations from practising psychologists too. Cyril Burt responded immediately to the Norwood Report:

Any scheme or organization which proposed to classify
children at the age of 11 or 12 according to qualitative mental
types rather than according to general intelligence is in conflict
with the known facts of child psychology.[2]

When the British Association devoted its 1947 conference to a
discussion of this problem, it became clear than many experts were
hostile to the tripartite system. S.J.F. Philpott neatly summarised
the feeling of the conference when he commented that the distinctions favoured in the Norwood Report

sounded suspiciously like the old Faculty psychology. . . . In
practice, the essential measure is of all-round ability. . . .
We need schools ranging in level from the typical grammar
school for children destined to go to the university down to
special schools for mental defectives.[3]

These criticisms undoubtedly help explain the difficulties which
the Labour administration was to encounter in implementing its
policies locally, but they did not deter Ellen Wilkinson. Although
she had not previously been to the fore in planning educational
policy she did identify education as a key area for the post-war
government and travelled to London to ask Clement Attlee for this
Ministry as soon as the 1945 election result was known. She claimed
two guiding aims, 'to see that no boy or girl is debarred by lack
of means for taking the course of education for which he or she is
qualified . . . and to remove from education those class distinctions
which are the negation of democracy.'[4] She saw the fulfilment of
the terms of the 1944 Act, the establishment of universal secondary
schooling and the raising of the school-leaving age as keys to the
realisation of these objectives, despite the fact that many within the
Party desired a wider programme.

At the end of the war a succession of publications made clear
the nature of Ministry policy. The *Guide to the educational system*
published as a pamphlet emphasised that

the key-note of the new system is that, so far as is possible,
all children should receive the type of education best suited
to their abilities and aptitudes. In order to fulfil this principle
in the field of secondary education it is intended that there
should be three main alternative types of education open to
children of eleven and over.[5]

It was made clear that in some cases a single school might offer all three types of education and that, in any case, 'free interchange of pupils from one type to another' was a key to the success of the system. This policy was spelt out in *The Nation's Schools*[6] before the election, and reasserted in December 1945, when a pamphlet on *The organization of secondary education*[7] made it clear that Ellen Wilkinson had no intention of tinkering with this aspect of Ministry policy. It was suggested that 'a unity of purpose' should underly the working of these separate schools and that no more than 25 or 30 per cent of pupils should be sent to grammar schools to avoid a dilution of standards. The failure of back-benchers such as Margaret Herbison and George Cove to force modifications of this policy in Parliament led directly to the major confrontation at the 1946 party conference. At that conference, when reminded that earlier conferences had committed Labour to multilateral secondary education, Wilkinson fell back upon a policy of parity of esteem. Despite her impassioned defence the conference went on to pass the resolution from the National Association of Labour Teachers that the Party should 'reshape educational policy in accordance with socialist principles.'[8]

Wilkinson's first act on taking over the Ministry had been to put the question of a possible postponement of the raising of the school-leaving age before the Cabinet.[9] Once she had received clarification that it would go ahead she pressed singlemindedly towards this objective, telling Parliament in the summer of 1946 that this part of the Act would come into force as planned in April 1947, 'whether or not the teachers were there.'[10] The *Times Educational Supplement* commented, with some justification, that the teachers certainly would not be there. Thus, the new Labour government found itself in a Catch-22 situation in respect of secondary schooling. The commitment to raising the leaving age was an old aspiration, its postponement again would have been unthinkable; but the timing meant tht ROSLA was achieved in economic circumstances which guaranteed the inferiority of the secondary modern schools in terms of staffing and accommodation, thus pre-empting at the outset that 'parity of esteem' and 'unity of purpose' which were the other main planks in party policy.

There were some on the Left who appreciated the dangers. G.C.T. Giles, who had recently retired as President of the NUT, argued in his book, *The new school tie*, that the common school on the American and Russian model offered the best hope:

At the secondary stage a more fundamental change is needed. It is here that a long history of class distinction, of inequality and of segregation has left the deepest blemishes. It is here that the 'educational pyramid' is most obvious. Public schools, secondary schools, technical schools, modern schools — here we have a regular graded hierarchy.[11]

He went on to argue that the existing system 'is quite out of keeping with the democratic, progressive spirit of the new Act, and still more at variance with the aspirations of the British people. Nor does it meet the needs of a planned economy and a rapidly expanding production.'[12]

If these were the tensions which existed within the Labour Party, it was clear to all that one step which could do much to alleviate inequality was the provision of adequate buildings. But in reality, so great were the difficulties when set alongside the pressing demands of the primary sector, that Attlee's administration could only respond to a series of crises. From the outset, the Cabinet committed itself to an emergency building scheme to make possible the raising of the school-leaving age in 1947. By the summer of the 1948 the Ministry of Works had provided over 5000 HORSA (Hutting Operation for Raising the School-Leaving Age) huts.[13] It was this provision which made it possible in December 1946 for Ellen Wilkinson to fight off the suggestion of the Ministerial Committee on Economic Planning that ROSLA be deferred. These huts were described by the RIBA as 'inconvenient in use, substandard in accommodation, uneconomical to heat, erected on playing space and unnecessarily costly,'[14] and it must not be forgotten that, almost without exception, they were provided in the inner cities and old suburbs to enable the conversion of old elementary schools. They contrasted with the 150 new secondary schools which were at work by 1951 and which, in the main, served the newer suburbs on the outskirts of the towns. The Bushbury Secondary Modern school at Wolverhampton, planned in 1949, is an excellent example of the attempt to cater for suburbanisation with buildings which compared with existing grammar schools but which made extensive provision for craft and technical subjects.[15]

These contrasts within the new category of secondary modern schools were to leave an inheritance which, during the 1950s and 1960s, deeply influenced the character of comprehensive reorganisation. But they did not go unremarked at the time. The first CAC Report on *School and Life* drew attention to the fact that

a number of schools have changed their name and are now
designated secondary modern. But as parents well know . . .
they are the same schools; . . . in personnel, premises and
equipment many of them fall far short of the level formerly
required of the secondary schools. Until good secondary
schools are available for all, we cannot escape from the
harmful competitive system whereby certain pupils are
admitted to well-staffed, well-equipped schools, and the
remainder treated as unsuccessful and sent to schools which
have merely changed their name . . . the recently erected
senior schools and junior technical schools are often pleasant
and well-equipped, but they are relatively few.[16]

These practical problems had implications for educational policy,
too, and undermined the viability of the tripartite system. One
commentator remarked that 'the reorganisation of the present
system on the basis of existing buildings . . . has driven a number
of educationalists to look with more favour upon some form of two-
type organisation of secondary education';[17] and as early as 1946
Ellen Wilkinson observed that 'more administrative elasticity
regarding schemes of reorganisation would seem to be desirable in
newly built areas and in recently developed housing estates.'[18]

There is some indication that the Ministry itself was not entirely
averse to this new kind of differentiation in secondary education
when its first building bulletin on new secondary schools, in 1950,
made clear that its new limit of £240 per place (against the £320
allowed in schools currently under construction) applied only to
secondary modern schools.[19] It was not until the appearance of the
second edition of this pamphlet that similar restrictions were placed
upon grammar and technical schools. In these ways post-war
building policy worked to deepen the contrasts in secondary
schooling, both between types of school and between differing kinds
of suburb.

Another significant factor during the late 1940s was the reverence
in which the grammar schools were popularly held. This was shared
by many members of the Labour Party, a considerable number of
whom owed their careers to the advantages bestowed by these
schools. In a speech at Leicester in 1946 D.R. Hardman, the
Parliamentary Secretary to the Minister of Education who remained
an important influence on the government's thinking on education
- until 1951, heaped fulsome praise upon the grammar school:

It is to be expected that until the secondary modern school has become firmly established in the educational tradition of this country, the over-riding standards of secondary education will continue to be set by the established grammar schools. Their spacious buildings, extensive playing fields, small classes and record of academic successes have all combined to produce an ideal of secondary education which has fired the popular imagination . . . . His Majesty's Government, far from intending to perpetuate the colourless and not infrequently repellent buildings and cramped conditions that characterize many existing senior schools, is determined that all secondary schools shall possess premises and amenities comparable to those enjoyed by grammar schools.[20]

This respect was shared by the educational press: in 1949 a *Times Educational Supplement* leader described the grammar school as 'one of the great successes of English education,'[21] while two years later there appeared an even more impassioned defence: 'The nation cannot do without them. It is their social function that is prized. These schools turn out an indispensable kind of citizen.'[22]

Creech Jones was the most prominent of several Labour parliamentarians who defended the grammar schools on the grounds that any weakening of their position within the state sector could only strengthen the links between the public schools and the professions. The Incorporated Association of Assistant Masters, many of whose members taught in these schools, caught the mood of the moment in a pamphlet, published in 1946, which called for experiment in secondary education so long as the nation 'hold fast to that which is good . . . nothing should be done to cripple the development of the grammar schools.'[23] This widespread support had important consequences: it meant that those within the grammar schools saw no need for curricular reform, even though their clientele was perceptibly changing, and it meant too that they were, for the time being at least, insulated against the threat of comprehensive reorganisation. In 1948 their position was strengthened when the government deferred to the grammar school lobby and empowered them to take exceptionally bright pupils at the age of ten. The *TES* commented: 'The exceptionally able invariably go in to the grammar school which thereby acquires additional prestige.'[24]

But the grammar schools were not exempt from their own internal problems which stemmed directly from the new situation in which they now found themselves. By 1949 it began to emerge that significant numbers of the pupils assigned to these schools by a selective examination were failing to stay the course: significantly, the problem was greatest in the industrial areas of the north. In that year, of 105,000 grammar school leavers, 25,000 left before the age of sixteen.[25] The IAHM took the view that the problem lay in the selection process itself rather than in the system, a view which won much support during the next few years. When pressed by T.W. Paling in the Commons on the extent to which this was a northern problem, George Tomlinson conceded that the nine authorities which had introduced pledges (legal agreements with prospective parents) were all in the old industrial areas.[26]

But this problem which impinged on some grammar schools was as nothing alongside the difficulties confronted by the whole technical sector in establishing its identity. By January 1949 there were over 3000 secondary modern schools at work, 1229 grammar schools but only 310 technical secondary schools.[27] The *Times Educational Supplement* noted that 'these few schools are very largely concentrated in highly industrialized areas . . . . Many are accommodated in the buildings of senior technical institutions.'[28] So common was the practice of siting these schools in existing accommodation that only three technical schools were at work in new premises by 1951, the year in which Tomlinson conceded in the Commons that the envisaged technical sector was not materialising.[29]

A few authorities threw themselves wholeheartedly into the provision of technical education. In Wallasey two schools were opened for children 'of very good ability who are interested in applying knowledge and skill to everyday life and work rather than in dealing with abstract ideas.'[30] After a two-year general course, boys specialised in building and engineering, although parents were told that 'the treatment of all subjects has a bias towards industry', while girls were offered commercial, pre-nursing and technical subjects. It was courses such as these which led the CAC to comment in 1947 that 'the present provision of technical education for women and girls seems to reflect a narrow and discarded view of women's place in our industrial and civic life.'[31]

But it was more usual for local authorities to organise on bipartite lines and to set up technical streams within the secondary moderns, as was the case at Lowestoft, or, as in Cheshire and Middlesex, in both grammar and modern schools. The headmaster of Middlesboro Technical Boys School complained in 1950 that this arrangement was being forced on schools, whether or not it was an item in LEA policy:

> the grammar schools find among their scholars some 20–30% who are quite incapable of benefitting from a predominantly academic education and who have been placed in schools which satisfy only the first of the three A's. The outcome is that many grammar schools have established courses in wood-work, metalwork and engineering drawing, not as recreational outlets but for examination purposes to satisfy the needs of their misfits.[32]

Where technical schools were set up, they often failed to attract entrants, since some LEAs deferred to parental wishes. In 1950 one London technical school offered 120 places but received only 72 applications for entry.[33]

As happened within the grammar school sector when problems appeared, many of those most closely involved attributed these difficulties to inaccurate diagnosis of abilities at 11 + rather than questioning the whole basis of tripartism. The annual conference of secondary technical heads and the ATTI both campaigned during the late 1940s for the improvement of test procedures, so that parental wishes would become less significant in placing pupils in the technical schools.[34]

But these problems did prompt some reconsideration of the whole nature of technical education. A growing lobby took the view that what should really distinguish schools in a tripartite system was their ethos, rather than curricular distinctions. As one correspondent to the *TES* argued:

> The main object of technical education at the secondary school level should be that of providing a unique approach to the process of learning designed to suit the practically minded boy.[35]

There were growing criticisms too of the widely contrasting provision in different parts of the country. The *TES* itself was also drawn, in May 1948, to raise questions which were going unanswered by the Ministry. What exactly was meant by technical education? What were its implications for girls? How could children be properly selected? This leader went on to call for a major reconsideration

of secondary technical education.[36] But within two years, the
editorial policy of the *TES* had moved to outright support for
tripartism, and in the process these reservations about what was
happening in the technical sector were forgotten.

By 1951, under these strains, the technical schools were beginning to bear a close resemblance to the grammar schools in
curriculum, and, where they existed, were seen as a second best
to the local grammar. They may not have succeeded in establishing
fully differentiated curricula, as was foreseen at the time of the 1944
Act, but the technical schools did preserve, and perhaps even
strengthened, the status hierarchy which existed within secondary
schooling.

There was, though, no ambiguity about the position in this
hierarchy of the new modern schools, although journals such as the
TES worked consistently to suggest a nobility of purpose. One leader
in 1946 harked back to the medieval period before the craft skills
of the common folk were destroyed by industrialisation:

> it is the noble task of the secondary modern school to give
> back to the ordinary people in a new setting the intellectual
> and emotional freedoms they have lost during the past 200
> years . . . . The modern school will never achieve this aim
> if it attempts to adapt or water down the academic tradition
> of the secondary grammar school . . . it must develop its own
> tradition, a more practical and craftsmanlike tradition.[37]

The way that this was to be achieved was through activity methods,
which were thought to be particularly appropriate for these schools,
and the *TES* worked hard to convince its public that this educational revolution was in fact happening:

> Because the new grammar school satisfied the more clerkly
> pupils for whom its education was devised (and efforts are
> being made to see that the other sort are no longer sent there)
> a reform of its method was clearly not required, whereas the
> reform of unacademic educational method (it was in fact a
> pale reflection of the academic variety and so entirely wrong)
> was urgently needed. Because the new activity methods . . .
> are bringing to all children the same happiness as has been
> for long enjoyed by the grammar school boy . . . they are
> wholly to be welcomed.[38]

But in reality the secondary modern schools were left to break as best they could from the old elementary school tradition despite poorer staffing ratios, less well-qualified staff and, in the main, inferior buildings. Many of them began, from the early years, to model themselves on the grammar schools to a surprising degree: by 1950, 62 of the 237 secondary moderns in the urban areas of Yorkshire were offering a second language.[39] Others, particularly those in rural areas, developed a strong rural bias: this was the case at Clyro in Herefordshire, where agriculture was made part of the school curriculum.[40]

It was impossible for these schools or their pupils to throw off the stigma of inferiority, which was all too often remarked in the educational press. One *TES* leader in 1951 concluded that 'what the secondary modern can do is to help its pupils in their difficulties.'[41] A correspondent summarised neatly the major difficulty under which these schools laboured:

> Yet another class, and the largest, will be the products of the modern secondary school, where material 'for leisure' is provided, since these boys and girls are not to be trained for any of the significant activities of society. Thus a State system of education is seen as subserving a threefold hierarchy, the place of a child within which is to be decided at an age not later than 13.[42]

It was in this context that the first tentative moves towards comprehensive reorganisation were made. The vast majority of local authorities opted for some form of bipartite or tripartite organisation and even those under Labour control believed firmly in the value of the grammar school. Many within the Party were in sympathy with the view of George Cove that the need for multilateral schools stemmed from the desirability of giving more children access to a grammar school type of education. But the Party had been committed, since 1942, to the encouragement of multilateral education, and, as had been the case before the war, grassroots support for the common school remained strongest among the National Association of Labour Teachers, which was particularly strong in London.

It was hardly surprising, therefore, that Middlesex and London were among the first authorities to plan for multilateral schools, although it must be noted that in both cases the initial schemes permitted the survival of some existing grammar schools. In

Middlesex it was soon noted that 'the potentialities of the group who did not proceed to grammar schools were infinitely greater than had been supposed, and modern schools should be encouraged to be both flexible and dynamic so that their achievement ceiling might continuously rise.'[43] After Labour gained control in the 1946 local elections, plans were drawn up for small multilateral schools. In the event, after much negotiation, Middlesex was given permission in 1949 to proceed with plans for two experimental schools, Mellow Lane and Mount Grace.

Proposals from the LCC were met by similar caution from the Ministry. Ellen Wilkinson had told the Association of Education Committees in 1945: 'We are not all born the same . . . . I hope the L.E.A.s who propose to start such schools will think out thoroughly the practical problems involved.'[44] So, the eight experimental schools which were set up in London between 1946 and 1949 were judged to be an acceptable experiment: they were based on old central or senior schools and allowed the 25 county grammar schools already at work in the area to continue. The full London plan, published in 1947, was to prove more contentious since it involved the establishment of 103 comprehensives, some of which were to incorporate grammar schools.[45]

As plans for some form of multilateral schooling came in from a growing number of local authorities (Coventry, Southend, Oldham, Reading, Bolton and the West Riding all produced development plans of this kind), there was some classification of issues and a hardening of party lines during the late 1940s. In some places, such as Middlesex after the 1949 local elections, and Ashford, Conservative Party sympathisers began a staunch defence of the local grammar schools, and by the time of the 1950 general election this had become an item in Conservative policy. The Ministry of Education under George Tomlinson fell back increasingly on a policy of encouraging small-scale experimentation rather than wholesale reorganisation: Tomlinson reassured the Commons, in his first Parliamentary question time, 'I want to encourage variety.'[46] Under him, authorities planning for comprehensive education were expected to think in terms of 6- and 7-stream entry schools which would be large enough to develop viable sixth-forms. When the Ministry advised Middlesex in 1949 that 5-stream schools were too small, Brian Simon retorted in the correspondence columns of the *TES* that a major justification for the reorganised schools was that they would encourage sixth-form entry among children from social groups which had never previously had the chance to stay on.[47] It became clear during these years too that the Ministry saw far more scope for experimentation in rural and suburban areas, a view which had found support before the war when the Spens Report had advocated that multilateral schools were most suitable for 'sparsely populated districts'. In 1945 Windermere grammar school became the nucleus of a small multilateral school, and by 1947 the *TES* claimed that several rural modern schools were running grammar streams for their more able pupils. None the less, it remained possible for the *TES* to comment approvingly when Labour left office that 'it is extremely doubtful whether Mr. Tomlinson ever once lifted a hand' to encourage the establishment of more comprehensive schools.[48]

The very nature of this early comprehensivisation provided fuel for its critics. The *TES*, which was to become an increasingly outspoken advocate of tripartism during the following years, attacked the very first LCC plan for five schools in 1946 with the argument that failure was inevitable in the existing situation:

> the opposition is by no means negligible . . . 'expanding some existing central schools it is unlikely that these schools would, especially in the beginning, attract many pupils of very high intellectual ability, and for that reason would not be fully comprehensive'. Such an admission is hardly calculated to win the support of those who continue to oppose the creation of comprehensive schools on the ground that they will lead to a lowering of educational standards.[49]

In the same year a leader commented dismissively on the experimental nature of comprehensive education that 'there is no proof, no certainty, only opinion.'[50] Supporters of the common school were forced, in this situation, to fall back increasingly on the argument that the inculcation of a sense of community was as important as academic standards, a point which was conceded in the official LCC plan in 1947 which set out to provide 'for all pupils equal opportunity for physical, intellectual, social and spiritual development which while taking advantage of the practical interests of the pupils should make the full development of personality the first objective.'[51] *Labour and the New Society*, published in 1950, emphasised that 'a person in one job has no right to regard a person in another job as inferior. All labour has its dignity . . . . Attendance at the same school emphasizes the fellowship of all members of the community.'[52] This helps explain the strength of what has been called 'the overreaching ideology of citizenship'[53] which impinged on all secondary schools at this time and influenced deeply discussions on the curriculum. For critics, this meant no more than the imposition of an artificial homogeneity. Eric James, High Master of Manchester Grammar School, argued in the *TES* that the common school would lead to 'grave social, educational and cultural evils . . . . It may well be a national disaster.'[54] In an influential book, which appeared in 1949 he went on to suggest that the best system of secondary education would be that which offered equality of opportunity to receive an education of appropriate content,[55] and, predictably, it was at this time that the problem of accurate diagnosis of children at 11 + became central to the debate on the structure of secondary education. The first interim report of the NFER, published in 1950,[56] focused on this issue, and in November of the same year Max Morris commented scathingly:

> The tests select for a predetermined number of places. The number of children capable of 'logical reasoning' (*vide* Norwood) miraculously fits the number of grammar school places provided by LEAs. A discipline which is capable of such manipulation is hardly likely to inspire confidence in its scientific objectivity.[57]

In this context, it is hardly surprising that comprehensive reorganisation got off to a faltering start. The precedents of these years were to be critical for the 1950s and 1960s. The primacy of the urban grammar schools was clear from the outset. There was a readiness, on the part of the Ministry and local administrators, to tolerate the coexistence of grammar and comprehensive schools. The pragmatism which saw comprehensives as particularly suitable for rural areas and new suburbs was to become an enduring feature of reorganisation. The failure of the labour movement to develop a single, agreed policy towards the organisation of secondary education helps explain why only a handful of comprehensive schools were at work by 1951, and meant too that the seeds of future problems were sown during the late 1940s.

The private sector remained above and outside these problems, despite fears early in the war that it would find difficulty in surviving. The Fleming Committee, which reported in 1944 was set up largely in response to pressure from within the public schools, and the two alternative schemes it proposed for closer contact between the state and the private sector seemed at the time to be a lifeline for the public schools.[58] The more radical proposal saw as many as 25 per cent of the places in boarding schools being offered as free places to LEA pupils for whom a residential education was appropriate.

At the end of the war few authorities began to operate schemes of this kind. Hertfordshire began to offer bursaries to admit volunteers to some of the well-known schools. In August 1946, Ellen Wilkinson set up a committee to work out the practical implications of the Fleming Report, announcing her wish 'to see a progressive development of boarding education for all pupils.'[59] Dulwich school began to use the local 11 + as its own common entry. By 1949 the headmaster was able to claim that open competition had saved his school, since there was now a test 'taken on equal terms by primary school boys, preparatory school boys and our own juniors.'[60] By the same year 20 LEA pupils had entered Christ's Hospital and the headmaster felt sufficiently confident of the success of the scheme to reflect on the new, wider social catchment of his school:

> Those who come from the higher social classes . . . slip more readily into ideas of public service, respond more easily to school discipline, and accustom themselves a little more rapidly to boarding school life. The ex-primary school boy is apt to be more individualist, to realize more fully the need for application and perseverence in his school work, and is much less likely to become a mere member of the herd . . . . Many boys used to become bilingual . . . But to the influence of masters and of other boys has now been added the all-pervading voice of the BBC and the problem has greatly diminished. When it occurs it is deliberately faced and tackled.[61]

This passage occurred in one of the series of articles in the *TES* whose intention was clearly to stress the viability of the public school system in the post-war world and to suggest that the Fleming proposals were being acted upon, in some areas at least. Warm support was given to the Fabian Society's *Next steps in education*, which came out strongly in favour of the 25 per cent free place arrangements suggested by Fleming.[62]

But it became clear, towards the end of the decade, that the vast majority of public schools were not working the new scheme. In

1948, of the 580 places offered in public schools to LEAs only 155 were taken up.[63] Difficulties of selection, allied to the prohibitive cost of maintaining pupils at boarding schools, proved too great a deterrent. In 1949 the *TES* was forced to acknowledge that cooperation was small, reporting that 'there is a virtual deadlock between local authorities and public schools in all but a few places.'[64]

Instead, there was a striking upturn in private education during the late 1940s with many small unrecognised schools springing up in private houses to cater for a demand the existing public schools could not meet. Patterns of employment meant that there was a growing number of parents who could consider the expense, while some LEA development schemes seemed, at least, to threaten the local grammar schools. In this situation a public school education began to seem particularly attractive. Not only did the schools themselves sense a new wave of confidence, but it became possible to argue that the new situation within the state sector strengthened their duty to remain apart. H.L.O. Flecker, the Chief Master of Christ's Hospital School, invoked the national need when, in 1950, he wrote of the grammar schools:

> Unfortunately they are now the object of many attacks . . . .
> Holidays are shortened to the elementary level, a serious loss
> to the sixth-form master needing time for reading and research
> . . . . Under some local authorities the grammar school is
> being submerged in the comprehensive school. In these
> circumstances the public schools are an oasis of freedom.[65]

It was considerations such as these which were used to justify the renewal of a divided and differentiated educational system in England immediately after the war.

One of the most striking features of the period is the extent to which the media, especially the eductional press, committed themselves to preferential treatment for existing elite institutions. The *TES* returned repeatedly to a defence of selective education, claiming in 1947 that 'the grammar schools can feel that their great work within the general scheme is thoroughly appreciated and will not want friends and defenders;'[66] and arguing in 1950: 'when it is urged that all schools should be endowed proportionably with the resources of the greatest, it is a matter that should be thought over seriously. It must be asked whether it is possible and again whether it is desirable . . . . Any special advantages they have carved out for themselves should be left to them, for they use them well.'[67] Central to this view was the argument that these schools had the duty of selection for leadership: ' "Elite", were it not debased, would be a good democratic word. It means chosen, which is what democracy's leaders are.'[68]

This belief in differentiation extended also to the question of gender. When the *TES* ran a series of articles on inequality in man in order 'to give equalitarians some arguments to meet', extended coverage was given not only to the need for a tripartite system, but also to the case for distinguishing between the sexes.[69] F.A.E. Crew wrote:

> Demands for the general acceptance of the view that the biological differences between male and female are relatively insignificant when compared with their similarity in respect of social value disturb the biologist. Here biological dissimilarity is most marked. The female of a viviparous species, the young of which mature exceedingly slowly, is enchained with the umbilical cord of posterity. In a society tailor-made for the male she endures the severe handicap of her womb. When married her reproductive and productive functions are usually in conflict and only by withholding herself from her children can she . . . hope to exercise to the full such native talents (not different from those of the male) as she possesses. Biologically she is of more importance than the male. Socially she is not.[70]

Although the coming of the modern schools saw a marked shift towards co-education at secondary level, there remained powerful forces in society which looked to schooling to preserve the discrimination of gender roles.

In England after 1945, a variegated system of secondary education quickly emerged. All political parties were now committed to educational advance, so that, as was argued in *Unpopular education*, the class character of educational politics which was endemic to the inter-war years disappeared. If the 1940s settlement was 'overwhelmingly statist,[71] as was argued in that work, the egalitarian aspirations of the Labour Party did not result in any significant diminution of social class differences in the educational provision. Quite apart from the geographical disparities in 11 + pass rates, which tended to work in favour of the South-East, contrasts in buildings, equipment and staffing, to say nothing of the length of school life meant that the 30 per cent who attended grammar school received almost half of the expenditure allocated to the secondary sector. As Vaizey has shown: 'The award of a grammar school place at the age of eleven was equivalent to more than doubling the resources devoted to that child if it had gone to a modern school.'[72]

What made this contrast particularly significant was the fact that, in view of the pattern of schooling described in this chapter, it resulted in stark contrasts between old and new suburbs, and between social classes. Further, the resurgence of the public schools, situated predominantly in the south of England, served only to heighten the disparities. By the time the Labour Party left office in 1951 it had succeeded in presiding over a massive expansion of secondary schooling which in practice confirmed the distinctions in an already divided educational system.

References

1. Council for Curriculum Reform, *The content of education* (ULP, London, 1945).

2. *TES*, 6 September 1947.

3. Ibid.

4. Labour Party Conference Report (London, 1945), 189.

5. Ministry of Education, *A guide to the educational system of England and Wales*, Pamphlet no. 2 (HMSO, London, 1945), 23.

6. Ministry of Education, *The nation's schools*, Pamphlet no. 1 (HMSO, London, 1945).

7. Ministry of Education, *The organisation of secondary education*, circular 73 (London, 1945); see also R. Barker, *Education and politics, 1900-1951* (Clarendon Press, Oxford, 1972), chapter 5.

8. A.R. Roulstone, 'Educational selection and the Labour Party, 1945-73', M.Ed. dissertation (University of Birmingham, 1974), 12.

9. N. Middleton and S. Weitzman, *A place for everyone: a history of state education from the eighteenth century to the 1970s* (Victor Gollancz, London, 1976) 317-18.,

10. *TES*, 6 April 1946.

11. G.C.T. Giles, *The new school tie* (Pilot Press, London, 1946), 70.

12. Ibid., 77.

13. H.C. Dent, *1870-1970: century of growth in English education* (Longman, London, 1970), 127.

14. Ibid.

15. M. Seaborne and R. Lowe, *The English school: its architecture and organisation*: vol. II, *1870-1970* (Routledge & Kegan Paul, London, 1977) 186-7.

16. CAC, *School and life* (HMSO, London, 1947), 16.

17. D.W. Oates, *The new secondary schools and the selection of their pupils* (Harrap, London, 1946), 55.

18. *TES*, 6 July 1946.
19. Ministry of Education, Building Bulletin no. 2, *New secondary schools* (London, 1950), 2.
20. *TES*, 12 October 1946.
21. *TES*, 2 April 1949.
22. *TES*, 5 January 1951.
23. IAAM, *The nation's secondary schools* (London, 1946), 10.
24. *TES*, 6 March 1948.
25. *TES*, 27 July 1951.
26. Ibid.
27. *TES*, 1 December 1950.
28. Ibid.
29. R. Edwards, *The secondary technical school* (ULP, London, 1960), 44; see also *TES*, 20 June 1951.
30. *TES*, 1 December 1950.
31. CAC, *School and life*, 16.
32. *TES*, 10 March 1950.
33. *TES*, 2 June 1950.
34. *TES*, 31 May 1947, 29 May 1948 and 11 May 1951.
35. *TES*, 22 January 1949.
36. *TES*, 22 May 1948.
37. *TES*, 30 March 1946.
38. *TES*, 13 May 1949.
39. *TES*, 30 June 1950.
40. *TES*, 25 May 1951.
41. *TES*, 6 July 1951.
42. *TES*, 23 March 1946.
43. Middlesex Education Committee, *Primary and secondary education in Middlesex, 1900–1965* (London, 1965), 62.
44. I.G.K. Fenwick, *The comprehensive school, 1944–1970* (Methuen, London, 1976), 54.
45. LCC, *Replanning London schools* (London, 1947).
46. *TES*, 15 March 1947.
47. *TES*, 12 March 1949.
48. D. Rubinstein and B. Simon, *The evolution of the comprehensive school, 1926–1972*, 2nd edition (Routledge & Kegan Paul, London, 1973), 39–40.
49. *TES*, 1 June 1946.
50. *TES*, 21 June 1947.
51. LCC, *Replanning London schools*.
52. Labour Party, *Labour and the new society* (London, 1950), 21.
53. Centre for Contemporary Cultural Studies, *Unpopular education* (London, 1981), 61.
54. *TES*, 1 February 1947.
55. E. James, *Essay on the content of education* (LSE, London, 1949).
56. NFER, *The allocation of primary school leavers to courses of secondary education* (London, 1950).
57. *TES*, 24 November 1950.
58. Fleming Committee, *Public schools* (HMSO, London), 1944.
59. *TES*, 24 August 1946.
60. *TES*, 17 June 1949.

61. *TES*, 24 June 1949
62. *TES*, 10 June 1949.
63. *TES*, 24 July 1948.
64. *TES*, 10 June 1949.
65. *TES*, 3 November 1950.
66. *TES*, 21 June 1947.
67. *TES*, 23 June 1950.
68. *TES*, 20 October 1950.
69. *TES*, 8 July 1949.
70. *TES*, 29 July 1949.
71. Centre for Contemporary Cultural Studies, *Unpopular education*, 64.
72. J. Vaizey, *The costs of education* (George Allen & Unwin, London, 1958), 101–2.

4

The New Scientism and
Higher Education

In 1950, reflecting gloomily on contemporary trends in higher
education, the *Times Educational Supplement* described what was
happening as 'the nationalisation of learning'.[1] Whether this
analogy with governmental policy in other areas was justified is
doubtful, but it is true that the post-war years saw a new
preparedness on the part of the state to involve itself directly in the
planning of higher education.

This was hardly surprising in view of the extent to which the
war had both disrupted the work of the universities and made new
demands on them. The number of students had slumped from
50,000 at the outbreak of war to 35,000 by 1943, and in many cases
whole departments had been evacuated from the major cities to areas
at less risk from bombing raids. At the same time the highly
technological nature of modern warfare forced university research
departments and industry into a closer liaison from which only a
few universities (notably Cambridge, London and Birmingham)
emerged with much credit. As the UGC commented in 1947:

> The hard experience of war had demonstrated plainly in many
> fields the essential value to the community of university
> trained men and women . . . The need for the services of such
> people would not become less with the end of the war, and
> in comparison with many other countries, our output of
> graduates at the pre-war rate appeared disconcertingly low.[2]

The view that closer and more effective links must be forged between
industry and the universities was not new. During the 1930s the
Cambridge University Appointments Board had set up an enquiry
on graduates in industry. Results published during the war

showed that less than a third of graduates of that university were entering industry.[3] In 1942 Nuffield College turned its attention to the same problem. Two years later the UGC informed the Chancellor of the Exchequer: 'the estimated fall in the number of Arts graduates already amount to not less than 15,000, while fundamental scientific research had almost come to an end.'[4] The UGC went on to argue that any plans for post-war reconstruction would necessitate 'a large permanent increase in the university student population'.[5]

As had been the case with earlier phases of expansion, there were many in the university world who feared the effects of too great a distortion of what were claimed to be traditional functions. L.A. Reid was one who argued for a humane, liberalising education:

> There is the gravest danger in regarding immediate and urgent needs as the only really important ones. . . . The urgency of practical ends is tending to cause the educational one to be elbowed out, so that even normally 'educated' graduates are becoming more and more cogs in the industrial-economic machine, instead of persons with character and independence of judgement and outlook.[6]

As the full horrors of Nazi domestic policy became clear in 1945, similar arguments that the universities had a duty to inoculate future political leaders against the dangers of unbridled scientism gathered ground.

The closing months of the war saw a growing consensus that expansion was necessary. The AUT's *Report on university development*, published in 1943, called for a 50 per cent increase in the student population, and in the following year the Association of Scientific Workers, the British Association and the National Union of Students all lobbied for an increase in numbers, as did Sir Ernest Simon in an influential book published in the same year.[7]

This expansionism was sustained by several official reports. The McNair Report, calling in 1944 for three-year courses of training for teachers and the establishment of more advanced courses in technical colleges for intending youth workers, foresaw an annual need for 15,000 newly trained teachers and 300 youth workers.[8] But it was the 1945 Percy Report of *Higher Technological Education* which crystallised the contemporary debate on the nature of the expansion that was needed.[9] There was nothing particularly original about the Percy proposals: in December 1944 the *TES* publicised a conference organised by the LCC at which most of the main recommendations were anticipated.[10] But the Percy Report was of enormous significance for the way in which it indicated growth might be achieved. It came out strongly for a clear distinction between the universities and the technical colleges, defining differing tasks for them:

> It will be essential to distinguish between the functions of Universities and Technical Colleges . . . Industry must look mainly to Universities for the training of scientists, . . . it must look mainly to Technical Colleges for technical assistants and craftsmen. . . . The practical distinction in the relation between academic study and works experience . . . corresponds with a distinction of principle between two aspects of technological education. Every technology is both a science and an art. In its aspect as a science it is concerned with general principles . . . in its aspect as an art it is concerned with the application of . . . principles to . . . problems of production and utilisation. . . . Universities have regarded it as their duty to select and emphasize the science aspect, and Technological Colleges the art aspect.[11]

By promoting this distinction to one of principle the Percy committee was led to reject the idea of a technological university, which would 'deflect development', but went on to suggest the promotion of a small number of technical colleges which would work 'to a standard comparable' to degree courses. Regional Advisory Councils were to be set up under the supervision of a National Council of Technology which would take over from London University the task of external validation. This report was prophetic: it enunciated the binary principle twenty years earlier than is generally recognised and it laid down the blueprint for post-war expansion. As had been the case in the late nineteenth century, this growth was to involve no serious threats to the status hierarchy within English higher education.

But this was not how the Percy Report was viewed at the time. It was warmly applauded by the *TES* for attacking

> the fundamental snobbery running through the whole social system which tends to regard those who deal with organisation and finance as superior to those who deal with research and production . . . Nowhere has that snobbery, which brought the country to the brink of disaster in 1939, been

more clearly reflected than in the educational system.[12]

Similarly, at the 1945 annual conference of the ATTI, T.J. Drakeley welcomed the report, arguing that 'the loss of British industrial prestige was due to the superior status of technology in competitor countries'.[13]

The case for expansion was strengthened by the appearance of the Barlow Report on *Scientific manpower* in 1946. This anticipated a doubling of the output of science graduates within a decade, and went well beyond the Percy Report in calling for the upgrading of the five university colleges and the foundation 'of at least one new university . . . There is nothing sacrosanct about the present number of universities in the Kingdom and we are attracted by the conception of bringing into existence at least one university which would give to the present generation the opportunity of leaving to posterity a monument to its culture.'[14] The Report also asked for the development of two or three Institutes of Technology, preferably in University cities, to conduct research to doctoral level.

No organisation played a greater part in advancing 'the Percy philosophy' in preference to expansion on lines suggested by Barlow than the University Grants Committee, which now began to play a far more active part in the planning of English higher education. Although the first response of the Committee was that the Barlow recommendations involved 'changes at the universities which can only be described as revolutionary', by 1947 it was able to report:

> the universities were able to assure us in 1946 that . . . they would be able to accommodate a total of 88,000 students within the following ten years. They have already done so much in this direction that the situation contemplated by the Barlow Committee does not immediately arise. In these circumstances the establishment of new institutions could no longer be regarded as a necessary means to the policy of expansion . . . greater progress can be made by concentrating the limited men and materials upon the development of existing institutions.[15]

It was widely accepted that the post-war expansion would necessitate a more powerful role on the part of governments. In May 1946 the Barlow Report had hinted at the need to strengthen the UGC, and only two months later the Vice-Chancellors' Committee conceded that 'the government has not only the right but the duty of satisfying itself that every field of study . . . which ought to be cultivated is in fact being adequately cultivated and that resources . . . are being used with full regard both to efficiency and economy.'[16]

At the end of July the Chancellor of the Exchequer announced the widening of the terms of reference of the UGC, which would now 'assist in the preparation and execution of university development plans', over and above its traditional role of advising Parliament on the level of funding needed by the university sector.

The Grants Committee set to with a will. In 1947 the quinquennial system of funding was reintroduced, and the first earmarked grants were made. A number of UGC subcommittees were set up to advise on specialist subjects, and by the end of 1947 its permanent staff had risen from 5 to 22. One immediate outcome was a strengthening of the social sciences, as the UGC committed itself to 'the spread of research into economic and social questions'.[17] And there was money to back these policy initiatives. By 1951 the social sciences were being encouraged through earmarked grants to the value of £400,000, while the overall level of governmental support for the universities continued to rise dramatically. The annual grant, which had stood at £4 million before the war, was doubled in 1945, and rose in steady increments to £20 million by the 1952–3 session, as the universities became increasingly dependent upon direct funding from the state. In return, government felt justified in participating more fully in manpower planning. The appearance in 1947 of an Advisory Council on Scientific Policy and of a Technical Personnel Committee within the Ministry of Labour were indicative of a new determination to oversee investment in higher education.

A further argument was used by the UGC to justify its new supervisory role. Until recent times, with recruitment to universities coming mainly from the 'upper classes', 'the general education of the university student could be left to look after itself'. But the post-war expansion meant vast numbers of first-generation university entrants: thus, 'owing to the change in the social background of students', greater care had to be taken to see that the inculcation of expertise was done 'without risk to the whole man'.[18] In these terms the UGC committed itself to the oversight of what was to prove a lengthy period of expansion: it was only when the engines were put into reverse in the 1970s and the Committee found itself planning for contraction, that its interventionism was seen generally to be controversial.

By October 1950 there was a total of 64,000 full-time students in English universities, of whom 15,000 were at Oxbridge and

18,500 at London. Almost a half of these were following arts and social science courses, although a growing proportion (20 per cent in 1950 as against 15 per cent in 1939) were studying pure science, and the proportion of applied science students had risen to 1 per cent. Despite this growth the demand for trained scientists and engineers remained 'at an insatiable level' during these years, and this had widespread ramification.[19] The FBI began to run courses and conferences on graduates in industry and this opened the door to a career in management for arts graduates, sustaining career distinctions within industry which were already well established. The difficulty in attracting personnel resulted in a salary surge for scientists in industry, which in turn precipitated a long-term shortage of qualified mathematicians and, to a lesser extent, scientists for employment as schoolteachers. The fact that about 75 per cent of students were now in receipt of financial support from LEAs or other sources explains the growing trend to move in order to follow courses in higher education: by 1950 only 37 per cent of undergraduates remained in the parental home while pursuing their studies.[20]

By 1950 there were over 900 state scholarships awarded annually (treble the pre-war figure) and a further 10,000 new awards each year by LEAs. These apparently rosy figures disguise what was seen at the time as a major crisis. The Ministry's circular 234, which advised LEAs on the payment of grants to students, was not mandatory, so that widely differing practices grew up. Many authorities refused to pay the maximum annual grant of £215. The Bristol authority adopted a policy of financing only the most promising students to study away from home: the rest were encouraged to use the local university.[21] The Durham LEA publicised its concern about the wastefulness of grant support when, in 1951, 112 of 662 award holders failed to complete their year's work satisfactorily.[22] Despite questions in the Commons and lobbying from the AUT and NUS, irregularities persisted until 1953. It is difficult to be sure how far these variations reinforced regional contrasts, but we can be sure that (as was the case at 11 + where there were widely differing pass rates across the country) students were at the mercy of the policy of their local authority. Despite this, some commentators remained opposed to mandatory awards. The *TES* gave full support in 1950 to a Ministry working party which 'rejected the slogan "fit for a place, fit for an award" . . . it can hardly yet be maintained that . . . the fact of a candidate's admission alone justifies spending public money on him.'[23]

Consequently, although several universities devised schemes to ease the problems of first generation students (Birmingham, for example, produced its own pamphlet, *Introduction to a university*, in 1951), there was if anything an intensification of the hierarchy of English universities which linked particular universities with a particular clientele. Ernest Simon complained bitterly at a Manchester University council meeting in 1951, that the proportion of outstanding students at Manchester compared unfavourably with the pre-war years: 'That might be partly because Oxford and Cambridge, under the new scholarship system, were probably getting an even larger proportion of top scholars.'[24] The annual 'league tables' of Oxbridge awards heightened competitiveness by their very existence, and did little to suggest that expansion meant democratisation, as Table 4.1 shows.

Table 4.1 Oxford Awards

	School of Origin		
1945	Independent	Direct grant	Maintained
No. of schools winning awards	62	15	68
% awards won	59	11.6	29.3
1950			
No. of schools winning awards	65	24	91
% awards won	53	15	32

The *TES*, presenting these figures, concluded: 'It is clear that independent schools still obtain a very high proportion of the highest awards.'[25]

These problems of access to higher education were exacerbated by the demobilisation of ex-servicemen, who competed with eighteen year olds for places. Indeed, the government's Further Education and Training Scheme ensured that those being demobilised had the better chance of financial support. Between 1945 and 1950 a total of 83,000 FET awards were made, and just over a half of them (43,000) were taken up at universities.[26] This new source of competition made it more difficult for school-leavers to win university places, despite the expansion, and this factor too worked to the disadvantage of first-generation secondary school pupils. It became usual during the late 1940s for universities to encourage school-leavers to complete National Service before becoming undergraduates in an attempt to alleviate the problem.

The impact of FET awards on further education was even more traumatic, since these ex-servicemen fuelled a vast expansion of technical education. This was the first instance of further education acting as a safety-valve after the Second World War by soaking up the excess demand for places in higher education. These new recruits, anxious to compensate for the lost years of the war, enabled the establishment of degree level work for the first time in a number of technical colleges. The Acton Technical College, Battersea Polytechnic and the Royal Technical College, Salford were three institutions where particularly large numbers of students of FET grants led to a proliferation of courses leading to external degrees of the University of London.[27] By 1949, nearly 9000 full-time, over 11,000 part-time students and an even larger number enrolled in evening classes were reading for London degrees in technical colleges.[28]

These students represented only a small proportion of the total enrolment in further education, but they were a portent of post-war trends,. By the end of the 1940s a post-war investment of over £10 million in technical colleges had resulted in a student cohort of 2¼ million in further education, of whom over two million were part-time. This persistence of traditional patterns (the 1931 Clark Report had seen no need to break with the well-established practice of part-time technical education) meant that technical education was to remain doomed to inferior status, despite the proliferation of degree courses.

Another surprising source of post-war expansion was the presence of a large number of refugees from Eastern Europe. The manpower shortage was an important factor which encouraged the Labour government to establish two official immigration schemes which resulted in the arrival of a quarter of a million Poles and over 80,000 from other countries. The Polish Resettlement Act led to the establishment in April 1947 of the Committee for the Education of Poles in Great Britain. The second language courses for newly arrived immigrants which this committee requested were, in many cases, provided by LEAs through technical and further education colleges. This was to develop later into an important function of the further education system in response to subsequent waves of immigration. Beyond this, a Polish University College was opened in Kensington, entering students for London external degrees, mostly in applied science, and by 1950, at the height of the working of the settlement scheme, over 2500 Polish students were in receipt of grant support, 1000 at the Kensington College, the rest in English universities. Thus, in the late 1940s, the education system was firmly committed to the assimilation of ethnic groups towards whom there was a significant residuum of wartime goodwill, and in the process a further boost was given to the expansion of higher education.

There is no doubt that the post-war resurgence of technology worked to retard the long-term trend towards equalisation of opportunity between men and women. There were other factors at work too: only a tiny fraction of the FET award winners were female. There is clear evidence too that there remained considerable employer resistance to the appointment of women to posts in business and industry, so that the vast majority of the 5 per cent of female graduates who wished to enter these professions were deflected elsewhere. In this situation the Civil Service presented itself as the most promising career route for scientifically-minded women.[29] In the event, partly because of these factors, and partly in response to the demand from school leavers, women remained outnumbered in a ratio of 3:1 at English universities during these years.

These developments took place against the background of a continuing and lively debate on the needs of higher education. Many commentators were concerned about the kind of higher technological education best suited to a modern industrial democracy, and a plethora of reports and commissions ensured that the chimera of a technological university did not evanesce from public view. Within six months of the appearance of the Barlow Report a Parliamentary Scientific Committee foresaw an even quicker expansion, both within the universities which, if fully committed to expansion, could achieve 'a possible but unlikely total of 108,000', and within the technical colleges which might take up to 7000 students annually to a university standard of work, provided a bachelor's degree were offered.[30] The *TES*, concerned by the implications of a possible twenty new subjects being available to degree level, fell back on the philosophy of the Percy Report, commenting that any subject was acceptable at degree level only if it ensured not simply 'a high professional competency but also a larger and more liberal understanding of the nature of man and the purposes of society'.[31] It was in 1947, too, that an FBI report called for more industrial research in technical colleges and the closer cooperation of the colleges with industry.[32] A year later both the Institute of Physics[33] and Nuffield College[34] turned their attention to the supply of highly skilled manpower for industry, which was proving an increasingly intractable element in the contemporary manpower shortage. By the end of the decade the Ministry of Education, the FBI, the National Advisory Council, the Advisory Council on Scientific Policy, the Royal Society and the University Grants Committee had all made further proposals.[35] The UGC's *Note on technology in universities*, appearing in January 1950 gave an augury of governmental thinking which was confirmed in the 1951 White Paper on *Higher technological education*. This confirmed that advance would be through enhanced financial support to existing institutions and that serious consideration would be given to a national validating body ('A College of Technologists') for awards other than degrees.[36] So, despite a vigorous campaign by the *TES* during 1950 and 1951[37] to keep alive the Barlow proposal for a technological university, it was the conservative strains of the Percy Report which echoed more loudly at the close of the 1940s.

This was but part of a much wider debate on the whole functioning of the universities. The most universal criticism, and the one which had been made for many years, was that the universities failed to provide a cultural synthesis which would enable the student to see the functioning of society as a coordinated whole and to understand the signficance of his specialist, and all too often isolated study. Just as Abraham Flexner in 1930 had criticised the universities for their absorption in vocational studies,[38] Ortega y Gasset had demanded in the same year that universities should once again teach 'culture . . . the system of vital ideas which each age possesses'.[39] The cry was soon taken up in England. In 1932 A.N. Whitehead complained that isolated studies lacked 'fertility of thought',[40] and W.M. Kotschnig too lamented the passing of 'the unified conception of the university which characterised earlier periods.'[41]

This idea was repeatedly taken up during the years that followed, and by the end of the war a strong body of opinion had emerged in favour of experimentation. In 1943 the *Chicago Yearbook* called for a 'new humanism' in the universities,[42] and D.G. James suggested that the provision of specialists was not their prime function. Their first work, he argued, was 'to generate and sustain the free play of curiosity and discussion which may result in seeing many things together and not one or two in isolation'.[43] But the most portentous development of this year, indicative of much soul-searching in teaching circles, was the publication of the *Report on university developments*. It urged the immediate reform of degree courses, the provision of first-year courses 'in groups of correlated subjects', and laid stress on the need for 'more widespread study of the structure and evolution of society, of the social significance of the various subjects of study, and of the main problems of philosophy'.[44]

In 1944, J. Macmurray called for 'the unification of Arts and Science',[45] and Bonamy Dobree made a similar appeal for a rethinking of university curricula.[46] Two years later, C.H. Waddington saw it as the prime duty of universities to set before their members a system of thought which is universal;[47] and in 1947 G. Templeman complained that 'none of the modern universities has succeeded in establishing a satisfactory general honours course'.[48] So an increasing number of widely respected critics added their weight to what was fast becoming a movement. Their demands prefigured the refurbishment of degree courses in many universities and colleges, and underlay the development of plans for a new university which could tackle these problems from scratch.

The success of Stoke-on-Trent in becoming the home of this new university, which opened at Keele in 1950, derived from a unique concatenation of circumstances. The area had a long tradition of adult education work under the auspices of Oxford University, and this had generated aspirations for a local college. Several of those who had been involved in this work earlier in the century now found themselves in influential positions. R.H. Tawney was in 1945 a member of the UGC. A.D. Lindsay, who had also lectured in the Potteries, was Master of Balliol College. E.S. Cartwright, who had been a student member of Tawney's pioneer tutorial class in Longton in 1908, was for many years organising tutor for the Oxford University Tutorial Classes Committee, and became in 1945 secretary to the newly-formed North Staffordshire Committee for Adult Education. These were key members of the 'junta' which in 1946 devised plans for a distinctly local university, which would teach social science to members of the local adult education movement and those physical sciences which were of greatest relevance to the pottery industry. Protracted negotiations with the UGC made it clear that the only hope of acceptance lay in a curriculum which would address national rather than local needs. By 1949, when a charter was granted, a 'foundation year' of general studies was envisaged: subsequently students were to proceed to a three-year honours course which combined a range of differing subjects. It was only when the proposed courses offered this response to the wider debate on specialisation within the universities that the UGC, and the three sponsoring universities who were to permit the new college to award its own degrees from the start, relented.[49] The University College of North Staffordshire was an important precedent. It broke the monopoly of the London external degree which had blinkered earlier university colleges, and offered a model of a liberal education which was to be widely imitated as the new university movement gathered pace during the 1950s and 1960s.

But for the moment, there was a distinct feeling that expansion was going quite far enough. The *TES* commented in April 1951: 'It was natural to increase the ''output'' of the universities . . . The plan has largely succeeded but if it is pushed any further it will be pushed too far.'[50] Four months later, surveying the record number of undergraduates beginning the new academic year, the same journal added that 'it seems unlikely that they will be substantially exceeded in the near future. There may be a slight decrease. This is no bad thing. The universities must be allowed to get their breath.'[51]

But, as events were to prove, the late 1940s had only initiated a vast expansion of higher education. During these years, the shape it was to take was largely determined. Reservations about too great a restructuring or too great an expansion of the universities, together with the greater responsiveness of the state sector, ensured that the rising demand for higher education was catered for through a 'binary' system whose two halves had differing characteristics. Those within the universities defined national need within the familiar framework of a liberal education, assuming that their alumni, even if they did enter industry, would aspire to management positions demanding a wider perspective. The expansion of the technical colleges was fuelled far more by short-run demands, by new, unforeseen sources of students and by insistent demands of industry for trained manpower. In this situation, it is hardly surprising that the post-war expansion of higher education, kaleidoscopic as it was, involved hardly any erosion of the old status hierarchies. As the *TES* commented in 1951 on the failure to plan for a technological university: 'The new policy leaves things much as they were — the universities taking the high road and the technical colleges the low.'[52]

References

1. *TES*, 17 March 1950.

2. UGC Report, *University development from 1935 to 1947* (HMSO, London, 1948), 26.

3. *The Times*, 6 November 1945.
4. UGC Report, *University development*. 23-4.
5. Ibid.
6. *TES*, 16 September 1944.
7. W.H.G. Armytage, *Civic universities* (Benn, London, 1955), 281.
8. McNair Report, *Teachers and youth leaders* (HMSO, London, 1945).
9. Percy Report, *Higher technological education* (HMSO, London, 1945).
10. *TES*, 9 December 1944.
11. Percy Report, 5-10.
12. *TES*, 10 November 1945.
13. *TES*, 17 March 1945.
14. Barlow Report, *Scientific manpower* (HMSO, London) 17.
15. UGC Report, *University development*; 41-2.
16. R.O. Berdahl, *British universities and the State* (CUP, London, 1959), 70-1.
17. UGC Report, *University development*, 72.
18. UGC Report, *University development from 1952 to 1957* (HMSO, London, 1959), 39.
19. M. Sanderson, *The universities and British industry, 1850-1970* (Routledge & Kegan Paul, London, 1972), 352.
20. UGC, *Returns from universities and university colleges, 1950-51* (HMSO, London, 1952).
21. *TES*, 19 October 1951.
22. *TES*, 26 October 1951.
23. *TES*, 4 August 1950.
24. *TES*, 30 November 1951.
25. *TES*, 11 May 1951.
26. Ministry of Education, *Education 1900-1950* (HMSO, London, 1951), 101.
27. E. Robinson, *The new polytechnics* (Penguin, London, 1968), 19.
28. Ministry of Education, *Education 1900-1950*, 52.
29. Sanderson, *The universities*, 357.
30. Parliamentary Scientific Committee, *Colleges of technology and technical manpower* (HMSO, London, 1947), 9.
31. *TES*, 9 August 1947.
32. FBI, *Industrial research in technical colleges* (London, 1947).
33. Institute of Physics, *Education and the training of technologists* (London, 1948).
34. Nuffield College, *The problems facing British industry* (Oxford, 1948).
35. See in particular National Advisory Council, *The future development of higher technological education*, London, 1950; FBI, *The education and training of technmologists*, London, 1949; and the series of articles in the *TES* on technological universities in January and February, 1950.
36. White Paper, *Higher technological education*, HMSO, London, 1951.
37. *TES*, 10 March 1950, 17 March 1950, 2 June 1950, 21 September 1951, 7 December 1951.
38. A. Flexner, *Universities: American, English and German* (OUP, New York, 1930).
39. Ortega y Gasset, *Mission of the university* (Routledge & Kegan Paul, London, 1946), 64.

40. A.N. Whitehead, *The aims of education* (Williams & Norgate, London, 1932), 82.

41. W.M. Kotschnig, *The university in a changing world* (OUP, Oxford, 1932), 21.

42. *The 42nd Year Book of the National Society for the Study of Education* (Chicago, 1943), 452.

43. D.G. James, 'New notions about universities', *Universities Review*, 16, 1 (November 1943), 12.

44. AUT, 'Report on university developments', *Universities Review*, 16, 2 (May 1944).

45. J. Macmurray, 'The functions of a university', *Political Quarterly*, XV, 4 (1944), 278–80.

46. B. Dobree, 'Arts faculties in modern universities', in ibid., 345–7.

47. C.H. Waddington, 'The integral university', *Political Quarterly*, XVII, 2 (1946), 143.

48. G. Templeman, 'The modern universities', *Universities Quarterly*, 2, 1 (November 1947), 44.

49. R.A. Lowe, 'Determinants of a university's curriculum', *British Journal of Educational Studies*, XVII, 1 (1969), 41–53; J. Mountford, *Keele: an historical critique* (Routledge & Kegan Paul, London, 1972).

50. *TES*, 6 April 1951.

51. *TES*, 10 August 1951.

52. *TES*, 21 September 1951.

Part Two
Education for an Affluent Society, 1951–1964

5

The Coming of Affluence, 1951–64

The parliamentary majority of six won by the Labour Party in the 1950 election meant that another general election was likely sooner rather than later. Spurred on by promising Gallup poll predictions in the spring of 1951, the Conservative opposition harassed Attlee's government through a series of snap divisions in the Commons and succeeded in forcing an election by the autumn. Although more people voted Labour than had done so in 1945, and the party won the popular vote by 13.95 million to 13.7 million, it lost the election. During the next fourteen years it was the Conservatives who presided over the country during a period when affluence became a social reality.

It was a situation laden with contrasts. The new government was committed to the maintenance of full employment and, in the main, was prepared to operate the Welfare State established by its predecessor despite the enormous cost. But, at the same time, one of the major items in the Conservative election manifesto was a determination to attack unnecessary expenditure; it has been described by one historian as a government of business interests, which saw the solution to reconstruction in releasing all controls on land, commodities and trade as easily as possible.[1]

There were, too, contrasts of leadership. If Winston Churchill, returning to power at the age of 77, seemed to some to be a throwback to the politics of the Edwardian era, the cabinets of the 1950s and 1960s also contained such representatives of a more radical Conservatism as R.A. Butler and Edward Boyle. By a further irony, another noted liberal, Harold Macmillan, who led the Party from 1957 to 1963, was married to a Devonshire: by 1958 seven of his nineteen Cabinet ministers were related to him by marriage. In the following year he joked to his old school: 'Mr.

73

Attlee had three Old Etonians in his Cabinet. I have six. Things are twice as good under the Conservatives.'[2] During the 1963 leadership crisis, it was a landed aristocrat, Alec Douglas Home, to whom the party turned to lead it into the 1964 election. These political contrasts were matched at the economic level by the irony that affluence was achieved at precisely the moment historically when Britain's comparative decline against the more quickly growing economies of Germany, Japan and the USA began to accelerate. This chapter will focus upon those social and economic developments which bore most closely upon the educational provision during this period of contrasts.

Economic and Political Determinants

> The generation which came to maturity in the 1950s had been born in the Great War, schooled during the slump, conscripted in the Second World War and rationed for years afterwards. It had no inclination to forgo the security and comforts now within its grasp in the hope of long-term economic growth.[3]

This percipient passage by one recent historian goes far to explain the consensus politics of the 1950s, which stemmed largely from the evenly matched electoral strength of the two major parties, neither of which could afford to desert the middle ground. It explains too the popularity of the Conservative commitment to releasing controls and sponsoring economic growth, despite the fact that, at the moment of transfer of power, the Korean War diverted large sums towards the armaments programme and brought into question the wisdom of too swift an economic expansion.

This war was to prove only a temporary hiatus, and within a few years it became clear that the 1951 election was a good one to have won, since it coincided with an upturn in world trade and a decisive swing in the terms of trade in favour of Britain. In consequence, the years from 1951 to 1964 saw continuing uninterrupted full employment, with a 40 per cent increase in industrial output during the whole period. This newly achieved popular affluence was marked by the acquisition of consumer durables. In real terms, wages rose by 20 per cent between 1951 and 1958, and by a further 30 per cent before the Conservatives left office in 1954. A few crude statistics can be used to demonstrate succinctly how this enabled what was nothing short of a social revolution. Between 1951 and 1964 the number of cars on the roads rose from 2½ million to 6 million, as annual expenditure on cars and cycles soared from £90 million to £910 million. During this same period the percentage of households owning refrigerators rose from five to 37, owning washing machines from 11 to 52, and owning television sets from nine to 85. This new middle class aspired to mass schooling for its young people and could afford the necessary sacrifices. While there was a steady increase in the numbers of children in school in the 5–14 age range (from 6,409,000 to 7,528,000), the most striking advance was in the numbers staying on above the age of 15 (from 299,000 to 848,000), and this was matched by a corresponding increase (from 85,000 to 126,000) in the number of university students. This enhanced affluence enabled the beginnings of a revolution in schooling, through fuller participation in leisure pursuits and school visits than had been possible previously, and it also meant that the secondary schools could extend existing elite practice by looking to their new clientele to provide such items as school uniform and ancillary sports equipment. In these ways the nature of the educational expansion of the 1950s was largely determined by the economic upturn.

Of particular significance was the housing policy of the new administration. At their 1950 Blackpool Conference the Conservatives had hit, almost by accident, upon the figure of 300,000 as an annual target for housing. Under the energetic guidance of Harold Macmillan this objective was met within two years by releasing the curbs on private house building and through the 1952 Town Development Act which opened the way for the expansion of existing small towns alongside the twelve New Towns already designinated by the outgoing Labour administration. Private housing became central to the Conservative drive to unshackle private enterprise, a policy which was confirmed during the mid-1950s when Anthony Eden declared his commitment to the ideal of a 'property-owning democracy'.[4] But the chronic shortage of building materials meant that, in the process, important aspects of public investment, such as road building, the renovation of industrial plant and the building of hospitals and schools were necessarily impeded. It is no coincidence that the early 1950s witnessed ratepayers' protests in several parts of the country against what was seen as over-lavish expenditure by local authorities on new schools.[5]

Further, the housing drive itself which was in part justified on grounds of social need, was in reality aimed at those upwardly mobile elements of the lower-middle and working classes who could best afford homeownership. As one historian has observed, 'it has been estimated that more slums were being created each year in the early 1950s by disrepair and dilapidation than were being removed by slum clearance'.[6] It was a policy which heightened social distance between the inner-ring suburbs and the new homogeneous overspill areas of the 1950s. Thus, housing policy predetermined the relative success of schools in these contrasting environments. Even worse, by identifying from the outset the new middle-class suburbs, the policies of the 1950s meant that when, during the 1960s, overspill areas for the inner cities were sought, they were, almost necessarily, developed away from these high-prestige suburbs, and in many cases, such as at Telford or Chelmsley Wood in the West Midlands, in localities which were hopelessly inconvenient in relationship to foreseeable employment opportunities. So, both immediately and in the long term, the promotion of domestic house building during the 1950s had important implications for the English educational system.

A further consequence of this suburbanisation, which impinged directly upon family life and less directly on schooling, was the rise of commuting. Central London had known a declining resident population since the First World War. By the mid-1950s the daytime population of Central London (1¼ million) was five times as great as the resident population.[7] During these years this phenomenon was mirrored in all of the major conurbations. This meant that not only were umprecedented numbers of schoolchildren being drawn from homes where commuting was the norm for at least one parent (usually the male), but also that schoolteachers themselves became able to travel greater distances from home to work. In the long term this trend came to influence the ways in which the teaching profession perceived its role, and it meant too that increasingly teachers in working-class schools chose to reside elsewhere in middle-class districts.

The more general management of the economy also had an impact upon the education service during these years. The 'politics of consensus' stemmed largely from the evenly matched electoral strength of the two major parties, neither of which could afford to desert the middle ground. Consequently, in preference to mounting a direct attack on the public sector, a succession of Conservative Chancellors fell back on monetary controls and the management of demand. In the process, the 'pump-priming' of R.A. Butler in 1955 and of Heathcoat Amory in 1959 has been seen by some historians as the invention of the 'election budget' and less sympathetically by others as the worst possible examples of 'stop-go' economic policies which mortgaged the future for the sake of the present. If one result was the encouragement of domestic consumption at the expense of industrial investment (which was far greater in major competitor countries such as Germany, USA and Japan), another was the reinforcement of Treasury control over the spending Ministries, including Education. As Edward Boyle commented subsequently: 'It was always easier to get a bit more on the building programme for further education than for other things because of the Treasury doctrine that this affected economic growth most.'[8]

At times, Treasury influence was more direct. Selwyn Lloyd's 1961 'wage pause' came 'crashing in on such long-established income determining bodies as the Burnham Committee for teachers' salaries'.[9] There can be little doubt that this increasingly susceptibility of the Ministry of Education to Treasury policy impinged upon the Ministry's innovatory powers and resulted in tighter control of the local authorities.

It is worth remarking, too, the receding impact of foreign and colonial policy, which no longer divided the parties as it had done between the wars, and no longer loomed as large. One result was that domestic issues, such as education, assumed a new prominence in political debate. Labour, having introduced an atomic bomb under Attlee, and also having become the first administration of any colour to introduce conscription in peace time, could hardly revert to the isolation and pacifism which had marked large sections of the party during the 1920s and 1930s. Similarly, Churchill's diehard opposition to colonial independence movements was forgotten as Macmillan steered the Conservative Party to a vantage-point from which it could acknowledge and respond to the 'wind of change' which was blowing through Africa. By 1964, 13 of the 24 New Commonwealth countries had achieved independence. What, then, was left for the two parties to differ over and to spar about for electoral purposes? Increasingly, the structure of the education system and the pattern of secondary schooling provided part of the answer. A more direct spin-off from foreign affairs was the ending of national service in 1960, which had the immediate effect of standardising the age of entry to higher education at 18 + (and thus drastically influencing the attitudes and mores of the student estate), and also of bringing schools into a closer and more direct relationship with employers than had prevailed for some years.

The last great London smog occurred in December 1952 and

was estimated to have killed over 4000 people. In the aftermath, Enoch Powell as Minister of Housing and Local Government, introduced the 1956 Clean Air Act, and, as industrial pollution steadily receded during the following years, one of the last great environmental health hazards for English schoolchildren was removed. In combination with the improved diet of the post-war years, less atmospheric pollution meant that the school population of the early 1960s was the healthiest of the century. In 1962, J.A. Scott, Medical Officer of Health to the LCC emphasised in his annual report:

> the general improvement in the health of London school children. Of the children inspected during 1961, 99.2% were found to be in a satisfactory physical condition and there was a slight improvement in the number who were found to have defects. During 1961 . . . there was a further reduction in the average pollution of the air to the extent of about 7% in smoke and 4% in sulphur dioxide.[10]

The improvements were as dramatic and as significant elsewhere in the country.

During these years there were, too, political developments which cast a long shadow over the future. Perhaps most significant was the regrouping of the Labour Party which had spent much of the early 1950s in disarray. At the very moment that Bevan was making his peace with Gaitskell (marked by his preparedness to concede the principle of multilateralism at the 1957 party conference), the right-wing revisionists, most notably Antony Crosland, Roy Jenkins, Denis Healey and Douglas Jay, were at work devising a new vision of an egalitarian society. Their views involved an acceptance of the mixed economy, and the promotion of education, which the state might use to engineer a fairer society, to the centre of political debate. In this new vision, which Harold Wilson held before the electorate in 1964, education was to be efficient and technocratic.

> Wilson made the slow pace of scientific and technological advance the basis of his attack upon the Conservatives. It was not the inhumanity and vulgarity of the Affluent Society which Wilson attacked, but rather the amateurism responsible for the 'slow rate of economic growth in Britain'. The theme of the scientific failure could be ascribed to the outmoded

structure of British industry and to the deficiencies of the educational system.[11]

It was an approach which chimed with, but took further, Edward Boyle's attempts to show Ministry of Education policy as being drawn from the best consensus of professional opinion. The appointment of a professional economist, Geoffrey Crowther, to chair the CAC, and the establishment of new specialist departments within the Ministry, are evidence of this trend.[12]

But there were evident, at the same time, the first stirrings of a new radicalism within the Conservative Party which was to resurface during the 1970s and 1980s. A group of economists and young politicians, most notably A.T. Peacock, J. Jewkes, Enoch Powell and Geoffrey Howe, began to argue that the coming of affluence would remove the need for the kinds of welfare provision established under Labour during the late 1940s. Accordingly, it was possible to look forward to a time when the boundaries of state involvement might be pushed back. In an influential and prescient pamphlet in 1961, Geoffrey Howe argued that, as part of the shrivelling up of the Welfare State, parents should be provided with vouchers as

> a decisive step towards enlarging the responsibility of parents
> for the education of their children . . . With rising standards
> all round the traditional enthusiasm of the middle classes for
> educating their children at least in part at their own expense
> is certain to spread. There is moreover a substantial minority
> of angry parents, who see their children of moderate ability
> (having 'failed' the eleven-plus) deprived of any opportunity
> of grammar school education. There is good reason for
> believing that many such children would achieve more in
> grammar schools than the theoretically more able children
> from poor homes.[13]

It is impossible to understand educational developments during these years without some awareness of this economic context and of these political debates. They help explain the contemporary enthusiasm for a system whose defects appear obvious in retrospect, and, perhaps more important, they suggest that the coming of affluence did not mean the obliteration of those divisions which had been endemic to English society and to English schooling since the outset of industrialisation.

A Changing Population

During the 1950s, the population trends established immediately after the war were sustained and strengthened. The total population of the United Kingdom rose steadily from 50 million in 1951 to 54 million in 1964, and the birth rate, which had fallen back from the 1947 peak, rose steadily from the mid-1950s onwards to pass the one million mark again in 1964. And more of these children survived to enter the schools than ever before: by 1961 deaths during the first year of life had fallen to an unprecedentedly low 22 per 1000 live births. This trend was complemented by the increasing popularity of marriage (by 1964 half of the total population was married, a figure unprecedented in the twentieth century) and by a dramatic fall in the age of childbearing. In 1951 there were 29,000 recorded live births to mothers in the 15 to 19 age range: by 1964 the equivalent figure was 77,000.

There were parallel changes in the pattern of employment, as the number of women at work and the proportion of white-collar workers both increased dramatically. In 1950, 40 per cent of females of working age (i.e. between 15 and 64) were in employment: by 1965, almost a half (48 per cent) of this female population was at work. There was a similarly striking rise in the number of white-collar workers, from 31 per cent of the labour force in 1951, to 36 per cent in 1961 and continuing to rise steeply thereafter. These expanding opportunities, in a labour force which was itself increasing, have been described by one historian as 'a safety valve for the ambitious . . . giving millions of working-class children the opportunity to ''improve themselves'' and live up to the expectations roused by their better education.'[14]

What these trends also meant (and this too had implications for schooling), was a reinforcement of the general reliance upon towns and urban systems, linked to an ability to commute over quite unprecedented distances. While, as we have seen, the population of the London county area fell between 1951 and 1964, the conurbation outside this county area remained relatively stable in population terms. It was the London 'region' extending up to 50 miles in range and mostly outside the designated Green Belt area, which experienced an increase of over half a million in population, some of it in New Towns and some in old towns and villages which now became commuter suburbs. This part-planned and part-unforeseen development was experienced on a lesser scale in the smaller northern conurbations, but by 1964 was a key characteristic in the English pattern of suburbanisation.

While these changes went relatively unremarked by contemporaries, trends in emigration and immigration were immediately seized on by the media as the harbingers of major social change. Several events coincided to trigger new movements of population in the post-war world. War-time experience of travel, together with a strong sense of solidarity running through the British Empire made the Old Commonwealth an attractive target for increasing numbers of aspirant English. At the same time the 1948 Nationality Act and an acute shortage of labour led some prospective English employers to advertise in the West Indies. The 1952 MacCarran-Walter Act, which effectively ended Jamaican emigration to the USA, marked the start of a significant West Indian immigration into England. At the same time, the resettlement of India after partition created a large displaced Sikh community, which, in common with many adult males in the West Indies, had no significant employment prospects. In combination, these factors meant that during the 1950s there was some balance between immigration and emigration, although this fact did not prevent some elements of the popular press from pointing to a 'brain drain' on the one hand, and a major racial threat on the other. Despite disturbances in Notting Hill in 1958, and evidence of a sustained and steady growth in the rate of immigration, any effective governmental action was postponed until 1962, when the Immigration Act prescribed conditions and limits aimed to stem the flow of immigration. By ensuring that many subsequent arrivals were dependants, this legislation inadvertently ensured that immigration would impinge closely upon schools during the decades that followed: during these early years the vast majority of Commonwealth immigrants were relatively youthful, either at or yet to reach, child-bearing age. During the early 1960s the first educational responses were formulated, and this 'liberal hour' was marked by policies whose object was assimilation. The settlement patterns of these new immigrant communities, forced by economic circumstance and social prejudice to set up home in the least salubrious of the old suburbs, meant that such policies were doomed from the start.[15]

The assimilatory response was pressed both in a series of official policy documents by local authorities up and down the country. At the official level, the mood of the moment was neatly encapsulated by the Second Report of the Commonwealth Immigrants Advisory Council (1964), which stressed that if their parents were brought up in another culture and another tradition, children should be encouraged to respect it, but a national system cannot be expected to perpetuate the different values of immigrant groups.

This Report went on to argue that the number of immigrant children in each class should be restricted lest 'the whole character and ethos of the school is altered'. This view was promoted a few months later by Edward Boyle, who responded to the disquiet of white parents in Southall by telling the Commons in November 1964:

It is desirable on educational grounds that no one school should have more than about 30% of immigrants. . . . I must regretfully tell the house that one school must be regarded now as irretrievably an immigrant school. The important thing . . . is to prevent this happening elsewhere.[16]

Similarly, at the local level, it was usual during these years to interpret immigration as posing a greater demand for remedial teaching of one kind or another. In 1960 Birmingham became the first local authority to appoint a full-time teacher of English to immigrant children and, as the provision within that city quickly expanded during the following decade, it was paralleled by many urban authorities elsewhere. This strategy was given at least semi-official approval by the publication in 1963 of the pamphlet *English for immigrants* which also looked to the schools to promote the assimilation of immigrant pupils.

The Modernisation of the Media

During the 1950s and early 1960s the mass media began to change more quickly than ever before and to take on their modern form. As television grew swiftly in popularity each of the established media responded with changes in their own form and content. These changes impinged on schooling in two ways, directly, by influencing the habits and attitudes of young people, and indirectly by modifying popular perceptions of youth and schooling. In sum, it was possible by 1964 to discern the outlines of an identifiable 'youth culture' in a form in which it had never previously existed.

The traditional medium most threatened by contemporary

developments was probably the cinema. At the height of the post-war boom there were over 4500 cinema houses in Britain: by 1967 there were only 1800. The response of film producers was to modify the messages they were relaying. As one historian has commented, during the early post-war years, 'British film makers . . . like John Reith at the B.B.C., focussed on middle-brow, inoffensive material aimed at the new middle-class suburbs.' [17] During the early 1960s this pulp diet of American musicals, Biblical epics, Westerns and war films was supplemented by a taste for a new social realism as film-makers responded to a collapse of their market by aiming directly at the youths and young adults who increasingly formed the backbone of their audiences. Films such as *A Taste of Honey* (1961), *The Loneliness of the Long Distance Runner* (1962), *This Sporting Life* (1962) and *A Kind of Loving* (1962) all concerned themselves with the problems confronting young people in contemporary Britain.

Popular music underwent similar changes, although the radio remained its most important vehicle. During the 1950s the old-style 'pop', which was deeply under the influence of Hollywood and aimed at an adult audience, gave way to new styles, which, although still apolitical in stance (the songs of protest belonged to the late 1960s) were clearly aimed at the younger audience. So rock and roll, skiffle, traditional jazz and the synthetic confections of performers such as Cliff Richard and Adam Faith (the stars themselves became young during this period) marked the increasing subjugation of popular music to youth. David Thompson summarised it thus:

> Teenagers spent their new-found wealth (the consequences
> of full-employment and the well-paid youthful labour force
> it produced) on long-playing records of 'pop' singers, on
> transistor radio sets, scooters and cosmetics, and created for
> themselves a fantasy world of juke-box delights . . . Cultural
> bulldozers were at work.[18]

There is no doubt that these changes were in part precipitated by the spread of television which drew audiences away from the older media, forcing them to seek a new clientele. Initially, the style and content of television was determined by the commitment to social improvement and didactics of the BBC, the monopoly purveyor. But the inception of commercial television in 1955 began to change this. The new channel, which was chronically underfunded at the outset and seemed during the early months in danger of imminent collapse, was forced to seek out a new television audience among the working classes. This led directly to a contrast in class allegiances between the two channels which was well established by the end of the decade and has never since been entirely dissipated. This contrast has helped, during the intervening period, to sustain, among other things, the differing perceptions of schooling held by different social classes.

The potential of this medium for shaping the attitudes of young people was quickly realised, and in 1954 the Nuffield Foundation was prompted by the BBC's Audience Research Department to fund a research project. The outcome was the publication in 1958 of *Television and the child*, described as 'one of the most comprehensive studies ever done of the effect of any mass medium on children'.[19] Coordinated by Hilda Himmelweit, this study showed an awareness of the Pandora's box being opened by the new medium, even if its tone smacked at times of middle-class condescension:

> the influence of television on the 13–14 year old grammar school children is negligible . . . In general it seems the groups most influenced are children from secondary modern schools, especially those of only average and below average intelligence . . . Television does not reduce differences in outlook resulting from social class.[20]

This was also an era of fierce competition between newspapers, and by the end of the 1950s their control was focused in fewer hands as a succession of dailies (most notably the *News Chronicle*) disappeared from circulation and others changed hands. Increasing affluence led to a boom in the sale of popular magazines: several new publications in this field were targeted at young housewives, the most successful being *Woman's Mirror*, appearing first in 1956. There was a boom too in the market for children's comics, with the magazine *Eagle*, founded in 1950, being perhaps the last fling for middle-class didactics. Although it was the brainchild of a clergyman, and was clearly targeted at young middle-class readers, even this comic was not welcomed without some reservations, as a *TES* editorial indicated.

> There is nothing inherently depraving in a strip cartoon . . .
> Much of what is now set out in this way is vicious, much

more is vulgar. An attempt to produce a comic which is free from these abuses, such as is made in *Eagle* . . . deserves unprejudiced consideration . . . Although *Eagle* has the best intentions, it must also be asked if its effects will not be to prepare its readers for a later addiction to adult strip publications conducted on less worthy principles.[21]

A major fear in this was the influence of American comics on young people, widely available during and after the war, and appearing to some to open up the possibility of exposing young people to new levels of violence.

Much of the impact of these changes was only fully felt during a later period, but it is clear that deep-seated and irreversible changes were taking place which impinged directly upon the consciousness of young people and upon how they were perceived as a social group. Some of these changes were clearly the results of full employment, which enabled the young to find identifying styles of dress and leisure activity. As 'adolescence' became an estate within the body politic during the late 1950s, it is difficult to be sure whether the unprecedented economic power of young people made them the manipulators of the popular media or the manipulated. Certainly no account of the development of popular schooling during these years can neglect the growing interrelationship of youth and the media.

References

1. N. Middleton and S. Weitzman, *A place for everyone: a history of state education from the eighteenth century to the 1970s* (Victor Gollancz, London, 1976), 333.

2. A. Marwick, *Britain in the century of total war* (Pelican, London, 1970), 423.

3. V. Bogdanor and R. Skidelsky (eds), *The age of affluence, 1951–64* (Macmillan, London, 1970), 77.

4. A. Sked and C. Cook, *Post-war Britain: a political history* (Harvester Press, Brighton, 1979), 141.

5. M. Kogan, *The politics of educational change* (University Press, Manchester, 1978), 29.

6. Bogdanor and Skidelsky, *The age of affluence*, 62.

7. Marwick, *Britain*, 385.

8. E. Boyle and A. Crosland, with M. Kogan, *The politics of education* (Penguin, London, 1971), 103.

9. Marwick, *Britain*, 426.

10. *The Times*, 29 December 1962.
11. Bogdanor and Skidelsky, *The age of affluence*, 105.
12. Boyle and Crosland, *The politics*, 29.
13. Marwick, *Britain*, 432.
14. S. Pollard, *The development of the British economy 1914–67*, 2nd edition (Edward Arnold, London, 1969), 501.
15. Runnymede Trust, *Britain's black population* (London, 1960); I. Katznelson, *Black men, white cities* (OUP, Oxford, 1973); N. Deakin *et al.*, *Colour, citizenship, and British Society* (Panther, London, 1970); R.K. Kelsall, *Population* (Longman, London, 1971).
16. Deakin *et al.*, *Colour*, 173.
17. J. Tunstall, *The media in Britain* (Constable, London, 1983).
18. D. Thompson, *England in the twentieth century* (Pelican, London, 1965), 271–2.
19. H.T. Himmelweit *et al.*, *Television and the child* (OUP, Oxford, 1958), vi.
20. Ibid., 259.
21. *TES*, 21 April 1950.

6

Schooling under Stress, 1951–64

The Collapse of Bipartisanship

When I first became interested in politics, during the later years of the war, people were devoting a great deal of thought and effort to the question of how we could eliminate certain social evils in our society — such evils as poverty, squalor and large-scale unemployment. I have never wavered in my belief that the elimination of avoidable unhappiness ought to be one of the prime objectives of government. But we have come to realize more clearly in recent years that there is another more positive aspect . . . and this brings one back to education. We do not just educate children in order to get rid of the scourge of illiteracy, though we ought to remind people that in recent years average standards of reading have in fact risen. What we are concerned with in education is, first and foremost, the development of human personality. Here, as I see it, we have made very great studies in Britain since the war. It is impossible to ignore the very great effect which developments such as the introduction of free movement classes have made upon the post-war generation. I do not believe that this emphasis on individuality is in any way inconsistent with industrial efficiency . . . And surely the best possible motive for working harder is the widespread realisation that the products of hard work will become available in the form of a higher and more varied standard of living.[1]

These words of Sir Edward Boyle, speaking to Devon schoolteahcers in July 1958, encapsulate one face of education during the 1950s and early 1960s. There are certainly grounds for seeing this as an era of unprecedented educational investment and expansion, which enabled progressive ideologies and modern teaching methods to come to the fore. Maurice Kogan has written that

> the period 1945 to 1965 was one of expansion of the economy and of education and of the expectations of both. The thrust forward in education was the result of demographic expansion and of economic expectation, and educational politics were largely consensual in their belief in expectation.[2]

David Eccles and Edward Boyle, who succeeded him in 1962, are often seen as the two Ministers who did most to promote this educational renaissance.

There was, though, another face to the educational politics of this period. At parliamentary level there was in reality a collapse of the bipartisanship which had marked the immediate post-war period; this, together with significant developments in the power of central government, meant that the nature and the effects of this educational expansion were largely determined from the outset.

The intensification of inter-party contest over education can be traced back to July 1948, when Florence Horsburgh suddenly and unexpectedly rounded on Labour with the accusation that the comprehensive school was 'a monster of mass education, with children on the assembly-line'.[3] There were similarly ill-tempered exchanges in the Commons on the question of school meals in April 1951, and again on comprehensive education in July. But it was the appointment of Horsburgh herself to the Ministry of Education in October 1951 which signalled the collapse of a bipartisan approach. Her Circular 242 in December 1951 was intended to save £13 million by cutting back on LEA expenditure: it generated howls of protest. One Labour backbencher commented that the Tory Party 'has always found it easy to sacrifice other people's children'.[4] while the *Times Educational Supplement* observed:

> the first fruit of the Minister's pruning do not taste of hope. Already there are reports of nursery schools to be closed and orders for primary equipment shelved. . . . Might it not be better to raise the age of entering to the primary school? A cut in school life would come more easily at the beginning.[5]

Later, in 1952, when Horsburgh sent a reminder to LEAs of the need to comply with this programme of cuts, the same journal remarked, 'to ask harassed authorities if they have reckoned with circular 242 is like asking the motorist in the ditch if they have had an accident.'[6]

In February 1952, despite the hostility aroused by this first announcement, Circular 245 imposed restrictions on the school building programme, emphasising the competing demands of rearmament. The new mood of inter-party contest which these announcements generated was captured by Stephen Swingler, who told the Commons: 'It has become clear that education has been picked on as the first, and chief victim of the Government's Cold War on the Welfare State.'[7] A censure motion moved by the Labour Party reflected the growing disquiet of the Left with Conservative policy and is further evidence of the breakdown of an educational concensus. Criticism was to come in during the next few years from the Select Committee on Estimates and the Association of Education Committees, whose secretary, W.P. Alexander, called in July 1954 for a further £2 million annually to bring school buildings up to scratch.

Yet throughout the early 1950s the Treasury pressed the Education Ministry in particular to make still greater savings. Horsburgh was approached in October 1952, when, at one interdepartmental meeting, Butler was reported as arguing:

as a matter of general principle it is desirable that a greater proportion of the cost of the social services should be made by direct payments . . . on this principle it would seem reasonable that there should be a fee of 3/- or 5/- a week for all forms of secondary education.[8]

In response, Horsburgh's contingency plans included the possibility of shortening compulsory schooling 'at both ends'. A month later, Butler sent for Horsburgh and asked her 'to be ready to put forward specific proposals for charging fees, e.g. for all secondary school pupils or for all pupils over the statutory age of compulsory attendance'. In December, she was being asked to investigate the possibility of children 'being allowed to leave school at 14 at the option of their parents'.[9] In 1953, Butler returned to the issue, reminding Horsburgh, 'There is no time to lose. We must think in terms of major changes in policy as well as constant pruning.'[10]

During 1954 the Swinton Committee, set up to find ways of saving £100 million, placed the Ministry of Education under similar pressure. Although Horsburgh argued that level funding would in reality mean cuts, since the number of children being educated was rising swiftly, she was also ready to promise 'steps to reduce still further the number of children in schools under the age of 5 . . . I intend to impose restrictions . . . in the interest both of economy and of maintaining decent educational standards for the older children.[11]

By identifying the education of the young as a soft target, Florence Horsburgh was damaging those parts of the education service which might have done most to bring about a fairer distribution of educational resources. It was the social groups whose children stayed on at school and went on to higher education which were most favoured during the 1950s. As David Eccles put it during the 1951 election campaign: 'A Conservative Minister of Education will search for the boys and girls of ability and will so shape the system of education that every one of them has the chance and the schooling to go to the top.'[12]

In October 1954, Eccles succeeded Horsburgh and was quickly subjected to similar pressures by Butler. He told the Chancellor, in the summer of 1955: 'It is impossible to prevent the estimates in my Department from rising with the increase in the school roll and the expansion at the top of secondary schools and in further education, which is government policy.'[13]

Eccles was to prove far stronger than his predecessor in resisting Butler. The correspondence between the two men in the autumn of 1955 was the turning-point, and marks the start of the financial 'break-out' discerned by Brian Simon in his analysis of this period.[14] Butler was at first irritated that Eccles seemed to have countermanded his circular to local authorities demanding cuts in capital expenditure. But by the start of November, Eccles had reduced Butler to the point where he could do no more than advise the Education Minister to make a well-reported speech emphasising 'the importance of not trying to do everything at once'.[15]

The result was that during the late 1950s the government presided over a significant upturn in educational expenditure. But the continuing policy commitment to the identification and promotion of an elite and to the underpinning of economic growth meant that the bulk of this expansion was directed to older school pupils and those in further and higher education. In 1956 a rural reorganisation programme committed £5 million to the ending of all-age schools. Expenditure of £20 million on technical education was announced in response to the White Paper of the same year. In 1958 a £300 million programme was initiated to implement the proposals of the White Paper on *Secondary education for all*, and a further £15 million allocated for the expansion of teacher training.

By September 1959, the Conservative Party was committed to 'a massive enlargement of educational opportunity at every level'. The election manifesto foresaw big increases in training colleges, in the universities ('by at least one third') and in technical colleges. It promised 'to defend the grammar schools against doctrinaire socialist attack' and to 'bring the Modern schools up to the same high standard'.[16] A *Times Educational Supplement* leader observed, not unfairly, that 'anyone writing a history of the Conservative party would mark the years from 1951 as the period in which they became converted to the importance of education.'[17]

During the election campaign Macmillan pledged the abolition of primary school classes of over 40.[18] Labour saw 30 as a realistic target and drew attention to the needs of the handicapped and the state of slum schools.[19] Although both parties were, by this date, being drawn towards the acceptance of increased funding for education, there remained significant differences between them on the best distribution of resources.

The electoral success of the Conservatives ensured that further and higher education continued to receive the lion's share. Before 1964 there were a series of increments to the teacher training programme; the 1960 Albemarle Report on the youth service elicited a £7 million building programme within two years; and the announcement of £3500 million ten-year expansion plan in response to the Robbins Report was in stark contrast to the government's desultory response to *Half our future* which appeared in the same year, a contrast which drew critical comment from the *Times Educational Supplement* before the year was out.[20]

These political developments coincided in time with a series of organisational changes which were seen by contemporaries as relatively uncontroversial, but which, in retrospect, amounted to a significant enhancement of the power of central government to control the educational system. First, the establishment of specialist National Advisory Councils not only gave an air of expertise to Ministry decisions, but made it easier to present policies as emanating from a consensus of the best professional opinion. The National Advisory Council on Education for Industry and Commerce, established in 1948, produced its first report in 1950 and quickly became one of the main determinants of policy in the field of higher technological education, weakening, in the process the control held by the local education authorities in this area. Similarly, the recommendation of the McNair Committee that these should be a Central Training Council to oversee developments was met, first, by the setting-up of an interim committee in February 1947, and then by the establishment of the National Advisory Council on the Training and Supply of Teachers in 1949. This immediately began to concern itself with training and recruitment and quickly became a major influence on governmental policy in the field of teacher training.

Within the Ministry, the key areas of building policy was placed on a new footing during the summer of 1949 when Antony Part and Stirrat Johnson-Marshall were made joint heads of the newly-created Architects and Buildings branch. Its brief was to disseminate new ideas on school design while tackling the problem presented by the fact that LEA building projects varied greatly in cost in different parts of the country. Working through the media of building bulletins and modifications to the 'cost per place' regulations, this department effectively standardised and cheapened school building during the period of greatest expansion.[21] Its defenders have emphasised its role in disseminating 'a new concept of school architecture'.[22] The dangers were sensed immediately by the local authorities: in March 1950, W.P. Alexander, Secretary of the Association of Education Committees, wrote to Johnson-Marshall protesting that the Ministry was taking over the proper functions of the LEA architects.[23] The effectiveness of the Architects' Branch was attested within twelve months when an enquiry by W.H. Pilkington on behalf of the Cabinet Building Committee on Economy cast a critical eye over the new departmental arrangements and concluded that they were 'conducive to economy' and so effective that the approach and methods of the Ministry of Education might well be used as a model by other governmental departments.[24]

Before the period was out there were to be further accretions to the power of central government when in 1958, the Local Government Act eroded the privileged position of local education authorities by obliging them to share in a block grant based in part on an estimate of necessary local educational expenditure made for them at governmental level. Also, the announcement on 9 March 1962 of the Ministry's Curriculum Study Group (soon to be reconstructed as the Schools' Council), fortified the aura of expertise which attended ministerial pronouncements. Finally, in 1964, the subsuming of the UGC under the aegis of a reconstituted Ministry of Education, in accordance with the wishes of the Robbins Committee, marked another enhancement of the powers of the Ministry of

Education. Thus, this period became one, as Maurice Kogan has observed when the Department moved

> from being the holder of the ring between the 'real' forces
> in educational policy making, which had hitherto been the
> local authorities, the denominations, and the teachers and
> parents, to being the enforcer of positive controls, based
> increasingly on knowledge which the Department itself went
> out to get.[25]

The real significance of this development, in the light of the policy emphases outlined above, is that while most contemporaries saw the educational expansion as being 'benign', or bestowing a general good upon society, in reality government was working to heighten social class contrasts in the long term by focusing growth upon those upwardly mobile elements of society who were already to some degree advantaged. And these enhanced powers of the central authority made it possible to achieve this unintended end more effectively than ever before.

Patterns of Growth[26]

The extent to which this heightening of social contrasts occurred can be shown by a brief examination of the pattern of growth actually achieved.

Table 6.1 charts the growth of the student population in all kinds of institution. Between 1951 and 1964 there was an increase of over one million pupils in the primary sector and a similar increase in the numbers in receipt of secondary schooling. The period saw a steady, but not complete, elimination of the all-age schools and spectacular growth in further and higher education with, significantly, the vast majority of recipients of further education being registered as part-time students. The increase in the number of university students did not involve any appreciable amelioration of sex ratios, as female students remained outnumbered by three to one. Perhaps surprisingly, disparities between universities remained constant too, with women having less chance of admission to the more prestigious universities which gave the best chance of access to the major professions. In 1964, Cambridge continued to give only 10 per cent of its undergraduate places to females, Oxford 14 per cent, the large civic universities 25 per cent and the smaller civic universities 35

per cent — a striking coincidence between the popularly perceived status hierarchy of universities and the dominance of
men!

Table 6.1 Student population (in thousands)

	1951	1955	1960	1964
Maintained sector				
Nursery	22	23	22	24
Primary	3133	3964	3934	4203
All age	872	636	267	93
Modern	1127	1234	1638	1641
Grammar	501	528	673	726
Technical	72	87	102	89
Bilateral & multilateral	19	48	38	48
Comprehensive	12	16	128	199
DG Grammar	84	89	109	113
Private sector				
Nursery	0.2	0.3	0.3	0.3
Primary	61	79	89	88
Secondary	60	63	70	76
Primary & secondary	99	117	135	144
Further & higher education				
Full-time FE	53	63	133	152
Part-time day FE	306	402	553	651
Evening FE	1998	1891	1800	1908
Teacher training	22	24	31	61
University	85	82	104	125

Table 6.2 Schools

	1951	1955	1960	1964
Maintained sector				
Nursery	434	434	454	460
Primary	17470	15136	22207	22941
All age	5636	3528	1281	411
Modern	3301	3550	3837	3906
Grammar	1190	1180	1268	1298
Technical	396	302	251	186
Bilateral & multilateral	47	96	57	69
Comprehensive	13	16	130	195
DG Grammar	164	164	178	179
Private sector				
Nursery	8	11	10	9
Primary	603	709	789	774
Secondary	244	249	257	299
Primary & secondary	344	390	433	468

Table 6.3 Teachers

	1951			1955			1960			1964		
	M	F	T	M	F	T	M	F	T	M	F	T
Maintained sector												
Nursery			967	0	982	982	0	963	963	0	921	921
Primary			101,000	30,506	94,873	125,379	31,798	100,763	132,561	34,371	103,013	137,384
All age			31,933	9,013	13,520	22,533	3,570	6,056	9,626	1,307	2,108	3,415
Modern			49,613	30,471	25,412	55,883	38,850	32,856	71,706	44,020	32,743	76,763
Grammar			26,951	15,615	12,908	28,523	20,323	4,959	35,282	23,766	15,909	39,675
Technical			3,889	3,254	1,473	4,727	3,669	1,573	5,242	3,426	1,449	4,875
Bilateral & multilateral			1,056	1,581	936	257	1,073	753	1,826	1,430	1,002	2,432
Comprehensive			596	435	358	793	3,788	2,631	6,419	6,241	3,819	10,060
DG grammar			4,400	2,110	2,630	4,740	2,757	3,025	5,782	3,164	3,103	6,267
Private sector												
Nursery			24	0	32	32	0	31	31	0	22	22
Primary			4,814	2,730	2,869	5,599	3,278	3,037	6,315	3,356	2,934	6,290
Secondary			4,704	3,013	1,859	4,872	3,390	1,937	5,327	3,843	2,206	6,049
Primary & secondary			6,516	2,345	5,053	7,398	2,622	5,626	8,248	3,234	5,784	9,018

The number of schools grew correspondingly (Table 6.2). While 182 new comprehensive schools were opened during this period, it is worth reminding ourselves that this number was far outstripped by the 605 new secondary modern schools and 108 new grammar schools which were also established during these years.

Table 6.3 charts the steady growth of the teaching profession, and emphasises the gender contrasts between the primary sector, where women outnumbered men by three to one, and the secondary schools, where, in the main, there was a much greater balance between the numbers of each sex employed, although, of course, a significant number of these continued to work in single sex schools.

Table 6.4 Teacher-pupil ratios

	1951	1955	1960	1964
Maintained sector				
Nursery	22.75	23.42	22.84	26.05
Primary	31.02	31.61	29.68	30.59
All age	27.30	28.22	27.73	27.23
Modern	22.71	22.08	22.84	21.37
Grammar	18.59	18.51	19.08	18.29
Technical	18.77	18.40	19.46	18.26
Bilateral & multilateral	17.99	19.07	20.81	19.74
Comprehensive	20.13	20.18	19.94	19.78
DG grammar	19.09	18.78	18.85	18.03
Private sector				
Nursery	8.33	9.37	9.68	13.63
Primary	12.67	14.10	14.09	13.99
Secondary	12.76	12.93	13.14	12.56
Primary & secondary	15.19	15.81	16.37	15.97

These three sets of figures, when brought together, enable us to derive the teacher-pupil ratios for different kinds of school (Table 6.4), and the average size of schools. The 1950s and early 1960s did not see a significant amelioration of teacher-pupil ratios, although the stark contrasts between the private sector and the maintained sector, between primary and secondary schools, and between differing kinds of secondary school persisted throughout the period. These contrasts provide evidence of the way in which the middle classes continued at an advantage in respect of the distribution of resources during the post-war expansion. This was a period, too, when schools grew steadily in size, although the average figures given in Table 6.5 suggest the small scale and intimacy of schooling experienced by most children in comparison with the present generation whose schools are, on the whole, significantly larger. These figures indicate also that there was a contrast in size between the new comprehensive schools and all other types of school, a point which was often emphasized in the debate on secondary reorganisation.

Table 6.5 Average sizes of school

	1951	1955	1960	1964
Maintained sector				
Nursery	51	49	48	52
Primary	179	262	177	183
All age	155	180	208	420
Modern	341	347	426	420
Grammar	421	447	530	559
Technical	247	288	406	478
Bilateral & multilateral	404	500	666	696
Comprehensive	923	1000	984	1021
DG grammar	512	543	612	631
Private sector				
Nursery	25	27	30	33
Primary	101	111	113	114
Secondary	246	253	272	254
Primary & secondary	288	300	312	308

Changing patterns of expenditure reflect precisely the perceived priorities of this period (Table 6.6). While expenditure on nursery and primary education grew four-fold, secondary schooling, which in 1951 received less of the educational budget, had by 1964 far outstripped primary schooling, receiving over £100 million more from the state. The twelve times growth in the funding of further education and teacher education, and the increase in governmental funding to universities, from £15 million to £157 million annually, were even more spectacular.

Table 6.6 Expenditure on education (£ thousands)

	1951	1955	1960	1964
Nursery and primary	84,841	127,821	190,321	322,100
Secondary	60,931	93,004	190,409	436,700
Special schools	3,635	6,277	10,651	26,100
FE	15,016	22,374	52,777	185,000
Teacher training	4,142	5,377	11,297	53,900
University	15,000	27,000	58,100	157,000

It is well known that the likelihood of staying on at school was related to the type of school attended, as is shown by the percentages of fifteen year olds who elected not to leave (Table 6.7).

Table 6.7 Percentage remaining at school at age 15

	1953	1956	1959	1962
Modern & all age schools				
Boys	6.1	9.0	14.5	18.4
Girls	6.4	7.9	12.7	16.6
Maintained grammar schools				
Boys	91.5	98.3	98.9	101.2
Girls	82.9	94.8	95.8	97.2
All non-maintained schools				
Boys	85.1	84.8	91.2	81.2
Girls	82.3	82.6	87.1	76.8

These contrasts were far sharper at age 18. The returns for 1959, for example, show only 0.1 per cent of boys in secondary modern and all-age schools staying on to 18, and no significant numbers of girls; while for maintained grammar schools the equivalent figures were 22 and 12 per cent.

Table 6.8 Percentage remaining at school age 15 — regional variations

	1953	1956	1959	1962
Northern	19.8	22.6	26.6	24.2
Yorks (E. & W. Ridings)	24.0	26.4	28.6	29.9
North West	21.8	25.7	30.7	32.7
North Midland	22.7	26.1	29.5	29.9
Midland	21.2	24.7	30.2	33.2
Eastern	26.3	30.6	35.2	38.0
London & Middlesex	37.0	43.7	48.0	52.2
South East	33.7	39.1	45.1	47.7
Southern	29.7	35.1	39.6	43.1
South West	28.5	31.6	35.5	39.5

Less well recognised is the fact that patterns of school leaving varied widely by region (Table 6.8). During this period these regional contrasts sharpened, with children in London and the South-East having twice the chance of their northern contemporaries of staying on by 1964. If we bear in mind that these regional figures conceal significant differences between differing types of suburb, we are forced to conclude that there existed local pockets where the contrasts between extremes were even sharper.

Patterns of school leaving were linked inextricably with life chances and destinations (Table 6.9). These figures show clearly the advantages conferred by independent and direct grant schools in access to university, and they show too the extent to which Colleges of Education remained an escape route for those able grammar school girls who were unable to enter university. These figures, too, conceal significant regional variations, as is illustrated by linking destinations with region of origin (Table 6.10). Interpreted crudely, they show that in 1964 almost one tenth of the males who left school in the South-East went to university or college of advanced technology. At the other extreme, the chance of a female from the North of following the same route were close to 1 in 40. These bleak social contrasts, which could only be heightened by more local studies, suggest the true impact of the expansion of education between 1951 and 1964. Contrasts between regions, and between lifestyles, were intensified. Unwittingly, the bases were being laid for the deep regional antagonisms that were to emerge in the social unrest of the 1980s.

Contrasts in Primary Schooling

For the historian the development of primary schooling during the 1950s and early 1960s presents an enigma. On the one hand, there is clear evidence of a growing acceptance of a progressive ideology and of the introduction of new internal arrangements which militated for a more pupil-centred approach to learning. Equally, it is clear that many contemporaries were concerned that the growing impact of the 11 + examination, blighting teachers' attempts to broaden the curriculum, and of underfunding of the primary sector meant that, although there was a significant expansion at this time, it did not involve a major transformation of primary schooling.

The primary school building programme of the 1950s involved a reduction in the cost of schools and consequently in space per child. The 1945 building regulations were revised in 1951 and 1954, and new detailed cost controls were introduced in 1950. In the process the teaching space available per child fell back from the level of 1945 to that of 1936, and, although building costs in general were rising, cost per place fell from £200 in 1945 to £170 in 1950 and £154 in 1957. The Ministry called for 'exciting spatial arrangements'[27] and claimed that new primary school buildings

Table 6.9 Destinations of school leavers in 1964 (in thousands)

Destination	SM & all age		Grammar		Tech.		Comp.		DG		Independent (efficient)	
	M	F	M	F	M	F	M	F	M	F	M	F
University	0.02	0.01	10.39	5.42	0.33	0.04	0.30	0.21	2.60	1.24	3.66	1.06
CAT	0.01	0.01	1.31	0.27	0.12	—	0.08	—	0.13	0.05	0.15	—
College of Education	0.09	0.12	2.54	8.26	0.22	0.31	0.21	0.40	0.17	1.15	0.14	0.84
Other F/T FE	11.49	14.16	5.78	10.85	0.94	0.48	0.60	0.60	1.26	1.72	3.61	7.19
Temporary/employment[1]	0.30	0.36	1.67	1.50	0.15	0.05	0.09	0.20	0.20	0.18	3.73	3.19
Permanent/employment	194.22	177.87	39.73	34.96	9.16	5.96	20.09	17.74	3.19	2.65	6.50	4.74

[1] i.e. Awaiting entry to HE or FE.

Table 6.10 Destinations by region of origin 1964 (in thousands)

Leavers going to:	North		Yorks E. & W.		N.W.		N. Mids.		Midlands		East		London & Middlesex		S.E.		South		S.W.	
	M	F	M	F	M	F	M	F	M	F	M	F	M	F	M	F	M	F	M	F
Univ. & CAT	1.11	0.52	1.63	0.71	2.86	1.10	1.25	0.46	1.82	0.79	2.13	0.70	2.05	1.03	2.33	1.05	1.31	0.62	1.56	0.71
Coll. of Ed.	0.28	0.93	0.48	1.27	0.50	2.11	0.43	0.99	0.39	1.03	0.20	0.89	0.17	0.89	0.23	0.96	0.13	0.54	0.29	0.67
Other F/T FE	2.16	2.77	1.87	2.82	2.93	4.64	2.54	2.51	2.31	3.50	2.46	4.19	1.51	2.69	2.98	4.86	1.60	2.25	2.77	3.60
Employment	21.48	19.71	27.56	25.29	43.06	38.43	24.12	22.23	32.46	28.95	32.59	29.42	29.89	27.63	26.18	23.97	17.43	15.98	21.60	19.10

were enabling more space to be available for teaching by minimising corridors (and so tacitly accepting that children did not in general move around the school during the day, receiving most lessons from a single teacher) and by encouraging dual use, in particular the exploitation of halls as dining areas.

The response of the local authorities was to meet the demands of overspill housing and of the 'bulge' in the birth rate with more standardised design and prefabricated components. Hertfordshire, under John Newsom, met the needs of its four new towns and two LCC housing estates by building a hundred new schools by 1954 and a hundred more by 1961. The Hertfordshire initiative created ripples in many directions. One of them resulted from the appointment of two Hertfordshire architects, Henry Swain and Dan Lacey (the latter later to become Chief Architect to the Ministry of Education), to Nottinghamshire. Lacey had been in charge of the Hertford primary school development programme during the early 1950s, and now turned his attention to prefabrication as a means of pre-empting the effects of mining subsidence. The Intake Farm Infants School, Mansfield, designed in 1957, was the first model of the 'raft' construction school which became the basis of the Consortium of Local Authorities Special Programme (CLASP) involving 40 members, which designed schools for large parts of the north Midlands. By the mid-1960s eight such consortia were at work, pooling ideas on school design, and, more significantly in our context, standardising the design of new school buildings throughout the country.[28]

Within the Ministry, these developments in primary school design were seen as coinciding with the general adoption of a more progressive approach to teaching. In one account of contemporary trends, published in 1957, the Ministry claimed that

> a great emphasis is now laid on practical activities. Again, teachers wish to break down the class or form unit into several smaller working groups, each following a different aspect of the subject. This variety of subject and approach necessarily calls for new kinds of teaching materials, aids and equipment. . . . We see a school no longer as a mere machine for giving lessons, but as a social unit concerned with the all-round development of boys and girls.[29]

Similarly, two years later, the Ministry's handbook on *Primary education* claimed that 'primary education today is deeply concerned with children as children'.

Such statements were part of a sustained official rhetoric, which emphasised the extent to which the primary sector was responding to the new thinking of the post-war years. Certainly, the design of some of the best-publicised post-war primary schools, such as Amersham (1958) and Finmere (1959), which anticipated the open-plan designs of the following decade would support Malcolm Seaborne's view that

> what was new was the more general acceptance of the ideas of the 1930s, and their actual implementation on a larger scale than before. There is no doubt . . . that group work was much more widely practised in the primary schools of the 1950s and 1960s than before the war.[30]

But even in this area of school design, which provides some of the best evidence for a transformation of the primary schools, there were contemporaries who doubted what was being achieved. Peter Manning, who spent a considerable amount of time researching trends in primary school design for the Pilkington Research Unit, commented in 1967 that 'changes were clearly prompted by economic pressures and the average architect's knowledge of educational theory is rudimentary . . . forms are copied, though the educational reasons for them may not be understood very adequately.'[31] One of Manning's co-researchers pointed out, too, that the hundred or so new primary schools illustrated in the *Architects' Journal* between 1949 and 1961 were hardly representative. The majority were in or around London and many were designed by private architects rather than by the local authority architects who had the responsibility for the vast majority of new schools.[32]

If the post-war building programme resulted in stark contrasts in primary school building stock, there were similar contrasts in the conditions within schools. Throughout the 1950s and into the early 1960s the question of class size remained a thorny problem. Although the Ministry was able to report by 1960 that the average class size in primary schools was 33, there remained many very small rural schools, while at the other extreme there were still 23,000 classes containing over 40 pupils and 188 with over 50. In May 1960, the availability of statistics such as these led the Labour Party to initiate a Parliamentary debate on the crisis in primary schooling, bringing evidence of 46 Shropshire primary schools which were still using earth closets, 51 with chemical toilets, 35 with no piped water and 6 with no artificial lighting. One Labour backbencher observed;

'just as there are two nations in education, so also are there two nations inside the state primary schools: those in the modern buildings and those still in the pre-1900 buildings.'[33]

Many saw the problem of class size as intimately linked to the question of teacher supply, which also remained a problem. Although between 1951 and 1961 the teaching force grew by 27 per cent, while the number of pupils increased by only 21 per cent, the Ministry remained concerned that the majority of these new entrants were female. The official survey of *Education in 1961* showed that the general trend of younger marriage meant that about a half of all female teachers left within five years of the commencement of their careers. Since three out of every four primary school teachers were female during this period (see Table 6.3 above), this was a problem which bore particularly on the primary schools.

One outcome was a widely publicised Ministry campaign, launched in February 1961, to attract married women back into teaching. Its timing reflected also the fact that, with the switch from two-to three-year initial training, there would be no output of newly trained teachers in 1962, and the following twelve months was expected to be a particularly difficult period. So, the tradition, inherited from the Victorian era, that women teachers retired from teaching on marriage to focus on domestic duties died hard in the changing social climate of post-war England. A second result of these problems of teacher supply was that the threat of part-time primary schooling never entirely receded. In April 1951, a Commons debate on overcrowding in primary schools resulted in this leader comment in the *TES*:

> The Chancellor of the Exchequer revealed in his Budget Speech that some curtailment of the school age had been considered. Fortunately it was resisted for it is not yet necessary. But it should now be resolved that if at any time the choice has to be made it is better that children should enter school at five and a half or even six and be properly taught than that they should start at five in schools unfit to receive them.[34]

In May 1963 the same spectre of part-time education from three to seven was raised in the same journal and was perceived as one likely outcome of the persisting teacher shortage.[35]

Another key factor which militated against progressivism of any kind in the primary sector was the debilitating influence of the 11 +

examination. In 1959 Leo Abse used his maiden Commons speech to put in a plea for the primary schools, commenting that 'their whole curriculum is hopelessly distorted because of the 11 + exam'.[36] It was a problem which elicited much press comment during these years and which led to the whole selection process coming under steadily increasing attack. one retired grammar school head teacher (who was himself a defender of selection at 11 +) recounted in a letter to David Eccles (the then Minister) in January 1955 how

> a Lancashire girls Grammar School headmistress was inter-
> viewing her new entrants in September 1953. She asked one
> girl (*inter alia*) what had been her favourite subject at her
> primary school. The prompt reply was, 'Intelligence, Miss'!
> 'And how often did you do Intelligence, dear? asked the head-
> mistress. 'Every day, Miss', was the reply![37]

One direct side-effect of selection was the persistence of streaming in the primary sector, particularly in the larger schools in urban areas within range of the established city grammar schools. it was a practice which came under increasing scrutiny during the early 1960s. First, in December 1961, the NUT turned its attention to this problem, circularising primary schools with a discussion pamphlet setting out the case for and against streaming. By the spring of 1963 the educational press was becoming increasingly wedded to the destreaming movement. In March, the *TES* devoted a section to streaming in primary schools, commenting, 'the ques-tion now is whether streaming is any longer appropriate to the kind of teaching which is best in primary schools.' This article went on to describe 'a grassroots movement away from segregating children . . . a movement to break the grip which the academic requirements of secondary schools have on the curriculum, to turn instead to the methods used in infants' schools for inspiration.'[38]

This was an area in which it was possible to throw the weight of much recent research behind the destreaming movement, and Brian Jackson was one commentator who drew attention to the work of Yates and Pidgeon, W. Rudd, J.C. Daniels, C.J. Willig and A.B. Clegg, all of whom produced findings which threw doubt on the advisability of streaming.[39] So, by the early 1960s, 'expertise' was being brought to bear as never before on the problems immed-iately confronting the primary schools. At the same time, the educational journals were beginning to publicise the organisational arrangements which offered alternatives to streaming. It is no coincidence that the spring of 1963 saw the appearance of articles describing the adoption of family grouping in some infant schools, and of open plan arrangements in the new primary schools at Radcliffe and Balderton in Nottinghamshire.[40]

By the summer of 1963 there were clear signs of a response at central government level to this mood of progressivism in the primary sector. The NFER initiated a five-year enquiry into streaming and its effects, while Edward Boyle, having mooted the idea the previous autumn, announced the setting up of the Plowden Committee to undertake a comprehensive review of primary education, including streaming in its brief.

As ever, there were those who feared too much of a good thing. A *TES* leader in October 1963 reflected a residual scepticism about the prospects for primary schools, and reminded its readers that the threat of part-time schooling remained a real one:

> Once the school was a place of instruction. Now it is also a service point for the welfare state. How far are the two functions compatible! . . . A cynic might sometimes suppose that a primary school is judged nowadays not by how far its pupils can read but by how far the place is awash with paint.[41]

Such reservations were to be submerged by the end of the decade. But they remained beneath the surface and have returned to view more recently. They help explain why the progressive ideologies to which the primary schools were increasingly exposed during the 1960s did not lead to the complete rejection of earlier practices during the expansion of the 1950s.

The Expansion of Secondary Education

Although much has been written about attempts to dismantle the selective system, the 1950s and early 1960s were in reality the heyday of the grammar schools and the secondary modern schools. The number of grammar school pupils rose from half a million to 726,000, and the number of secondary modern pupils from 1,127,000 to 1,641,000. One hundred and eight new grammar schools were added to the 1190 already in existence, while 605 new secondary moderns were opened.[42] Many of the pupils were themselves first-generation recipients of secondary schooling (even in the grammar schools) and this fact helps explain the conservatism of these schools, in matters of curriculum and lifestyle. The grammar schools, particularly, saw themselves as suddenly acquiring a new clientele, and their response was to emphasise their traditional function and their long-term contribution to national life. Their task was perceived by many within them as conditioning the permanently changed student body to this task. For the secondary moderns, newly emerging from the elementary sector, the challenge to establish their worth was met by a conscious imitation of the grammar schools, despite a deal of rhetoric which proclaimed their distinctiveness.

In any account of secondary schooling during this period it is easiest to begin with the grammar schools (even though this ordering leaves one open to the charge of elitism), since so much else in the secondary sector was either derivative from or in response to their established pre-eminence. The mood of the moment in the grammar schools was neatly encapsulated in January 1952 by Frances Stevens, an educationalist, in a letter to the *TES*. She wrote:

> The last five years have caused in the grammar schools a major change. For the first time . . . many children whose parents wish them to attend grammar schools cannot do so because of their failure to pass the qualifying examination, while others whose parents have little regard for higher education find themselves in these schools. . . . The average level of intelligence may be a shade higher, but this is more than counterbalanced by the fact that the staff of a grammar school can no longer count on the strong . . . desire of both parents and children for something which their school had to give: perhaps it was partly a regard for scholarship, partly a concern for the establishment of certain patterns of behaviour and ethical standards, and partly, let us admit, a sense of middle-class superiority . . . In the old ethos of the grammar school was something worth preserving . . . with patience and skill a way can be found of transmitting it to these new 'first generation' pupils.[43]

One major problem confronting the grammar schools and their apologists was that their distribution was irregular: in Westmorland in the mid-1950s the grammar schools offered 42 per cent of the secondary school places available, while, at the other extreme, in

Gateshead, the figure was 9 per cent. Worse, there were disparities within single authorities. Alex Clegg estimated in 1953 that the figures for different parts of the West Riding varied between 15 and 40 per cent, while in Kent the proportions of grammar school places ranged from 12 to 33 per cent in different parts of the county.[44] In some cities, such as Birmingham, there were almost twice as many 'selective' places available for boys as for girls. There was also a widespread contemporary belief that the academic standards of urban grammar schools were moving ahead of those of equivalent rural schools. L.S.A. Jones, the headmaster of Burford Grammar School, undertook a survey of small rural grammar schools for the Oxford University Education Department in the early 1950s and concluded:

> social and economic changes have tended to remove the intelligentsia among pupils of these schools, especially those maintained by local authorities. Children of the professional and managerial classes are more often sent to independent than to local grammar schools and migration to urban areas has lost for country districts many of their most enterprising inhabitants.[45]

There were contrasts within the cities too. One investigation into secondary school selection in 1958 showed that children in the middle-class outer wards of Birmingham were five times as likely as pupils from inner-ring areas to gain a grammar school place.[46] These contrasts were quickly perceived and exploited by the opponents of 11 + selection. Within the Ministry of Education there was some concern on this issue, and David Eccles's announcement to the NUT in 1955 that in future LEAs would be expected to allocate between 15 and 25 per cent for grammar school places[47] was part of an official attempt to round off the rougher edges of grammar school provision.

There is no doubt too that the selective sector remained largely the enclave of the middle classes, as was pointed out by P.E. Vernon in 1957:

> so far from there being . . . 'parity of esteem' between different types of secondary school, there is a strongly established hierarchy, corresponding closely to the hierarchy of social classes. Despite the greater social mobility of post-war years, most professional and upper-business class parents . . .

feel that they are losing face if they cannot afford to send their sons to Headmasters Conference Schools. The rest of the upper middle-class families similarly prefer one of the direct grant or older grammar schools to the state grammar schools. To them and to the lower middle classes the failure of their children to achieve a place in any grammar school tends to be regarded as a social disgrace.[48]

Similar conclusions were reached in the same year by Halsey, Floud and Martin in their influential reader on *Social class and educational opportunity*.

The grammar schools continued to be staffed in the main during these years by graduates. One of the most prestigious, Manchester Grammar School, had a staff of over 80, two-thirds of whom were graduates of Oxford or Cambridge.[49] Oxbridge alumni remained the dominant element in most of the direct grant grammar school staffrooms. At Manchester only the physical education and manual training departments were staffed by non-graduates. At Watford Grammar School the staff were described as 'usually graduates of a British university who have taken an honours degree in the subject they now teach'.[50] For these grammar school teachers, the concept of 'parity of esteem' offered a real threat. As one *TES* leader put it, arguing for a greater freedom for the grammar schools in negotiating staff salaries:

> The spirit of 1944 has bad as well as god things to answer for. One of the bad was the thought that secondary education was the same all through, or ought to be. This principle reflected itself in policy towards maintained grammar school salaries and administration. Such policy has made service in grammar schools relatively less attractive. To some this will not matter: for them it can mean only that the modern school has come up the ladder. But things are not as easy as that. A weakening of the grammar school spreads to every other sort of school, the universities and every part of the national life.[51]

Against this background, it is hardly surprising that there was little or no curricular change in these schools during the period under review. As the senior history master of one country grammar school observed in the mid-1960s:

The actual content of the basic curriculum in the school has probably altered little in the last forty years . . . . The situation is dominated by the ever-present external examination system, wherein teachers are examined as well as pupils, and this limits flexibility and experiment to a certain extent. We are a long way from the child-centred education. . . . The nature of grammar school work, based as it is on the need to provide its pupils with a piece of paper on which arbitrary examination successes are neatly presented to a future employer, is essentially conservative in curriculum and teaching techniques.[52]

Similarly at Watford Grammar School, one member of staff described how

we put them through a pretty rigorous course following the traditional dual road of the sciences and the humanities. After five years they begin to specialize, some in sciences, some in history or languages, others in classics. . . . Academic work is the real basis of life in the grammar school and here we are quite uncompromising in setting the very highest standards of accuracy.[53]

The changed intake to these grammar schools, drawn from a wider social catchment, was seen to strengthen the need for this traditionalism rather than to lead to any major reconsideration of curriculum or teaching method.

With the coming of affluence and the greater availability of national and international travel, a new industry developed during the 1950s. By the middle of the decade a growing number of advertisements were appearing in the educational press for school holidays abroad — eight days in Paris for £13—14—0*d*, a winter sports holiday in Switzerland for £22—5—0*d* per pupil (both on offer in 1955).[54] It was the grammar schools which made the most use of these and similar opportunities, and their commitment to 'an immense variety of sport, clubs and other activities during the lunch hour, after school, at the weekend, and during the school holidays'[55] distinguished them from the secondary modern schools in which it was generally more difficult to establish and sustain such activities. By introducing their pupils to new leisure pursuits, and by permanently widening horizons, the grammar schools were able through their extra-curricular activities to provide what was, in effect, a social-class conditioning: it became an aspect of their work every bit as significant as the formal curriculum. Indeed, the very nature of the pursuits on offer was a token of a school's standing within the hierarchy of grammar schools. Most of the more prestigious direct grant schools for boys had a combined cadet force, imitative of the major public schools, and offering military training to some pupils.

Given their traditionalism and their continuing commitment to a particular lifestyle, it is hardly surprising that the grammar schools found difficulty in holding on to many of their first-generation pupils. As the 1950s progressed, the problem of early leaving loomed increasingly large for these schools. In January 1952 one grammar school headmaster was arguing publicly for fees to be charged of the lowest 25 per cent of the selective intake to deter those who might leave early:[56] a year later the Cumberland authority attempted to impose a fine of £10 on the parents of a girl who left Cockermouth Grammar School early to become a hairdresser.[57] The fact that isolated instances such as these were only the tip of an iceberg became evident when the CAS report on *Early leaving*[58] showed that at least 4200 pupils who were capable of pursuing advanced courses were leaving the grammar schools early. Although the *TES* thought this 'a terrible prodigality', an editorial went on to argue that 'important bodies like the trade unions should be glad that some able boys at least drop off the academic ladder halfway and so are not lost to their class, which one day will need their leadership.'[59]

A succession of sociological reports brought home the fact that it was the new recruits to the grammar schools from working-class origins who were at greatest risk of not completing even a five-year course. Floud, Halsey and Martin, J.W.B. Douglas and Jackson and Marsden all produced complementary analyses.[60] As Jackson and Marsden concluded, 'despite our formal legislation grammar schools remain 'closed' to society at large, in subtle but very firm ways which have as much to do with social class as with ability.'[61] It was a problem with which the grammar schools could never fully get to grips, and its increasing exposure strengthened the arm of those who were advocating the complete dismantling of a selective system of schooling.

The early leaving problem was of far less concern to the direct grant schools, the best known of which operated as regional 'super' grammar schools, attracting able middle-class pupils from a wide area. They bridged the gap between the state selective schools and the public schools: for them the 1950s were a golden era. After the

1944 Act the number of schools on the direct grant list was reduced from 235 to 164. In December 1956 David Eccles announced the intention to readmit a small number of schools, and their total went up to 179. The increase marked the determination of the government to secure the future of these schools, which by 1964 were educating 113,000 pupils, one-sixth of the number in the maintained grammar schools. At this time the direct grant schools provided 15 per cent of all school leavers aiming at university. They were allowed to charge fees, but were obliged to offer at least 25 per cent of their places without charge.[62] At some schools, such as Manchester Grammar School, subventions from the local education authority allowed up to a half of the pupils to receive a free education.[63] This enabled these schools to claim that they were genuinely meritocratic, although a survey carried out by the sociological society of Bristol Grammar School in the early 1960s showed a strong bias in that school towards the sons of professional, managerial and white-collar workers, and this was probably fairly typical of the direct grant sector as a whole.[64] Almost all of the boys' direct grant schools had third-year sixth forms by the early 1960s, compared with two-thirds of the maintained grammar schools, and this enabled the best known of them to win a large number of places at Oxbridge. Between 1956 and 1961 pupils from five schools (Manchester G.S., Winchester, Dulwich, St Pauls and Bradford G.S.) gained 714 places at Oxford and Cambridge.[65] It is notable that four of these were day schools, two (Manchester and Bradford) were on the direct grant list, and two more (Dulwich and St Pauls) had many of the 'super grammar school' characteristics of the direct grant sector. Although independent, they drew from a large, densely populated area, and at Dulwich in particular, a number of pupils were funded by the LEA. In our context, the strength of this direct grant sector during the 1950s and early 1960s has two major implications. It confirms the existence of a status hierarchy within the selective sector which was clearly related in a variety of ways to wider social stratifications; and secondly, the existence of these powerful and favoured elite grammar schools was to impinge directly on the progress of comprehensive reorganisation, both by providing arguments for the defenders of selection and by ensuring in almost every town and city that there was at least one selective school whose special position made it strong enough to hold out against comprehensive reorganisation which took place around it.

It is clear that, by the early 1960s, the continuing success of the grammar school sector meant that the parity of esteem promised in the aftermath of the 1944 Act was a dead letter. Professor R.K. Kelsall surveyed the Ministry's *Statistics of education* for 1961 and commented gloomily:

> In the last decade there has been an important overall improvement in the success of pupils at maintained grammar schools in England, when success is measured in terms of GCE passes . . . . Much less encouraging is that the social class gradient, if not always quite as steep as it used to be, is still very much to be reckoned with. The chances of working class children realizing their higher education potential are still very much worse than those of children from families higher in the social scale . . . . The English maintained grammar school is apparently not markedly more successful as a social melting pot than it used to be.[66]

Yet, despite this growing awareness of the failure of the selective sector to seek out and nurture working-class pupils in significant numbers, there remained strong and influential voices behind the grammar schools. When, in 1960, the Incorporated Association of Headmasters published a survey of the changing role and clientele of the grammar schools, a *TES* leader expostulated:

> More damaging to the grammar school is the apologetic air that pervades the document. It is as if these headmasters were half-ashamed of the traditional, currently unpopular features of the grammar school — strong study of a subject, intellectual vigour and the like . . . . Nothing that they say dispels the nagging suspicion that these unrewarding and unrewarded pupils might be better off in a comprehensive school. A document on the grammar school should surely do better than that.[67]

As we move on to examine the movements for reform and reorganisation during this period it is important to remember the continuing existence of a strong lobby for an elite sector committed to what was perceived as the maintenance of standards and the perpetuation of the best. For this lobby the grammar schools still had a vital part to play in the English educational system.

By contrast, it proved no easier during the 1950s than it had during the late 1940s to establish the secondary technical school.

In June 1954, a *TES* leader commented: 'Hardly more than 79,000 are in the technical schools. The figure is far too low.'[68] This was part of a sustained campaign by that newspaper to promote the one sector in a tripartite system of secondary schools which was failing to materialise.

The problem was immediately identified by David Eccles, on his arrival at the Ministry of Education, as one which was central to his government's strategy. In a long memorandum to Toby Weaver he confessed:

> I do not have a clear idea of the importance of these schools
> . . . The proportion of 5% of all secondary school children
> is so low that it shows this to be a national problem . . . .
> A good many children from homes poor in letters or in morals
> might find it easier to take GCE and go to a university via
> a technical school rather than via the grammar school. 11 +
> is early to show your paces if you come from a dumb or bad
> home. But you may have some practical abilities. This is one
> reason why technical schools attract me.
>
> There is another more profound. We have to triumph over
> the opposition between the technical society, which we cannot
> escape, and the human personality, which is the most valuable
> thing we know . . . we must find a way to interpenetrate a
> technical society with the humanities. I wonder whether this
> is not best done by accepting the technical revolution, put-
> ting its needs in the front window and allying them to a general
> education. We must both catch up with our century and
> preserve our Christian tradition.[69]

Toby Weaver's reply was equally revealing of attitudes within the Ministry towards secondary schooling. He stressed the need for different levels of training:

> The world of work may be crudely analysed, for the purposes
> of this discussion, into jobs at three levels, which are reflected
> in secondary school courses and organisation:
> i. Major professional and administrative jobs, for which a
> university degree or its equivalent is the normal qualification,
> which require in turn advanced courses up to the age of 18 at
> secondary school: I shall use the term 'fliers' to denote boys
> and girls who show at 11 + or subsequently that they are likely
> to achieve this level of educational and employment career;

ii. Minor professional and executive jobs (e.g. physiotherapist, production manager) for which a group of GCE passes at matriculation level or equivalent is the normal qualification, and which require in turn 'O' level courses up to the age of 16 + at secondary school: I shall call these people 'hurdlers', i.e. children who show at 11 + or subsequently that they can take a basic 5 year course in their stride;

iii. Clerical, craft, semi-skilled and unskilled jobs which require no prior paper qualification before entry into employment. These children will receive a four year course and the majority will leave school at 15 — though many children will obtain some qualification by part-time study. I shall call these people 'pedestrians'.

Weaver went on, against this background, to proffer his view that the secondary technical school should be

a selective school which is in no way inferior to the grammar school in quality of staff and buildings, age of recruitment, freedom to attract children of the highest intelligence, intellectual demands, standards of work, including capacity to prepare for GCE and advanced level courses, and the breadth of its vision and humanity.[70]

Weaver was offering a bleak but not inaccurate analysis of the underlying trends in secondary schooling during the mid-1950s. Not only was the distinction between different types of school being seen as increasingly hierarchical in nature, but those few separate technical schools which had been opened were more and more viewed as part of the selective sector, in reality functioning as low prestige grammar schools. By the mid-1950s there were more than 300 technical schools at work: within a decade almost half of these had disappeared, either resurrected as grammar schools (like the Doncaster Technical High School), or metamorphosed in schemes of comprehensive reorganisation.

The death knell was in fact sounded by David Eccles when, in May 1955, he announced in a talk to the NUT that only in exceptional cases would new technical schools be allowed, adding that he hoped 'the general policy will be to distribute technical courses over as many schools as possible'.[71]

Policy on the secondary technical school remained confused during the next few years, as pressure mounted from various quarters for the regeneration of technical education. The 1956 White Paper referred to 'the secondary technical school of tomorrow',[72] although it did not spell out precisely what form it might take. In March 1957, Lord Hailsham, during his brief tenure of the education office, told a gathering of head teachers of secondary technical schools that he saw 'a new future' for them, on a parity with grammar schools.[73] The lack of a clear lead from central government, allied to the pressure of a society which looked for a clear distinction between passes and failures at 11 + , meant that during these years the technical schools lost their way. By the early 1960s, David Eccles, during his second spell at the Ministry, had fallen back on a policy of deferring to local authorities on this issue. He told the Commons: 'I agree about the importance of technical education, but many local authorities prefer to give this in secondary modern rather than secondary technical schools. I would rather leave them that freedom of choice.'[74] Two years later, in 1963, one head of a technical school was complaining publicly that there was no longer any difference in syllabus between grammar and technical schools.[75] She was right: in less than twenty years the view which had underpinned the 1944 Education Act, that three types of mind needed three different kinds of secondary school, had become a dead letter.

But, for the majority of secondary school children the secondary modern school remained a reality between 1951 and 1964. The coming of affluence resulted in steadily increasing educational expectations for a growing number of people. During the 1950s the secondary moderns discovered that unprecedented numbers chose to stay on beyond the minimum leaving age, and that many of these pupils were anxious to enter for external examinations. Hardly surprisingly, these aspirations were strongest in the new and growing lower middle-class suburbs, so this sector, too, experienced a heightening of contrasts during this period.

Differing strategies were adopted to cater for these increasing aspirations in different parts of the country. In many areas the response was the establishment of small groups of fourth and fifth year pupils in secondary moderns working towards a few subjects in the new GCE examination. This practice distorted the staffing pattern in many schools and made it harder to reduce the size of classes lower down the school: in this way important contrasts between the opportunities made available to pupils developed also within individual schools. Elsewhere, specialism was thought to be more appropriate. From 1949 Southampton ran a scheme by which each of its 16 secondary modern schools was allocated one special course: seamanship, craftsmanship and secretaryship were included in the specialisms, and pupils were given the chance to opt either for one of these special streams, or for a course with no vocational bias.[76] In East Sussex, by the early 1960s, there was a formal scheme through which any secondary modern pupil with four or more 'O' level passes could transfer to the local grammar school. In Staffordshire and Derbyshire selected fifth form pupils from secondary moderns were sent on 'day-release' courses to their local technical colleges for vocational training.[77]

There was, too, a growing variety of examination routes for the more successful pupils in the secondary moderns, particularly during the early 1950s when it was not clear precisely how the secondary modern sector might develop. Many schools introduced their own leavers' certificates for the more successful pupils. In 1953 the Birmingham LEA devised a series of five-year courses for second-ary modern pupils, each vocationally oriented, leading to RSA qualifications. Elsewhere, the Pitman's typing and shorthand exams were used by some secondary moderns, and in 1954 the *TES* reported that over 700 secondary moderns had already approached the College of Preceptors to investige the suitability of its examina-tions for their pupils.[78] A year later the plan announced by the College for a 15 + examination for secondary modern pupils was attacked by one head teacher as 'an earlier inferior exam' which would widen the rift between the grammar and modern sectors.[79]

By the end of the decade, though, it was the new GCE examina-tions which were being seen, increasingly, as the criterion by which the success of the secondary moderns was to be judged. By 1960 nearly 22,000 secondary modern pupils were entering annually for GCE, and while 5000 of these passed in no subjects, over 2000 gained five or more 'O' levels. These figures enabled David Eccles to reassure the Commons that 'the advance made by secondary modern schools is very remarkable'.[80]

The response to these developments was a growing tide of opi-nion that, if the secondary moderns were to succeed in the long run, they needed their own nationally validated and recognised examination alongside the GCE. This was an argument pressed by the *TES* as early as 1952 and voiced repeatedly during the 1950s.

> The secondary modern, sooner or later, will have to dig down beneath the G.C.E. to find incentives for the general run of its pupils. What is wanted is some modest but accredited

standard that the ordinary pupil, if he works, can reach[81]

argued a leader article in 1954. As another correspondent put it:

> the object should be to put an end to the present soul-sapping
> attempt to turn modern schools (or the modern school stream
> in the comprehensive school) into an inferior edition of the
> grammar school and to give them something of educational
> value in their own right.[82]

This view, that ways must be found to prevent secondary moderns
from turning into the poor relations of the grammar schools, was
to be heard increasingly, and it had supporters both within the
Ministry and outside. In particular the 1958 White Paper, *Secondary
education for all: a new drive*, foresaw a big increase in senior courses
in the secondary moderns which 'must be enabled to be good in
their own ways'. Presenting this White Paper to the Commons,
Geoffrey Lloyd (the then Minister of Education) forecast enthusi-
astically that there would soon be over 1000 modern schools offering
GCE courses, adding that 'one of the main objects of the White
Paper was to bring about a massive voluntary raising of the school-
leaving age'.[83] The *TES* commented that at the heart of the
government's programme was 'a new deal for the secondary modern
schools',[84] which could resuscitate them from the inferior position
into which they had fallen since the war. From the Labour side
though, this was seen as a desperate attempt to engineer an increase
in the numbers staying on at school on the cheap. Ted Short dismissed the White Paper as 'a vicious little document, intended to
shore up a collapsing system and to frighten off any local authority
which has the flexibility to trying anything new'.[85]

As early as 1953, H.C. Dent had observed that 'the secondary
modern school is breaking up into a number of different types of
schools', adding that in the urban areas it was easier to tempt pupils
to stay on for GCE work and easier to set up specialised and
advanced courses.[86] By the early 1960s the contrasts were clear for
all to see. In the new and growing middle-class suburbs some spectacular successes were recorded. F.C. Willmott, head of the Sarah
Robinson Secondary Modern School in Crawley New Town,
reported his school's success in getting non-examinees to complete
a fifth year on vocationally-oriented courses. One Croydon head
teacher wrote:

Many parents in the area value education in school for its own sake. I knew that most of my children would come from homes where the family income was above the average, with all the accompanying cultural and social amenities. I knew, too, that I had to deal with the sense of shock and deprivation at 11 + failure and rehabilitate the children of ambitious parents.[87]

The *TES* reported that 'in some parts of the country a secondary modern school without a fifth form will soon be the odd man out. . . . We have not needed a Beloe to help us.'[88]

But elsewhere the picture was bleak by comparison. In 1956 a PEP report on *Secondary modern schools* confirmed that there were wide variations around the country, many having large classes and those in the old suburbs usually being accommodated in outdated and under-resourced buildings. Similarly, in 1963, a report compiled by Mark Abrams for the NUT on *The state of our schools* emphasised that, by the Ministry's own standards, two-thirds of the secondary modern schools were overcrowded, over half lacked specialists for work with backward children, 45 per cent lacked any dining room, and only a minority had adequate library or science facilities. In the same year, the Newsom Report highlighted 'the contrasts which exist between school and school. . . . The most striking thing . . . is the way in which individual schools differ.'[89] It is hardly surprising that, when the Newsom Report was debated in the House of Lords, Baroness Wootton dismissed the secondary modern schools as 'the dump which took the leavings'.[90]

The growing public awareness of these contrasts and problems in the less prestigious parts of the secondary sector was pregnant with significances for policy-makers. On the one hand, there was a continuing problem of teacher supply, as it became clear that the Burnham scale militated against secondary modern teachers, who, in the view of one commentator 'will feel not only underpaid but undervalued'.[91] This problem was also emphasised by William Taylor in his major survey of the secondary modern school[92] and by the Newsom Report, which drew attention to the high turnover of staff in some of the more difficult schools. This report also had something to say about the secondary moderns in the slum areas, and it is in these passages that we can discern the emergence of new emphases in educational policy:

Schools in slums do require special consideration if they are to have a fair chance of making the best of their pupils. They seem to us to need a specially favourable staffing ratio. . . . There is another aspect to the staffing ratio which also overlaps strictly education boundaries. There is no doubt at all about the need for a good deal of social work in connection with the pupils. Problems of poverty, health and delinquency are involved . . . The fact that 79% of the secondary schools in slums were seriously inadequate points to the need for a bold rebuilding policy.[93]

So, it is possible to discern various implications from the development of the modern sector of secondary schooling during this period. First, it is clear that the government of the day remained committed to the secondary modern until the early 1960s, and was increasingly ready to justify them with reference to the criteria usually applied to the grammar schools — numbers staying on and GCE successes. Secondly, it is evident too that the secondary modern sector became increasingly stratified, and in this respect reflected the growing divisions of urban and suburban society. The growing awareness of this stratification was seen to have policy implications, and the drive to increase the numbers training to teach as well as the continuing commitment to school building during the late 1960s both derived in part from the needs of the secondary moderns. Indeed, it can be argued with some justification that one of the roots of the policies of positive discrimination lay in the determination of government during the 1950s and early 1960s to make the secondary moderns work.

The Private Sector

Meanwhile, the public schools retained their privileged position despite a good deal of rhetoric which suggested that they would be subjected to a programme of reform, and some steps to bring them under closer governmental control. It was announced in July 1954 that part three of the 1944 Act, requiring the registration and inspection of independent schools, would come in to effect in 1957.[94] A public relations campaign was initiated by the Ministry to reassure the public schools, and in September 1955 Sir Martin Roseveare, Senior Chief HMI, explained to a conference of the Independent Schools Association what inspection would mean for them.[95] Implementation in October 1957 in reality strengthened the private sector, by enabling the weeding-out of some of the weaker and less prestigious schools and by formally legitimating the major public schools, which could now claim recognised status. The fact that this sector was entirely answerable to central government made it impossible for local education authorities to exercise any leverage over the private schools in their areas in any reorganisation schemes. So, the closer integration of independent schools and state schools foreseen by the Fleming Report was made even less likely by this development.

It is possible to discern an increasing identity of views between the two major parties on the public schools issue during these years. The appearance in 1957 of a Bow Group pamphlet, *Whose public schools?*, chimed with the views of Michael Stewart, a Labour Party spokesman on education, in advocating that the fee-paying element in the public schools should be progressively reduced to a half. It was a consensus opposed only by the far left. In the same year the *Socialist Quarterly* argued that any scheme based on the Fleming proposals could only result in public subsidies being awarded to the privileged.[96] Antony Crosland's influential book, *The future of socialism* (1956), promoted educational reform as one of the possible alternatives to nationalisation in future Labour Party policy. He vilified the public schools as

> the strongest remaining bastion of class privilege . . . a system of superior private schools, open to the wealthier classes, but out of reach of poorer children, however talented and deserving . . . I have never been able to understand why socialists have been so obsessed with the question of the grammar schools, and so indifferent to the much more glaring injustice of the independent schools.[97]

Crosland's views were increasingly echoed within the Conservative Party. In a Commons debate in 1961, Sir David Eccles, as Minister of Education, emphasised that 'a small minority of children coming from more or less the same kind of homes and receiving an exceptional kind of education is bad for our society'.[98] His Conservative colleague, Geoffrey Johnson-Smith, referred more pointedly to

> a kind of educational apartheid based on the financial ability of a number of individuals wealthy enough to segregate their children from the major part of the education system. It is

this educational apartheid, this . . . separateness, which has
. . . largely contributed to the remarkable class conscious
atmosphere which still pervades our society.[99]

Into the early 1960s publicity continued to be given to the small
number of cases where 'Fleming' schemes appeared to be working.
Mill Hill was one such school frequently cited for its arrangement
with the Middlesex LEA by which 20 per cent of its pupils were
11 + successes.[100] Another such was Rencomb College, whose
headmaster, A.O.H. Quick, claimed in 1963 that half of his pupils
were sponsored by the Gloucester authority.[101] It proved more difficult for the local authorities to forge effective links with the
boarding schools, although by the early 1960s the Hertfordshire
LEA was annually taking up two places at Eton, two at Winchester
and two at Rugby. At the same time, two public schools, Lancing
and The Leys, were running trial schemes for the admission of 13
year olds who seemed to have been wrongly allocated to secondary
moderns at 11 + .[102] However, in response to proposals from the
Governing Bodies Association and the Headmasters' Conference
that schemes such as these should be funded more systematically,
David Eccles concluded in the Commons that he could see 'no
reason to use public money to subsidize the transfer of boys from
one system to another'.[103] It was an inertia which protected the
private schools and the social groups which benefited most from
them. The failure to hammer out effective reform policies proved
to be of more importance during these years than the succession
of public pronouncements that ways should be found to bring the
public and private sectors into a closer relationship.

So, in reality, the public schools were able to confirm the life-
chances of pupils of varying abilities, but drawn almost exclusively
from financially and socially advantaged backgrounds. One research
study published in 1963 by P.L. Masters and S.W. Hockey confirmed that, as in the past, the public schools succeeded in gaining
places in higher education for young people who would not have
won grammar school places. They found that 'the conclusion is
inescapable that the public schools do contain a high proportion
of genuine 11 + failures', adding that their work served merely to
'reinforce the findings already to hand from secondary modern and
comprehensive schools that there are considerable "reserves of
ability" in this country'.[104]

There was, though, one very significant way in which the public
schools responded to the changing social and economic situation

of the country during this period. Although they continued to recruit from the social groups which they had served throughout the twentieth century, there were significant changes in job opportunities to which they could hardly fail to respond. The end of Empire meant a dramatic decline in the chances of employment abroad. Although the Civil Service in general continued to grow, and the public schools retained a firm grip on recruitment, especially to the Foreign Office, the Colonial Service disappeared as a major employer of the old boys of public schools. At the same time the business community made a major attempt to promote industry as a career route for public school alumni. In 1955, on the suggestion of the headmaster of Monkton Combe, the Industrial Fund for the Advancement of Scientific Education in the Schools was set up. Within two years 141 industries had allocated over £2 million for the provision of science teaching facilities in public schools. The Public Schools Appointments Bureau responded to this initiative with a number of conferences funded by industry. These developments had, as Ian Weinberg pointed out at the time, 'a major impact both in the public schools and in the direct grant grammar schools'. Not only were more public schoolboys studying science at sixth form level, but, Weinberg reported:

> the public schoolboys who do not go to university, and who a generation ago would have gone into the city or out to the colonies, seem to be going into business. This is an important and dramatic shift. . . . Traditional occupations such as the civil service and the Church are now recruiting many grammar school boys. The public schoolboys seem to be moving to greener pastures and the grammar schoolboys to be moving to the spaces they create . . . If it is a secular trend in Britain that businessmen are becoming more central, then it does not seem that public schoolboys will be left out in the cold.[105]

Weinberg identified precisely an important contemporary trend. One of the sources of the rise of a set of 'business values' which were to dominate political discourse during the 1980s was the subtly changing orientation of the private sector during the 1950s and 1960s.

What was unchanging about the private sector was the ethos which these schools set out to generate. For those within the schools, closer links with industry and commerce reinforced rather than weakened the demand for the inculcation of a particular lifestyle.

That lifestyle was vividly portrayed in 1953 in an account in the *TES*, of a visit to a preparatory school. It offers an effective and not unfair summary of the experience of thousands of boys who passed through the private sector during these years. I have chosen the example of a boys' school to reflect the extent to which these schools, whether wittingly or not, ensured the continuing male domination of the English elite into the later twentieth century:

> The curriculum was formal, the lessons academic; but the boys were given plenty of chances to speak. The air was friendly and relaxed. The boy who drummed out the subjunctive might have his knees on the seat. With many of the masters the attitude to pupils was man to man. Here, perhaps, the dash of sport that spices a preparatory school was seen at its best. If the master who had just taken you at the nets is prepared to give his mind to mathematics you may as well give yours too, especially if he is the sort, as at this lucky school, who can get you Hutton's autograph.[106]

References

1. *TES*, 18 July 1958.
2. M. Kogan, *The politics of educational change* (University Press, Manchester, 1978), 37–8.
3. P. Wann, 'The collapse of Parliamentary bipartisanship in education', *Journal of Educational Administration and History*, 3, 2 (1971), 28.
4. Ibid.
5. *TES*, 18 January 1952.
6. *TES*, 27 June 1952.
7. Wann, 'The collapse', 32.
8. PRO Ed. 136/892.
9. Ibid.
10. PRO Ed. 136/890.
11. PRO Ed. 136/896.
12. *TES*, 22 October 1954.
13. PRO Ed. 136/894.
14. B. Simon, 'The Tory government and education, 1951–60: background to breakout', *History of Education*, 14, 4 (December 1985), 282 and 287–8.
15. PRO Ed. 136/894.
16. *TES*, 18 September 1959.
17. Ibid.
18. *TES*, 16 October 1959.

19. *TES*, 2 October 1959.

20. *TES*, 1 November 1963.

21. On this see particularly S. Maclure, *Educational development and school building, aspects of public policy 1945–73* (Longman, London, 1984), esp. Ch. 4.

22. M. Seaborne and R. Lowe, *The English school*, Vol. 2 (Routledge & Kegan Paul, London, 1977), 162.

23. P. Gosden, *The education system since 1944* (Martin Robertson, Oxford, 1983), 11.

24. Maclure, *Educational development*, 78.

25. M. Kogan (ed.), *The politics of education* (Penguin, London, 1971), 30.

26. The figures presented in this section are derived from the *Statistics of Education* compiled annually throughout this period by the Ministry of Education.

27. Ministry of Education, *New primary schools*, Building Bulletin no. 1 (HMSO, 1949), 5.

28. Maclure, *Educational development*, Ch. 5, and Seaborne & Lowe, *The English school*, Ch. 11.

29. Ministry of Education, *The story of post-war school building* (HMSO, 1957), 2.

30. M. Seaborne, *Primary school design* (Routledge & Kegan Paul, London, 1971), Ch. 5.

31. Seaborne & Lowe, *The English school*, 169.

32. Ibid.

33. *TES*, 13 May 1960.

34. Ibid., 20 April 1951.

35. Ibid., 24 May 1963.

36. Ibid., 30 January 1959.

37. PRO, Ed. 147/205.

38. *TES*, 1 March 1963.

39. Ibid.

40. Ibid., 15 March 1963 and 14 June 1963.

41. Ibid., 4 October 1963.

42. See tables 6.1 and 6.2 for details.

43. *TES*, 4 January 1952.

44. P.E. Vernon (ed.), *Secondary school selection* (Methuen, London, 1957), 17.

45. *TES*, 17 August 1962.

46. *TES*, 28 March 1958.

47. P. Gosden, *The education system since 1944* (Martin Robertson, Oxford, 1983), 31.

48. Vernon, *Secondary school selection*, 20–1. See also A. Yates and D.A. Pidgeon, *Admission to grammar schools* (NFER, Slough, 1957) on this issue.

49. R.E. Gross (ed.), *British secondary education* (OUP, Oxford, 1965), 160.

50. Ibid., 178.

51. *TES*, 1 August 1952.

52. Gross (ed.), *British secondary education*, 274.

53. Ibid., 182.
54. *TES*, 23 September 1955.
55. Gross (ed.), *British secondary education*, 202.
56. *TES*, 11 January 1952.
57. Ibid., 13 November 1953.
58. CAC, *Early leaving* (HMSO, London, 1954).
59. *TES*, 31 December 1954.
60. Floud, J., Halsey, A.H. and Martin E.M., *Social class and educational opportunity* (Heinemann, London, 1957); J.W.B. Douglas, *The home and the school* (Macgibbon & Kee, London, 1964); B. Jackson and D. Marsden, *Education and the working class* (Routledge & Kegan Paul, London, 1962).
61. Jackson and Marsden, *Education*, 221.
62. E. Allsopp and D. Grugeon, *Direct grant grammar schools*, Fabian research series no. 256 (London, 1966), 3.
63. Gross (ed.), *British secondary education*, 149.
64. Allsopp and Grugeon, *Direct grant grammar schools*, 6.
65. Gross (ed.), *British secondary education*, 150.
66. *TES*, 15 March 1963.
67. Ibid., 30 December 1960.
68. Ibid., 25 June 1954.
69. PRO, Ed. 147/207.
70. Ibid.
71. *TES*, 20 May 1955.
72. *Technical education* (White Paper) (HMSO, London, 1956).
73. *TES*, 7 June 1957.
74. Ibid., 21 July 1961.
75. Ibid., 5 May 1963.
76. Ibid., 6 February 1953.
77. Ibid., 13 April 1962.
78. Ibid., 27 August 1954.
79. Ibid., 8 July 1955.
80. Ibid., 7 April 1961.
81. Ibid., 28 May 1954.
82. Ibid., 29 October 1954.
83. Ibid., 30 January 1959.
84. Ibid., 5 December 1958.
85. Ibid., 30 January 1959.
86. Ibid., 11 September 1953.
87. Ibid., 23 February 1962.
88. Ibid.
89. Department of Education and Science, *Half our future* (HMSO, London, 1963), 186–8.
90. *TES*, 16 August 1963.
91. Ibid., 10 February 1956.
92. W. Taylor, *Secondary modern school* (Faber, London, 1963), 49–50.
93. *Half our future*, 24–5.
94. *TES*, 9 July 1954.
95. Ibid., 9 September 1955.

96. Ibid., 13 December 1957.

97. Quoted by A.H. Halsey in 'The public schools debate', *New Society* (25 July 1968), 120–2.

98. H. Glennester and Richard Pryke, *The public schools*, Young Fabian pamphlet no. 7 (1964), 3.

99. Ibid.

100. J.C. Dancy, *The public schools and the future* (Faber, London, 1963), 22–8.

101. *TES*, 3 May 1963.

102. Dancy, *The public schools*, 27–8.

103. Ibid., 30.

104. *TES*, 17 May 1963.

105. I. Weinberg, *The English public schools* (Atherton Press, New York, 1967), esp. Ch. 6.

106. *TES*, 3 July 1953.

7

Comprehensive Schooling:
A Revolution Postponed

It is impossible to understand fully the reorganisation of secondary schooling as it occurred in England from the 1950s onwards without considering the nature of contemporary suburbanisation and the socio-economic changes that accompanied the onset of affluence. The new overspill housing estates of the post-war era became living and constantly changing suburbs. They were peopled initially by young families, new to the experience of home-ownership, with aspirations that their children should attain higher levels of education than their parents had done, so that they might be enabled to take advantage of the job opportunities created by the new affluence. This social group provided a large part of the clientele of the 'first-phase' comprehensive schools, which were built in the main to serve the overspill housing estates.

It is ironic that, within a generation, these new suburbs found themselves in a relative decline as new middle-class overspill areas and dormitory towns appeared further away from the urban centres, often in leafy and prestigious market towns and villages which, during the 1960s and 1970s, became the domain of the new middle classes. In this process the early post-war suburbs experienced a gradual, and at first barely perceptible erosion in status in response to subtle changes in the age and occupational groupings of their residents. The large, 'first phase' comprehensive schools located in these suburbs, which had enjoyed a brief heyday during the 1950s and 1960s, underwent a parallel fall in prestige. These contrasts between suburbs and schools were intensified by the drift to the South of young professionals, which resulted in deepened contrasts between differing regions of the country and, in the 1980s, in a growing sense of alienation between North and South. In retrospect, this historical process has an almost inexorable quality: it predetermined the nature, the social functions and the fate of the comprehensive schools from the outset, yet at the time it was largely unconsidered by those involved in the debate in the structure of secondary education in England.

What did present itself as a key issue for those involved during the early 1950s was the question of the reliability of selection at 11+ . In 1952, particularly, a succession of reports commented on the use of intelligence tests for transfer at 11+ . In April the *TES* drew on the research of P.E. Vernon to argue that 'teachers have long felt doubts about the tests. . . . The verdict of the psychologists has now been delivered, and it is bound to alter the place the tests take in selection for secondary schools.'[1]

In November the University of Bristol published a collection of *Studies in selection techniques for admission to grammar schools*, and a month later it was the turn of the NFER whose pamphlet on transfer to secondary schools was described in one press comment as 'a report which frankly admits that objective tests are inconclusive.'[2] These publications reflected a growing concern among educatioal psychologists, some of whom were becoming increasingly sceptical of theories of fixed intelligence. The Scottish Mental Survey, conducted during the late 1940s, had highlighted the relationships between family size and intelligence, and this received wide publicity in England during the early 1950s, several influential articles being authored by J.D. Nisbet.[3] In July 1953, A.F. Watts of the NFER published a book, *Can we measure ability?*, which threw more doubt on the objectivity of selection procedures. Alice Heim's *Appraisal of intelligence*, which appeared in 1954, was another monograph from within the psychological profession to offer a sceptical view of the received wisdom, although Brian Simon's book on *Intelligence testing and the comprehensive school*, presented a blanket indictment of the influence of psychologists, particularly those involved in the testing movement, on the structure of English secondary schooling.

The initial response of educational administrators and local politicians was defensive, seeking ways to make selection fairer and more efficient rather than abandoning it entirely. The Bournemouth LEA sought ways to supplement its objective tests at 11+ , and the Northumberland authority looked to improved selection procedures to end the problem of early leavers in grammar schools.[4] Perhaps most radically, in January 1953, Hertfordshire announced that intelligence tests would no longer be used in allocating pupils to different types of secondary school: 'The plan is to ring the changes in selection techniques so as to reduce their backwash in the primary schools.'[5]

By 1955, similar schemes, dependent upon the recommendation of primary school headteachers allied to written examinations were being tried in Yorkshire, and the Lincoln authority was reported as using wide range of criteria (including health and personality) to allocate pupils to secondary schools.[6] Initiatives such as these found favour with the *TES*, which in 1953 reported recent research by Halsey and Gardner which showed that the middle classes were disproportionately represented in some London grammar schools and that once in the grammar schools, middle-class pupils tended to achieve the best results. The *TES* concluded:

> the moral would seem to be that if selection favours boys of higher social class it does so with a good reason, for they are more likely to make a go of the grammar school course. The wisdom is confirmed of these local authorities which look beyond intelligence scores in their secondary selection.[7]

Keith Fenwick has shown, in his work on this period, that the trade unions (and the teachers' unions in particular) were loath to commit themselves fully to support of comprehensive reorganisation during the early 1950s, while the IAHM, always a champion of the grammar schools, was overtly hostile.[8] Although some elements within the Labour Party worked hard to keep the topic of secondary organisation before the public, the electoral defeat of 1951 committed the Party to a lengthy period of introspection, during which internal dissentions severely weakened its power to promulgate clearly defined policies. Further, there were some Labour Party members who had strong reservations on the question of comprehensive schooling. In July 1951 the *TES* reported that several Labour members of the LCC were unhappy with their own Party's plans to open comprehensives: 'Numbers of Labour members were disturbed by the prospect of building these huge schools. In its recent pamphlet the party had underlined the view that a comprehensive school need not necessarily be large.'[9]

Florence Horsburgh and her successor as minister, David Eccles, were both committed to a policy of cautious pragmatism, placating elements within the Conservative Party by repeatedly proclaiming their commitment to the grammar school, but also ready to co-exist with 'politically uncommitted groups of teachers and educationists'[10] by allowing a limited number of reorganisaton schemes from local authorities to go through where the conditions seemed right. Horsburgh told one questioner in the Commons in 1954 that 32 out of 36 proposals for comprehensive schools had met with approval.[11]

Conservative ministers had a difficult path to follow during the early 1950s, since much party opinion was becoming violently hostile to the idea of the common secondary school. The *Report on secondary education* prepared as a policy document by the Conservative and Unionist Teachers' Association in February 1954 stated flatly:

> This report will be found to have nothing to do with Comprehensive Schools except to condemn them, since they render, themselves unable to make adequate provision for the vital differences among pupils.
>
> Selection becomes a first consideration of this report, and there is no vestige of apology for it. It is based alike on sound educational argument and honesty of thought. Mistakes in selection are relatively few in number and light in substance.[12]

This report went on to advocate that there should be a pass rate of not less than 20 per cent to the grammar schools and 10 per cent to technical, that the pay of grammar school teachers should be enhanced, and that a separate examination alongside GCE should be devised for technical schools.

As well as this groundswell of opinion within the Party, the severe economic pressure under which R.A. Butler as Chancellor placed the Ministry of Education during the early 1950s undoubtedly militated against the development of any effective policy. During these years the Ministry took the view that it was the job of local authorities to sort out their own best policy, and accordingly enquiries or complaints were frequently deflected away to the LEAs.

The arrival of David Eccles in the autumn of 1954 with 'a brief to refurbish the government's image'[13] led immediately to attempts within the Ministry to articulate a policy on secondary education. A.A. Part, the Assistant Secretary, prepared in November a long typescript, pointing out that the increasing birth rate, together with the increasing doubts about the accuracy of 11 + selection, argued for a generous provision of grammar school places. On the comprehensive school issue he commented:

Some claim that it provides the type of secondary school organisation best fitted to the requirements of a democratic community. . . . Others fear the effect of size alike on children, teachers and the head . . .

Time alone will show how far these hopes and doubts were justified. The decision of 123 out of 146 local education authorities not to include such schools in their development plans show that they share the doubts. There are, however, comprehensive schools already approved, or under construction and . . . already in use. This limited experiment will at least have the healthy effect of bringing the argument about these schools from the realm of sometimes over-dogmatic theory to the more profitable sphere of actual educational experience.'[14]

This memorandum was circulated within the Ministry prior to a Minister's meeting on secondary education policy which took place on 23 February 1955. At this meeting the senior officials of the Ministry and senior members of the schools inspectorate (who were particularly vocal) warned Eccles of the dangers of closing grammar schools in favour of comprehensives, which posed new and as yet unresolved problems. One senior HMI commented,

the problem of Miss Greene, headmistress of Kidbrooke [a comprehensive school], is at least two-thirds that of looking after guiding and the staff: the comprehensive idea has presented altogether new problems to the Kidbrooke staff, who look anywhere they can for guidance.[15]

What emerged clearly in this meeting was strong opposition within the Ministry to any suggestion that pupils might have to be coerced into attending a comprehensive school. The Eltham case, in which the Minister had recently kept open a London grammar school despite the opening of the Kidbrooke comprehensive nearby, was held up as a shining example, and it was noted approvingly that the Birmingham Labour Party had promised that some bright children from homes near their planned new comprehensive schools would be given the chance to attend one or other of the city grammar schools. Such a policy was seen as having benefits for the comprehensives, and the Permanent Secretary, Gilbert Fleming remarked; 'there is some evidence to suggest that, for example, Kidbrooke, will be educationally better for not having absorbed all the grammar provision in its area.'[16]

Another outcome of this meeting was that the Ministry adopted a target figure of between 1200 and 1500 pupils as a reasonable size for new comprehensive schools, thus confirming the rule of thumb to which it had been working since the late 1940s.

Later in the spring of 1955 David Eccles made clear, in a speech to the NUT conference at Scarborough, that his Ministry remained committed to the grammar school and looked to the expansion and development of the secondary modern schools as the best response to demographic trends. His reservations about the size of the comprehensive schools and the competence of head teachers to deal with unprecedented managerial problems made him reluctant to consider sanctioning more than few comprehensive schools.[17] This policy was given the seal of Prime Ministerial approval in May, when the Joint Four approached Antony Eden with a letter arguing:

> we would, as educationalists and citizens, but not as political partisans of any kind, plead that there should be no sacrifice of any schools which have established their power to give good service and are making a worthy contribution to our country's education; rather we would press that such schools have all possible encouragement and support in the continuance of their work.[18]

Eden's reply went through several drafts in the Ministry, gradually increasing in warmth towards the Joint Four in response to Eccles's comment: 'this is a sensible letter and I hope that you will draft a warm reply.'[19]

In the event, the formal Prime Ministerial response, which went out on 20 May, broke no new ground in terms of policy, but confirmed what had in reality been the Ministry line for several years:

> The Conservative Party fully supports the aims of the Education Act of 1944 with its emphasis on the needs of individual children. We strongly agree that what matters in education is the development of the child's talents and personality, not the forwarding of a political theory. . . . May I say that my colleagues and I take very real encouragement from the knowledge that our aims coincide so closely with those of a responsible and important body of men and women in the

educational world such as your Committee represents.

In secondary education our view is that a variety of schools is needed to match the increasing opportunities of the modern world. We are prepared to see experiments with comprehensive schools where all the local conditions are favourable and no good school is swallowed up, but we agree with your committee in being opposed to the hasty and wholesale adoption of schemes for the establishment of such schools.

We believe it is vital to build up secondary modern and technical schools so that they offer an attractive range of vocational and other courses. We wish to see the grammar schools preserved and strengthened. [20]

Accordingly, enquiries which reached the Ministry in 1955 on the question of selection for secondary education were either deflected away to the local authorities, or met by a stolid defence of tripartism. In March, when John Profumo enquired on behalf of a constituent as to the status of Moray House intelligence tests for admission to grammar school, he was told by Denis Vosper, Parliamentary Secretary to the Minister of Education,

When a child is about the age of 11 years, it is necessary for a Local Education Authority to decide on the type of secondary education for which he is best suited (whether grammar, technical or modern). Local education authorities usually, identify the child of modern or 'technical' ability by a series of objective tests, the series usually comprising an intelligence, an arithmetic and an English test. The Moray House series of tests are widely used in this connection. In addition many authorities take into account the record of the child during the primary school years and, where possible, the wishes of the parents.

These arrangements are not prescribed by any regulations of this Ministry, but they are clearly sensible and by and large effective. Local Education Authorities are, in general, very much alive to the need to make their assessment of the child's ability as complete as possible. [21]

Similarly, in April 1955, David Eccles explained, in a letter to a parent:

I do not think that the idea of fixing a 'national standard'

for grammar school admissions — even if it were possible —
is the right way. . . . What really matters . . . is to try to
ensure that no child that may have failed to gain admission
to a grammar school at the age of eleven should be debarred
on that account from achieving his or her ambition.[22]

This then was the rationalisation employed by the Ministry
throughout the 1950s to cope with a swiftly changing situation. The
considerations which led Horsburgh to defend existing grammar
schools early in the decade were to lead inexorably, within a few
years, to the governmental effort to make a success of the secondary moderns. This was the political reality confronting any local
authority which made proposals for the reorganisation of its
secondary schools along comprehensive lines. Allied to a press which
was at best sceptical concerning the appropriateness and the
prospects of comprehensive schooling, this governmental attitude
ensured that the 1950s saw no dramatic reconstruction of the
structure of secondary education.

Throughout the decade, though, proposals did emerge from a
steadily growing number of local authorities which involved a
greater or lesser degree of commitment to the abolition of selection
at 11 + , at least in those localities where no existing grammar school
was threatened. The few authorities which came up with proposals
for comprehensive schools during the early 1950s — notably
Staffordshire, Coventry, London, West Yorkshire and Manchester
— were marked less by a shared ideological commitment than by
the fact that they had all identified quickly growing new suburbs
in need of some secondary provision. Only in London, where the
National Association of Labour Teachers had been active for many
years, was it possible to discern a deep-seated conviction among
many Labour councillors of the need for radical change; but here,
as elsewhere, pragmatic considerations were paramount.

A plan from Staffordshire for 63 comprehensive schools, which
emerged in 1951, was quickly dismissed as 'quite fantastic' by
one of the county's grammar school headteachers, and resulted
in ministerial permission for three purpose-built comprehensive
schools to serve the quickly growing overspill suburbs of
Wolverhampton.[23] They began work in 1955. In 1953 a proposal
from Coventry LEA for two suburban comprehensive schools was
accepted by Horsburgh with the proviso that 'it should be seen as
strictly experimental.'[24] Similarly, the Calder High School in the
West Riding and the new schools at Hayes and Potters Bar in

Middlesex, were all functioning as comprehensives by the mid-1950s, were all situated in quickly expanding suburbs and coexisted with nearby grammar schools.

It was not until the spring of 1954 that any significant public controversy developed on the comprehensive schools issue, and, predictably, the occasion for this was the realisation that London's first purpose-built comprehensive, Kidbrooke, threatened the existence of the Eltham Hill Girls Grammar School, whose parental body mounted an effective publicity campaign. The ministerial veto of the London plan was warmly welcomed by the *TES* which commented that 'by putting her foot down over Eltham Hill the Minister has acted wisely and well . . . has acted responsibly in checking an irresponsible policy.'[25]

Four months later the same journal was equally enthusiastic about Horsburgh's refusal to allow the Bec Grammar School to be expanded into a comprehensive:

> She has not forbidden the local authority to experiment with comprehensive schools. There are about ten on the stocks which do not demand interference with existing grammar schools. . . . In fact, London parents are being given freedom of choice by the Minister.[26]

The rejection of plans from the Manchester authority in the following year, to establish three comprehensive schools in Wythenshawe, has been seen by one historian, Keith Fenwick, as evidence not only of the government's continuing determination to restrict the extent of comprehensive reorganisation, but also of the ability of the leading Labour members of a local education committee to pursue a policy to the brink of success despite the lack of unanimity among local Party members on this issue.[27]

The net result of these conflicts and tensions was that, when the Ministry was asked in the summer of 1955 to furnish a list of those comprehensive schools already at work, it could find (only after considerable difficulty) no more than 14 in England.[28] As Stephen Swingler pointed out in the Commons, questioning whether the Ministry was prepared to give any encouragement to comprehensivisation, there were fifty local authorities with new grammar schools under construction in July 1954, but only four comprehensive schools being built.[29]

This pattern of events induced strangely differing responses in the two major political parties. Within Labour the failure to achieve any significant impact in an era when an increasing number of schools was being built led first to a redoubling of effort and, within a few years, to a major consideration of the nature of any planned reorganisation programme and of its presentation. Within the Conservative Party, the whole comprehensive schools issue was relegated to a minor position in the deliberations of the late 1950s and early 1960s.

The publication of the Labour Party's *Secondary education for all* in 1951 signalled a formal commitment to comprehensive schooling, which was confirmed at the 1953 party conference, where Alice Bacon (speaking for the NEC) directed the Party towards local action within an overall framework which remained under the control of the Conservative Party. A year later, in a major debate at the party conference, the comprehensive ideal won 'the full and passionate support of delegates.'[30]

Meanwhile, in the educational press comprehensive schooling was increasingly being presented as offering an insidious threat to the English way of life through its being identified with communism. In this connection the advocate who attracted most attention in the early 1950s was Brian Simon, whose public statements were widely reported and often subjected to bitter attacks. One *TES* leader, sparked off by a speech made in London by Simon, commented: 'However much Communists may wish it were otherwise, children differ widely in intelligence, quickness to learn, retentiveness, imagination and industry — nor was this discovery made with the advent of intelligence tests.'[31] In a spirited response, Simon argued that 'the extent of educational opportunity must always be a political question of first importance. Miss Horsburgh . . . has recently stated that the present government does not intend to allow even a single area to develop a complete common school system.'[32]

This popular identification of 'root and branch' comprehensive reorganisation with the left wing of the Labour movement was one of the catalysts which led some members of the Labour Party to step back during the late 1950s from the advocacy of a thorough-going restructuring of secondary education towards more pragmatic proposals which would be more attractive electorally. There is no doubt, too, that a second catalyst to this revisionism was the defeat of the Party at the hustings in 1955. After the election a Labour Party study group was set up to prepare a new policy. The outcome was *Learning to live* (1958), a publication which placed its emphases upon flexibility and pragmatism. At the time of the publication of this report Hugh Gaitskell confirmed publicly this softening of

Labour Party policy, claiming that under any future Labour government there would be no insistence that all children should attend the same kind of huge, impersonal school.[33] This produced no outcry within the Party, which was at this period largely preoccupied by the problem of the public schools. Rather, Gaitskell's remarks were complemented by the pronouncements of other party gurus. Antony Crosland's *The Future of socialism* (1956) and Roy Jenkins's *The Labour case* (1959) were key tracts in the revision of Labour Party thinking on education and ensured by the end of the decade that any foreseeable Labour government would stop well short of a full-blown implementation of the comprehensive ideal. As Jenkins explained, the commitment was now to paring away the rough edges of inequality, rather than eradicating social contrasts entirely: the comprehensive school would include

> children now classified into the different types of grammar, technical and modern. It does not imply that these children will be taught in the same classes and all do the same work. They must be divided according to intelligence and aptitude . . . but the division will be less sharp and less final.[34]

This redefinition made it possible for Labour to make education a key plank in its platform. In 1961 the Party's *Signposts for the sixties* emphasised that greater equality of educational opportunity was central to any programme of national regeneration. At the annual conference in 1960, Harold Wilson had already advanced the idea of a 'scientific revolution' and in the years that followed this was linked increasingly to the Party's policy on comprehensive schooling. Wilson's famous 'Science and Socialism' speech to the 1963 party conference stressed the need for educational reform as a prerequisite for technological development. This subordination of the comprehensive principle to the drive for economic growth meant that what had been an electoral liability throughout the 1950s was now reworked by the party leadership into a political asset. But, in this process, the pragmatic approach now promised by Harold Wilson meant that the complete restructuring of secondary schooling along comprehensive lines — towards which many party members had aspired during the 1950s — could not come about in the foreseeable future. This 'revisionism' within the Party meant that Labour was in reality committed by the early 1960s to legitimating what was already happening on the ground, and had effectively stepped back from a determination to eradicate the selective schools.

By contrast the Conservative Party was at first distracted by other educational issues during these years, and it was only during the early 1960s that, among some sections of the Party at least, a softening of policy on comprehensive schooling was discernible, making possible the relative rapprochement of the two major parties on this issue which marked the mid-1960s.

During the mid-1950s it was increasingly technological education which gained the attention of the Conservative Party, as was clear from the debate at the 1955 annual conference, and the 1956 White Paper on *Technical education* which announced a 'large-scale programme of capital expenditure' aimed at 'attracting many more students and placing them in the right courses.'[35] In the following years, spectacular Russian successes in space, featuring Leika, the first space dog, and Yuri Gagarin, the first cosmonaut, served only to heighten this resolve. The 1955 Conservative Party manifesto emphasised 'our intention to reduce the size of classes, to reorganize all-age schools in town as well as country, to replace slum schools and greatly to expand technical education.'[36] By the end of the decade, other issues, too, were preoccupying the Party. Edward Boyle drew attention to the fact that

> during the period immediately following the 1959 election, the eleven-plus issue tended for a time to fade from view. This was partly due to the fact that, during David Eccles' second term of office, other matters were receiving greater prominence: the teacher shortage and the need for continued expansion of the colleges of education: the promotion of wider opportunities in further education, following the publication of the Crowther Report; and the pressure for university expansion, to match the dramatic growth of numbers becoming qualified in the sixth-forms.[37]

In 1958 the Party pinned its hopes, in *Secondary education for all: a new drive*, on the future of the secondary modern school. It may have been the enthusiasm with which this initiative was launched (backed by a £300 million spending programme), which led to the first stirrings of disquiet that perhaps the Party was not giving enough credence to the prospects of the comprehensive schools. In 1959 a Bow Group pamphlet conceded that 'the comprehensive school may sometimes be preferable to a rigid system of allocation',[38] and a year later *The Times* reported some Conservative backbenchers as believing that 'the value of the Kidbrooke type of school should be more realistically recognized in the Conservative Party.'[39]

As an increasing number of local authorities came up with reorganisation proposals during the early 1960s, the Party moved, under the influence of David Eccles and Edward Boyle, from its out-and-out defence of the grammar schools towards a more pragmatic position. By 1963, Boyle was attacking one of his own backbenchers, Sir Kenneth Thompson, who claimed that accurate selection at 11 + was possible.[40] In July, he reassured the annual conference of the AEC that he welcomed the abolition by the LCC of a written examination at 11 + .[41] He told an audience in Oxford that he knew and sympathised with 'the great anxiety which the 11 + examination causes to a great number of children and their parents.'[42]

It was during this same summer of 1963 that Harold Wilson offered the reassurance that the grammar schools would be abolished 'over my dead body'. It was these pragmatic responses by both major parties to the swiftly developing events of the early 1960s which signalled what has been described as 'the new educational settlement of the 1960s'.[43] It was a settlement which ensured that the spread of comprehensive education would take place within, and as part of, a deeply divided educational system rather than as its replacement. It was to be a settlement which sealed the long-term fate of the comprehensive sector.

This fate was also in part predetermined by the continuing scepticism of the educational press, particularly the *Times Educational Supplement* during the later 1950s and early 1960s. From 1952 until 1969 this journal was edited by Walter James, described by a more recent *TES* columnist as 'an elitist who opposed comprehensives and the expansion of higher education'. He recruited his staff direct from Oxbridge and used the *Supplement* as a proving-ground for young journalists, and to promote the arts. Patricia Rowan has described how one young recruit 'was encouraged to write full-page features on jazz clubs or Proust, though on reflection it might have been better to report on leaky school roofs in the north-east.'[44] Under James, a succession of editorials and articles showed scant regard for the prospects of the comprehensive schools. In January 1955, for example, publicising Robin Pedley's *Comprehensive schools today*, which was then the most up-to-date survey of current practice, the *TES* commented caustically:

They get the worst of both worlds . . . there remains little point in comprehensive schools . . . There is no evidence to show that comprehensive schools are classless societies; the physical proximity to each other of different types of pupil does not ensure that their social ties will be any closer than if they went to different schools.[45]

In the autumn of that year, full publicity was given to the publication of a Joint Four pamphlet on *The organisation of secondary education*, which dismissed comprehensive schools as experimental, too large, and committed to an internal selection which resulted only in children being grouped 'in the stratum of their immediate locality.'[46]

Over the next few years a succession of leader articles and editorial comments in the *TES* rehearsed these and similar arguments in what was nothing short of a campaign against the comprehensive ideal. In November 1956 it was the experimental nature of these schools that came under attack:

It cannot be emphasized too strongly that nothing has yet been *proved*. A letter on another page . . . sets out the examination results of a comprehensive school. They are excellent. But even evidence of this sort ought to be treated with a normal reserve. These results show too that this particular comprehensive school has done admirably with most unpromising material. But schools of other kinds do that too. And we still need to see what the comprehensive school can do with really promising material. Nobody has yet dispelled the doubts about its suitability for the average child.[47]

During the following year, the editorial tone became increasingly hostile. In February 1957 a leader article attacked the continuing preference of the Labour Party for comprehensive schooling:

It is time that the folly was halted. We have all been far too tolerant. There are enough comprehensive schools already here and there for any testing that needs to be done. New ones should not be countenanced until the worth of the first has been established.[48]

Two months later the *TES* reported gleefully a speech given to the NUT by Dr W.P. Alexander, Secretary of the AEC, in which he argued that the abolition of selection at 11 + would be illegal.[49] In February 1958 a feature on 'Comprehensive Schools' was given a chilling editorial introduction:

'Give us three or four years and we shall have something to tell you.' This was what teachers in comprehensive schools said when they started. For many of them the time is now up. For some it was up long ago. So the next seven pages give them a chance to describe what it is like.[50]

Similarly, in January 1959, a leader article was violently anti-comprehensive in tone, arguing that 'the head, like the school, must be pulled now one way, now the other. It is a school without a clear purpose.'[51] By contrast, this leader went on to argue, the selective sector had a clearly identifiable aim: 'The grammar school stands, as no other school can, for the cultivation of the intellect. That is its main bent and purpose and it pursues it single mindedly . . . That some pupils in some schools are not of this timber does not affect the argument.'[52]

During the early 1960s this editorial defensiveness extended even to an assault on those elements in the press that were prepared to reflect a growing scepticism with respect to the finality of selection for schools of differing types. In February 1962, for example, the *Observer* argued that the Ministry should take a more active line in seeking alternatives to 11 + selection:

If Sir David believes that all parents should be free to send children to the school of their choice he should put his newly created Research and Intelligence Branch to work to see how best to end selection at 11. The experts have told us that eleven plus selection is moribund. But like many other institutions it lingers on making a mockery of education and engendering in society the 'we' and 'they' complex.[53]

This was argument for which the *TES* had no time at all, commenting, 'The tripartite system could work, and we have the physical framework of it. Let us stop assuming that education can alter nature.'[54]

If this media hostility did much to damage popular perceptions of the comprehensive schools from the outset, it could not prevent the steady expansion of this sector during these years. It was an expansion which marked the almost inexorable response of local authorities to the continuing growth of the suburbs.

Initially, caution was the watchword in many parts of the country. In January 1955, for example, the Buckinghamshire authority announced that it would build a school for Eton and Slough 'which can be used at will in the comprehensive, bipartite or tripartite system. The intention is that parents shall [sic] decide.'[55]

This proposal of a comprehensive school primarily for eleven + failures, which would accept children successful in the 11 + examination if their parents so wished, was seen by the *TES* as 'bristling with difficulties of architecture and organisation, but it still seems no bad thing to let parents have their say.'[56] In fact, this proposal from Buckinghamshire was precisely in line with the policy enunciated by Florence Horsburgh in the Commons a year earlier, when she had said that

> she was prepared to sanction the building of some comprehensive schools but, because she regarded them as experimental, she preferred that they should be constructed so that they could be organized later as separate schools . . . She pointed out that it would be as well where possible to build the school in blocks so that it could be divided if that were thought advisable in future.[57]

The design of several of the first purpose-built comprehensive schools reflected this uncertainty over the future. The first comprehensive school in Birmingham was opened at Great Barr in 1956 and was divided into self-contained upper, middle and lower schools. In the same year the Woodlands School in Coventry opened: this was divided into separate blocks on a 'house' system.[58] Both approaches were justified on the grounds that they pre-empted many of the problems associated with over-large schools, but both could be adapted to suit alternative modes of secondary organisation should the comprehensive 'experiment' be abandoned. Indeed, the planning needs of these pioneer comprehensive schools received very little official consideration before the mid-1960s. As Stuart Maclure has shown,[59] the Ministry remained preoccupied by the problems of planning and adapting the grammar schools (the Ministry's Development Group funded a series of projects focused on grammar school design), and no building bulletins were produced which dealt with purpose-built comprehensive schools. It was left to the local authorities to find their own best solutions, guided only by occasional ministerial statements, and the result was that the comprehensive schools built during this period did not, by and large, reflect any unity of purpose.

During the late 1950s it was the small rural grammar schools which were at greatest risk of being swallowed up in reorganisation schemes. In the autumn of 1956, confronted by an annual bill of over £20,000 for bussing pupils, Westmorland announced an extension of its comprehensive scheme, involving the closure of three of its eight grammar schools.[60] At the same time, the Kent Education Committee published an account of the *Problems of secondary education in Kent* and reported almost unanimous support for the county's tripartite system of secondary schooling. In Leicestershire, a largely rural county with only a few small industrial townships, an energetic Director of Education, Stuart Mason, was able to announce in 1957 the introduction of a two-tier system of secondary schooling. Politically, this involved quite brilliant sleight of hand on Mason's part, since the position of the local grammar schools was protected by assuring them pride of place among the county's new high schools, and no reference was made to the comprehensive principle. None the less, the *TES* commented that the Leicester plan 'will have to succeed in no uncertain fashion if it is to displace the present system, which is proving itself adaptable to the needs of our age.'[61]

It has recently been hinted that the Leicestershire Plan resulted from a ministerial initiative. Robin Pedley, as an aside in a book review, recalled that 'In 1955 I was asked by the then Minister . . . Sir David Eccles in person, to consider inviting an interested LEA to launch a two-tier comprehensive scheme as an experiment . . . within a year just such a scheme was born in Leicestershire.'[62] It is a claim that will require fuller investigation by future historians, and it suggests that the Ministry may not have been as supine on the question of comprehensive reorganisation as the currently available records suggest.

There were still, during these years, occasional well-publicised ministerial vetos of comprehensive reorganisation schemes. In 1959, for example, Geoffrey Lloyd, the then Minister, rejected proposals which came in from the Darlington authority.[63] In the spring of 1961, when Stephen Swingler mounted another attack from the Labour backbenches, David Eccles (now restored to the Ministry) was able to report the approval of 29 new comprehensive schools during the previous eighteen months, although he took care to reassure opinion within the Conservative Party with the observation that 'I think Mr Swingler, just to get the record straight, might like to know that in the same period I have approved 460 other types of secondary schools, including 57 grammar schools. Nonetheless, I am in favour of reasonable experiment.'[64]

It has been estimated that, between 1960 and 1964, over a quarter of all LEAs made significant changes to their selection procedures in response to the comprehensive lobby.[65] These were the years when several of the larger city authorities moved decisively towards comprehensive schooling. In February 1962 London announced that fifteen of its remaining 20 grammar schools would merge with neighbouring schools 'to form comprehensives or a new kind of twin school.'[66] This heralded the coming of the split-site comprehensive, which was to become an increasingly popular device applied by several LEAs to the older suburbs during the following ten years. In London, initially, this arrangement was defended by Labour members of the education committee as no more than a readjustment of the 1947 plan to cope with the problems of a declining population in the inner city. In this year the Ministry estimated that the 152 comprehensive schools already at work in London were catering for over 50 per cent of the secondary school population, while both Coventry and Bristol were not far behind. Before the Conservatives left office, major reorganisation schemes came in from Sheffield, Leeds, Hull, Manchester and Liverpool. Proposals from Bradford for a two-tier system were approved by Edward Boyle in 1964 and this became the first English city to dispense entirely with selection at 11 + in its maintained schools. It is worth remarking, though, that the presence of a prestigious direct grant school in Bradford ensured that some pupils, at least, were creamed away from the non-selective schools. It was this anomaly, to be replicated in other towns in the next few years, that led the Labour Party to see the direct grant sector as an appropriate target to attack in the mid-1970s.

Thus, by 1964, the picture on the ground was a mixed one. A quickly growing number of local authorities were at least tinkering with the comprehensive principle, which was coming to be seen as increasingly appropriate for urban as well as suburban and rural areas. But still in many areas there were no plans for comprehensivisation: over 100 local authorities had no comprehensive schools and no plans to introduce them in 1962. But the tide was now running swiftly in favour of comprehensive reorganisation at the local level.

The reasons for this change were complex, but it is possible to identify some of the more significant. First, the concern among psychologists at the implications of 11 + testing, which, as we have seen, was growing during the early 1950s, became even more widespread later in the decade. Benn and Simon have shown how, in 1957, major reports from both the British Psychological Society and the NFER threw further doubt on the validity of intelligence tests.[67] During these same years a growing awareness of the research of Basil Bernstein, which explored the relationships between social class and academic achievement, served only to undermine further the concept of fixed intelligence upon which the vast majority of selection procedures depended. A growing army of sociologists of education was at work also during the 1950s and early 1960s, establishing the power of environmental factors in determining children's capacity to benefit from formal education. Among the most notable were Halsey, Floud, Douglas, Mays, Jackson and Marsden. All of this chimed too with Vaizey's work which emphasised the investment function performed by schooling for society. A deeper underlying question is the problem of why the vast weight of educational research during this era was so overwhelmingly pointed in the same direction, being at least environmentalist in orientation and fundamentally optimistic concerning the power of properly regulated schooling systems to bring about social change. There can be little doubt that this newly self-conscious educational 'expertise' was reflecting not only the currently fashionable English attitudes to post-war reconstruction, but also an international phenomenon, since much contemporary work in North America and continental Europe addressed similar issues.[68] It may be this coincidence of national with international preoccupations which enabled this research to exercise so great a sway on both local and national policy-makers.

A second factor which helps explain the rate of change at the local level was an increasing self-assurance among the teaching profession which, in the 1950s as never before, was ready to involve itself in political contest. Ian Fenwick has shown how the teachers' unions moved fairly swiftly during the late 1950s from a halting recognition of the comprehensive schools towards a serious attempt to consider their prospects.[69] This reflected the growing numbers of unionised teachers who were employed in comprehensive schools. Hardly surprisingly, the union which responded most quickly was the NUT which organised a series of conferences for teachers in comprehensive schools and in 1958 published *Inside the comprehensive school*, a collection of essays by practising head teachers.

But the most compelling factor was the quickening pace of suburbanisation, which impinged upon the vast majority of secondary schools. Over 5 million new homes were added to the housing stock between 1946 and 1964, and a further 2 million before the end of the 1960s.[70] The new suburbs thus created forced a major accommodation problem upon the local education authorities, and many responded with plans that were more radical than might otherwise have been the case. In Birmingham, for example, when the Sir Lionel Russell, Chief Education Officer, reported on the provision of schooling in 1964 and was asked to offer suggestions on the extension of comprehensive schooling, he emphasised that the greatest need for such schools was in the new housing estates on the east side of the city and in the central area, where a major redevelopment proposal was under way.[71] This emphasis was mirrored elsewhere in the country.

It was already becoming clear to some contemporaries that, because of these links with suburbanisation, the comprehensive schools were something of a misnomer, and that what was taking place was in reality a sharpening and clarification of the stratifications of English society as it entered the era of universal secondary schooling. In January 1957, R.R. Hancock, the President of the Incorporated Association of Head Masters, observed tellingly that:

> If the motive for the comprehensive school was some cosy theory of social integration it had to be remembered that in urban areas comprehensive schools with geographical catchment areas would vary widely from one another in social content and accordingly in public esteem.[72]

The work of D.V. Glass, and in particular his collection of essays on *Social mobility in Britain*, published in 1954, placed the problem of suburbanisation firmly on the agenda for educational researchers. Two years later, Flann Campbell, who had studied under Glass at the LSE, published a study of the impact of suburbanisation upon the London grammar schools. He observed that 'The migration of population to the suburbs has been a feature of most large urban communities in Britain during this century, and London has been particularly affected because of the enormous size of its built up area.'[73] He identified a steady decline in the proportion of London grammar school pupils coming from middle-class homes as one direct result of this suburbanisation, and reported that, by contrast, the suburban grammar schools had become, if anything, increasingly socially exclusive during the post-war era. For Campbell, the comprehensive school offered some hope of providing 'a partial solution to the problem of a secondary-school entry that fluctuates in both quantity and quality'.[74] One perceptive correspondent to the *TES* took Campbell's analysis a step further and argued that while he had conclusively shown how the migration of the middle class to the suburbs affected the class composition of schools, his research could also help explain why support for comprehensives was strongest in the 'largely middle-class dormitory areas which are insufficiently endowed with grammar schools'.[75]

The implications of these social changes for the comprehensive schools were compounded by the fact that, without exception, during the 1950s and early 1960s these schools used streaming as an internal selection device. It was unthinkable that they might have done otherwise: the more vocal middle-class parents placed great pressure on these schools to ensure that their children did not 'suffer' in competition with grammar school pupils from too close proximity with low achievers, and there was, during this period no developed and articulated lobby for destreaming. The result was that these comprehensive schools quickly became, if anything, a more effective agency than the grammar and secondary modern schools for sifting pupils from differing social backgrounds, as 'reliable' middle-class pupils who would not have achieved selection in an 11 + examination tended to become 'upwardly mobile' within the streamed comprehensive, while those pupils from working-class backgrounds which were less supportive of the aims of the schools were more readily moved into 'non-academic' streams. This factor meant that even where the new comprehensives served large rural catchment areas or socially mixed suburbs they were unlikely to alter radically the long-term trend for English secondary schools to confirm their pupils' life-chances rather than change them.

So, the social function of those comprehensive schools which began work before the mid-1960s was largely determined by the nature of post-war suburbanisation. They were forced to work within an existing system rather than as its replacement. Although selection procedures came under increasing scrutiny, the media continued to extol the virtues of the grammar schools, which remained paramount in terms of prestige. Further, as the number of comprehensive schools increased in the early 1960s, the extent of their identification with particular suburbs became increasingly clear. In the newer dormitory suburbs, some comprehensives offered an acceptable alternative to a grammar school education for the new middle classes. By contrast, the 'inner city' comprehensives which began to appear after 1960 could never be more than an alternative secondary modern for the working classes. Whilst the aspirations of the Left that comprehensive schooling might work towards a fairer society may seem naive when seen in retrospect against the wider social trends of this period, what no one foresaw was that the comprehensive schools might help to confirm the stratification of English society. That they were, within a generation, to assume this function, was largely predetermined by the distortion of the comprehensive ideal which took place between 1951 and 1964.

References

1. *TES*, 4 April 1952.
2. *TES*, 12 December 1952.
3. J. Nisbet, 'Family environment', *TES*, 26 June 1953; and Nisbet, 'Family, environment and intelligence', *Eugenics Review*, XLV (1953), 31–42.
4. *TES*, 7 December 1951.
5. *TES*, 9 January 1953.
6. *TES*, 9 September, 16 September and 23 September 1955.
7. *TES*, 3 April 1953.
8. I.G.K. Fenwick, *The comprehensive school, 1944–1970* (Methuen, London, 1976), esp. Ch. 4.
9. *TES*, 20 July 1951.
10. Fenwick, *The comprehensive school*, 65.
11. Ibid., 72.
12. PRO Ed. 147/206.
13. B. Simon, 'The Tory government and education, 1951–60', *History of Education*, 14, 4, (December 1985), 287.
14. PRO Ed. 147/206.
15. PRO Ed. 147/207.
16. Ibid.
17. PRO Ed. 147/209.
18. Ibid.
19. Ibid.
20. Ibid.
21. PRO Ed. 147/205.
22. Ibid.
23. *TES*, 2 November 1951.
24. D. Rubinstein and B. Simon, *The evolution of the comprehensive school, 1926–66* (Routledge & Kegan Paul, London, 1969), 50.
25. *TES*, 26 March 1954.
26. *TES*, 9 July 1954.
27. G.K. Fenwick, *The comprehensive school, 1944–1970* (Methuen, London, 1976), 99–103.

28. PRO Ed. 147/208.
29. *TES*, 23 July 1954.
30. Simon, 'The Tory government', 289–290.
31. *TES*, 31 October 1952.
32. *TES*, 14 November 1952.
33. M. Parkinson, *The Labour Party and the organisation of secondary education, 1918–65* (Routledge & Kegan Paul, London, 1970), 84.
34. R. Jenkins, *The Labour case* (Penguin, London, 1959), 96, cited in Centre for Contemporary Cultural Studies, *Unpopular education, schooling and social democracy in England since 1944* (London, 1981), 73.
35. Ministry of Education, *Technical education*, Cmd. 9703 (HMSO, London, 1956), 35–6.
36. Fenwick, *The comprehensive school*, 104.
37. E. Boyle, 'The politics of secondary school reorganisation', *Journal of Educational Administration and History*, 4, 2 (June 1972), 32.
38. Fenwick, *The comprehensive school*, 119.
39. Ibid.
40. Ibid., 112.
41. Ibid.
42. *TES*, 1 March 1963.
43. CCCS, *Unpopular education*, Ch. 4.
44. P. Rowan, writing in S. Maclure *et al.*, 'The *TES*, 1910–1985', *TES*, 27 September 1985.
45. *TES*, 7 January 1955.
46. *TES*, 23 September 1955.
47. *TES*, 16 November 1956.
48. *TES*, 15 February 1957.
49. *TES*, 26 April 1957.
50. *TES*, 7 February 1958.
51. *TES*, 9 January 1959.
52. Ibid.
53. *Observer*, 11 February 1962.
54. *TES*, 16 February 1962.
55. *TES*, 28 January 1955.
56. Ibid.
57. *TES*, 2 April 1954.
58. M. Seaborne and R. Lowe, *The English school*, vol. 2 (Routledge & Kegan Paul, London, 1977), 192–5.
59. S. Maclure, *Educational development and school building, 1945–73* (Longman, London, 1984), 240–1.
60. *TES*, 12 October 1956.
61. *TES*, 12 April 1957.
62. R. Pedley writing in *BJES*, 34, 2 (June 1986), 200.
63. C. Benn and B. Simon, *Halfway there* (Penguin, London, 1970), 52.
64. *TES*, 28 April 1961.
65. Rubinstein and Simon, *The evolution*, 88.
66. *TES*, 9 February 1962.
67. Benn and Simon, *Halfway there*, 47–8.
68. J. Mc V. Hunt, *Intelligence and experience* (Ronald, New York, 1961) provided a review of recent North American research in this area.

69. Fenwick, *The comprehensive school*, Chapter 6.

70. Times Newspapers, *The British economy: key statistics, 1900–1970* (London, 1971), 13.

71. W.A. Webb, 'The development of the ideal of comprehensive education in the City of Birmingham', MEd dissertation (Birmingham, 1986).

72. *TES*, 4 January 1957.

73. F. Campbell, *Eleven-plus and all that* (Watts, London, 1956), 36.

74. Ibid., 40.

75. *TES*, 15 March 1957.

8

Higher Education, 1951–64

The mainsprings of the expansion of higher education during this period are not far to seek. There was an important demographic factor of which planners and politicians were aware. The high point of live births in 1947 and the relatively high figures of the following years had clear long-term implications for the demand for places in higher education. Of more immediate impact during the 1950s was the trend, quickly evident after the establishment of universal secondary schooling, for more young people to stay on at school beyond the period of compulsory schooling and then to seek one form or another of higher education. This reflected both the increased affluence of the fifties and the growing realisation that the economic transformation towards the service industries and the professions demanded a more highly educated workforce. Between 1951 and 1964 the numbers employed in distributive trades and other services rose from 8½ to 10½ million.[1] So, while it was widely and accurately anticipated during the late 1940s that the numbers of university students would decline once the demobilised ex-servicemen worked their way through (the figure actually fell from 85,314 students in 1950–51 to 80,602 in 1953–54), it was soon realised that this was no more than a lull in what was to prove a long-term expansion. The number of school-leavers with two or more 'A' levels rose quickly from 25,000 in the mid-1950s to over 60,000 by 1964. The result was a quick fall in the percentage of this group going on to university, from 80 per cent in 1956 to 65 per cent in 1961. This, in turn, led to what was described by one observer as 'a spillover of well-qualified young people no longer able to go to university who went instead to colleges'.[2]

This pattern of expansion goes some way towards explaining the nature of developments in higher education during these years. In a swiftly developing situation the existing universities committed themselves to expansion and to some internal changes. But, since they could not — or did not — do enough to meet this sharp increase in demand, other institutions (most notably the technical colleges and the teacher training colleges) began to offer a 'compensatory' higher education. As this process increased in scale, the pressures for some redesignation, at first of only the more successful of these colleges, and later large numbers of them, became irresistible. So, it appears in retrospect that the 'binary system' which has been the subject of much public debate since the mid-1960s, arose as much from almost inexorable demographic and economic pressures as from decisions taken in the aftermath of the Robbins Report, although there can be no doubt that the issue of precisely which institutions should be brought under the aegis of the UGC was crucial in defining the nature of the 'binary controversy'.

Equally significant for the historian of these developments are a cluster of questions concerning the developing social functions of English institutions of higher education during this period. What patterns of access to differing institutions became discernible and how precisely did these colleges and universities relate to the job opportunities and career prospects of a quickly changing economy? What curricular changes took place to accommodate this new situation, and how powerful were existing 'elite' models of a humane curriculum in retarding change in the new or quickly expanding institutions. How did all this link with patterns of population movement and the process of suburbanisation? And how far is it possible to discern a developing status hierarchy of institutions of higher education with implications for the wider stratification of society? In describing the changes which took place in higher education, it is hoped that this chapter may provide the materials for at least a partial response to some of these questions.

The 1950s saw dramatic changes in the catchment of the civic universities which meant that they became more truly national in character. Before and immediately after the war almost a half of their students lived at home. Many of the rest were attending their regional university. It became increasingly clear during the early 1950s to both university dons and local authority administrators, that one reason for this was the wide disparities between authorities in the award of grants to students. It was shown by one piece of investigative journalism in 1952 that Swansea was making 75 awards annually for every 10,000 in the age group 5 to 14, Leeds, at the other extreme, was making only 5.[3] Further reports in 1954[4] and 1956[5] confirmed that wide varieties in level of support were commonplace. This publicity contributed directly to the greater availability of awards. When in November 1956 the head of Mexborough Grammar School complained that eight of his pupils had won university places but been awarded no grant by the West Riding authority, a question was put on their behalf in the Commons. The response confirmed that the authority was 'technically in the right', although the *TES* saw this as a clear example of the authority's 'scandalous niggardliness. . . . The proportion of children in this area who receive grants is far lower than in comparably rich and populous areas — Lancashire, Surrey or Middlesex for example . . . The West Riding owes an explanation.'[6]

There was a growing consensus that students should be supported through university. S. Hirst, the Director of Education for Middlesborough, told a meeting of the Association of Education officers in 1953 that 'the rational view appeared to be that all those "able to profit" by a university course should have the chance of taking one, irrespective of means. The natural corollary was that it should be free.'[7] The outcome was that by 1957–58 four out of every five students at the English universities were in receipt of some kind of financial support, and only a quarter of all students lived in the parental home.[8] For the first time it became possible for significant numbers of the growing army of first-generation university students to move away from their own home area. It was a luxury shared to a lesser degree by the teacher training colleges and hardly at all by the technical sector.

The enhanced financial accessibility of the universities and university colleges during this period served only to sharpen the debate on whom they should educate. There were many who feared the effects of any democratisation of access, and this frequently surfaced in the argument that existing selection procedures were a guarantee of standards. In March 1951, for example, Eric James, the head of Manchester Grammar School claimed publicly: 'most headmasters and headmistresses would agree that nearly all those who are really fitted for a university education . . . do in fact obtain one somewhere.'[9] A year later the *Times Educational Supplement* reflected on the fact that, despite the coming of universal secondary schooling, maintained secondary schools could win only 32 per cent of the Oxbridge scholarships available, a figure very comparable with those of the pre-war years.[10] The *TES* concluded that: 'it may be . . . that this is a statistical sign of the decline of

standard at the grammar schools which economic causes may have
brought about.' Similarly, the Political and Economic Planning
Group Report *Choosing university students*, which appeared in
November 1953, put in a plea that universities should retain the
power to select their students rather than be dictated to by examination grades earned in the new examinations.

When, in 1956, *The Times* annual review of Oxbridge graduates
revealed, for the first time, schooling as well as College, the newly
available evidence was seized on by the *TES* leader writer as con-
firmation of his worst fears:

> At Oxford HMC schools gained 69 firsts to 60 from all the
> rest of the schools in the country . . . Should we not have
> expected the village Hampdens to have stolen a march? Might
> not the masses have revealed a flush of buried talents and left
> the classes far behind? Not at all . . .
>
> The results do seem to suggest what has long been
> suspected, that the family and home background has most
> to do with intellectual prowess . . . The cultivated parent, the
> well-stocked library, the well-chosen dinner parties — how
> useful they are to a boy of parts, and how unamenable they
> are to universal distribution by egalitarians. . . . Although
> all this is tentative, this year's results should produce second
> thoughts in those social engineers who think that by a radical
> reorganisation of the educational system they can redress
> nature's balance. . . . These simple facts seem to escape the
> educational politicians who are prepared to scrap established
> school systems and spend millions of pounds in a hopeless
> attempt to abolish inequalities of nurture, which are bound
> to elude their grasp.[11]

A year later, the same journal found it 'reassuring' that each year
up to 2500 young people were gaining qualifications which fitted
them to enter university, but were unable to find a place: 'Minimum
qualifications do not amount to much: there is no saying how they
square with Faculty demands.'[12]

Such views were acceptable to a sufficiently large number of dons
for there to be little chance that the continuing upturn in demand
would result in any real democratisation of the university system
during the late 1950s and early 1960s, although some commentators
became increasingly frustrated at the prodigality of the system. One
grammar school headmaster commented in 1958:

I have heard recently that in the third year of the Honours School of Maths at Bristol there are only 5 left out of an original first year group of 30 and at Exeter only 6 out of about 20. In 1957 Exeter is said to have sent down about 150 first year students, and even more in 1956 . . . whatever the explanation, such a policy does not seem likely to produce the increased supply of qualified scientists and mathematicians which we are repeatedly told is so urgently needed.[13]

Not only did the universities continue with policies which debarred significant numbers of entrants from honours degree courses, and resulted in many others failing to gain a degree at all, but also there was in practice little relaxation of the stranglehold held by the major schools on the more prestigious universities. A succession of reports confirmed that year after year about a half of the entrants to Oxbridge came from independent schools. In 1957 the Kelsall Report showed that while 42 per cent of the Oxford intake and 53 per cent of that of Cambridge was drawn from the private sector; only 6.5 per cent of the girls entering Oxbridge came from working-class origins.[14] When, in 1961, the *Oxford Magazine* published a survey of the backgrounds of students, it found wide disparities between colleges, with Trinity ('known as Oxford's top social college') admitting over four-fifths of its students from independent schools, while, at the other extreme St Peter's Hall drew less than a third of its students from the same source. The Master of St Peter's, The Revd Thornton-Duesbury, pointed out that the college's high proportion of science students meant more recruitment from state schools, while direct grant schools such as Manchester Grammar School, which contributed a significant number of pupils, were not listed as independent schools.[15] One contributor to the *TES* during these years thought this to be a situation in which 'non-academic public school men are keeping out the direct grant and grammar school scholar from Oxbridge'.[16]

Further studies during the early 1960s showed that of the 27 boys' schools which won most open awards to Oxbridge only five were direct grant and two state grammar schools: the rest were independent.[17] These researches detected significant contrasts by both region and gender in recruitment to Oxford and Cambridge. The 30 per cent of the population resident in the North won only 23 per cent of the available places, while girls were far more likely to be drawn from local direct grant schools than boys:

One possible explanation for this is that girls from professional families are more likely to attend a local direct grant day school whereas the sons more usually go to independent boarding schools . . . The curious anomaly of the Oxford and Cambridge system is that it perpetuates sexual apartheid in the scramble for highly prized places, but once the initial discrimination is over, permits men and women to study for identical degrees.[18]

The statistics presented by the Robbins Committee in 1963 showed that the pattern of admission to Oxford and Cambridge was in stark contrast to that of other universities:

Table 8.1   *University entrants by type of school attended*[19]

| | Type of school | | | | |
	Maintained	DG	Independent	All entrants	Numbers
Men					
Oxbridge					
1955	31	12	57	100	3709
1961	30	16	54	100	4002
Other univs.					
1955	72	10	18	100	9647
1961	72	13	15	100	13638
Women					
Oxbridge					
1955	39	21	40	100	533
1961	47	22	31	100	593
Other univs.					
1955	66	14	20	100	4638
1961	76	10	14	100	6666

The Robbins Report showed too that there was a further contrast between the universities and technical colleges, since the colleges remained largely regional with the vast majority of their students being drawn from state schools and many following part-time courses.

This segmented pattern of higher education had important implications for recruitment to the professions, industry and commerce, and led many commentators to perceive a sad waste of national talent. A Commons questioner in March 1963 elicited the information that recruitment to Branch A of the Foreign Office (one of the upper echelons of the Civil Service) was 94.2 per cent from Oxbridge and 5.3 per cent from other universities. Alan Thompson, the Labour member for Dunfermline asked:

Does the Minister really think that 5% is drawing on the reservoir of talent in the English, Welsh and Scottish universities? Is one in five of successful applicants from state schools really representative of the number of boys attending these schools?[20]

It is significant that, within higher education, despite a growing awareness of the injustices inherent in this situation (particularly after the coming of universal secondary schooling), the major debate of this period was concerned with curricular change rather than with the thorny question of access. The themes and tensions which had marked the debate on the curriculum of the new University College of North Staffordshire in the late 1940s were rehearsed and repeated throughout the following decade, and had an enormous impact on the work of existing institutions as well as on the planning committees of the new universities. The issue was crystallised in the UGC Report on *University development, 1952-57* which argued that fifty years previously, when recruitment was largely from the upper classes, and leisure was freely available to students, it could be assumed that 'the general education of the university student could be left to take care of itself . . . the university could concentrate on turning him into an expert without risk to the whole man.'[21] This view was thought to be no longer tenable because of changes in the social background of students, and the premature specialisation of sixth-formers since the introduction of the GCE. The twin threats of over-specialisation and memorisation of detail must be met, the UGC, emphasised, by always keeping in mind the fact that:

it is the first duty of the university . . . to teach him how to think. For this purpose he must be given not only competence in one field of knowledge, but access to related fields and a general appreciation of the art of learning. He must be helped to acquire interests outside his special subject.[22]

The report went on to advocate the introduction of more interdisciplinary courses, of non-examined options which would introduce students to new subjects, and the creation of more free time for students as essential steps to counter the problem of over-specialisation.

This debate on the breadth of curricula was linked intimately with and went on at the same time as one on the most appropriate training for technicians. Here, too, the UGC had marked out its position clearly in the *Note on technology in the universities* issued in 1950. This document drew a clear distinction between the practical training of the technical colleges and the more fundamental education appropriate to a university department.

> This is a difference . . . not in status or grade but in kind
> . . . In general the university courses should be more widely
> based on higher standards of fundamental science and con-
> tain a smaller element of training related to immediate or
> special work in industry . . . This corresponds with a distinc-
> tion between two types of recruit required by industry. . . .
> While there may be some degree of overlapping in the func-
> tions of universities and of some technical colleges, the distinc-
> tions between the technology proper to universities and that
> of the technical colleges ought to be recognized more clearly
> in planning future change.[23]

Notions such as these remained current throughout the period under review and helped to define the nature of 'the binary controversy' as it developed into the 1960s. Equally, the currency of these ideas meant that advocates of a radical reappraisal of technical education often met with a stormy reception. In 1956 Professor R.W. Revans, newly appointed to the Chair of Industrial Administration at Manchester, argued at the British Association meeting for 'a rational analysis of industrialists' decisions . . . If one wants to be a philosopher king in industry, why not study industry rather than Xenophon or Tacitus?' Such philistinism was immediately attacked in the columns of the *TES* as '. . . a deceptively plausible argument . . . Such a study would hardly supply the qualities of vision and judgement required in industry.'[24]

So, the expansion of the 1950s and 1960s took place against the background of a vigorous and continuing debate on the appropriateness of the courses on offer to a swiftly changing industrial society.

Retrenchment remained the order of the day within the universities during the early 1950s. The UGC, preoccupied by the spectre of unemployment among arts graduates, saw in 1952 no prospect of 'a substantial rise in numbers . . . Some indeed think it desirable to stabilize their numbers at a somewhat lower level.' Yet, in the event, the number of university students was 81,000 in 1954–55, and climbed steadily to over 100,000 by the end of the decade. Growth was most dramatic in the small and relatively new university colleges, four of which were awarded Charters by 1957. Within a decade their enrolment had doubled. These four (Southampton, Hull, Exeter and Leicester) were the last English institutions to use the London external degree as a stepping-stone to full university status. It was an expansion which elicited widely differing responses from the academic community, differences which surfaced in an explosive debate at the 1955 Home Universities Conference. Conservative estimates made by Guy Chilvers of Oxford University and Professor R.G.D. Allen of the LSE suggested that a small permanent increase of 1000 university places would be enough to meet the 'bulge'. The opposition to this view was led by Lord Simon of Wythenshawe, who won much support for his argument that England's survival as a great power depended upon an increased number of university students, a vast building programme and a greater emphasis upon the education of technologists. Within a year the UGC had committed itself to a permanent target of 106,000 by the mid-1960s, a figure which was to be revised upwards to 124,000 in February, 1958. In January 1960 a further revision anticipated 170,000 university students by 1970. By 1963 the Robbins Committee was able to look forward with confidence to the time when over half a million would be embarked on full-time courses in higher education.

The fact that the first phase of university expansion, during the late 1950s, was confined to existing institutions and was greatest in the smaller and newer universities meant a restructuring of the English university system, which now became far more national in its scope. As recently as 1938–39 Oxbridge and London had between them educated two-thirds of the undergraduate population. By 1958 this figure was below a half, and falling. The trend for increasing numbers of students to move away from their home areas meant that the civic universities ceased to be largely 'regional' institutions: the increase in the number of post-graduate students (to 11 per cent by 1957–58) served only to reinforce their acceptance as part of a national system of universities.

One immediate reaction to this growth in the size of the universities was the fear that the sense of community, which was widely regarded as one of the strengths of these institutions in England, might be lost. In May 1960 Lord Simon commented that a few institutions 'were getting rather near the great universities of the United States' and two years later the Vice-Chancellor of Cambridge university expressed his concern that the Treasury 'was preferring student expansion to the advancement of knowledge'.

It was this fear, allied to the steady increase in the demand for university places, which ensured the acceptability of local initiatives for the foundation of new universities. The impact of C.P. Snow's *Two cultures*, which highlighted the relevance of the debate on curricular reform, made it certain that each of these new institutions would attempt, in one way or another, to break from the traditional single honours course which typified the existing civic universities.

The demand for a university at Brighton, which was resuscitated at a public meeting in the Royal Pavilion in July 1956, was originally made at the start of the twentieth century. By the mid-1950s the case was reinforced by inexorable demographic pressures. As Professor W.G.B. Balchin, Dean of Science at University College, Swansea explained:

> whereas the nineteenth century experienced the growth of the great urban centres in the Midlands and in Northern England, the twentieth century witnessed the growth and expansion of population in southern and eastern England. In the latter areas the present inhabitants undoubtedly have less ready access to university facilities than elsewhere. The general need for new foundations in south and east England clearly emerges.[25]

It was a view shared by the UGC, on whose behalf Viscount Hailsham told the House of Lords on 22 May 1957 that a university at Brighton might relieve congestion in existing universities. This was the first official hint that the lobbying of W.G. Stone, the energetic Director of Education for Brighton, might meet with success. A year later, in February 1958, Heathcoat Amory, as Chancellor of the Exchequer, announced the go-ahead for a University of Sussex, and anticipated a subvention of £15 million in 1960-61 for the planning of new universities.

The immediate result was not only the establishment at Brighton of an Academic Planning Board, to ensure that the new institution would meet national as well as local needs, but also the generation of a plethora of plans for new universities, reflecting a buoyancy and optimism which was suddenly fairly general at the close of the 1950s. No self-respecting township was without its planning committee, and proposals poured in from Bournemouth, Chatham, Chester, Coventry, Essex, Folkestone, Gloucester, Cheltenham, Grantham, Hereford, the Isle of Man, Kent, Lancaster, Norwich, Plymouth, Shrewsbury, Stamford, Stevenage, Swindon, Thanet,

Whitby, York. It says much for the power of a particular model of university life within England, deeply influenced by Oxbridge, that the seven proposals which did emerge as the basis of new universities during the 1960s all resulted in semi-rural campuses associated with townships which were remarkable as much for their historical associations as for their links with British industry.

Those towns which had already devised plans for a local college were in the best position to make a clear case to the UGC. In York, where the idea of a university was current as early as 1946, the York Academic Trust had been at work throughout the 1950s, anticipating that 'when the demands of science and technology have been more fully realized, the UGC would . . . turn its attention to the humanities . . . to the kind of work which the Trust is carrying out.'[26] So, when the trust presented its case formally to Sir Keith Murray, Chairman of the UGC, in June 1959, it was able to articulate clearly the claims of York:

> The archaeological, historical and architectural survivals from the past make it an admirable centre for research in, and teaching of, *the traditional humanities*. But possessing all the administrative machinery and public services of a great city on a scale small enough to be readily comprehensible, it can also make a valuable contribution to the study of subjects like local government and sociology; what may . . . be called the humanities of the twentieth century.[27]

At Norwich, too, proposals for a local university had been in the air since the First World War and this fact meant that the announcement of a possible increase in the number of universities was seized upon by the Norwich Chamber of Commerce. In this instance, the precise nature of any new academic enterprise was less clearly articulated, and when, on 19 April 1960, the UGC announced its approval in principle for universities at York and Norwich, it insisted that the Norwich Promotions Committee should be complemented by an academic planning board along the lines of that at York. The claims of East Anglia as a region were to be met, provided perceived national curricular needs were paramount.

Once initiated, the process of agreeing new universities proved a difficult one to stop. No sooner were York and Norwich approved, than it became clear that the gap between governmental target figures and the capacity of the university system was increasing. By the time the UGC's 1962–63 allocations were announced, a shortfall of 17,000 was anticipated within ten years, leading the UGC to the view that: 'in view of the possible gap in the early 'seventies and of what appeared to us to be a further inevitable expansion thereafter, we felt it prudent to make immediate firm provision for a further four new universities.'[28]

Despite attacks from academics such as W.H.G. Armytage, whose advocacy of a university of Scunthorpe was based on the view that the new campuses 'were not within engagement distance' of an industrial complex,[29] and despite a growing lobby for the renewal of the inner cities in which new universities could play a part, the more traditional English view of a university as an academic community continued to win out. It was backed by fears that the urban universities were becoming increasingly nine-to-five institutions, and by the argument that these small new institutions needed to be in environments which enabled space for future growth.

In Essex, as had been the case at Brighton, the demographic pressures of the south-east were seen by the Promotion Committee set up in January 1900, as vital to its case:

> Inquiries made of schools maintained by the Essex Authority show that there have been a number of boys and girls who, though qualified to enter a University, have failed to gain a place in recent years, and there are undoubtedly others of good ability to whom the existence of a University close at hand . . . would act as a spur.[30]

In this case, the strength of local industries and the proximity to London were stressed by the Promotion Committee, and it needed the active discouragement of the UGC to abandon plans for a Chelmsford site in favour of Wivenhoe Park, Colchester. The UGC took the view that Chelmsford would have been an unsuitable location for the university to build a strong corporate life in view of the rival attractions of London.

Similarly, in Kent, where schemes for a university had been circulating since the war, the strong support for a university came initially from Broadstairs, Margate and Ramsgate, which could boast a joint population of over 100,000 and the prospect of immediately available student accommodation. But by April 1960, the County Council was persuaded of the superior claims of Canterbury, whose historical associations were seen as appropriate for a university town. Although the nature of the curriculum awaited

clarification, industrialists quickly added their support to the financial backing promised by the county. During 1960, Pfiser, a local
manufacturing chemist, A.E. Reed, paper manufacturer and
T.E.G. Baker, an engineering firm, all promised subventions.

The third new university to be sanctioned by the government
in May 1961 was to be at Coventry, a decision to which *The Times*
responded querulously:

> Will the students like being sent to Coventry? Is Coventry
> more than a city mainly remarkable for car factories and left-
> wing shop stewards? In reality Coventry has . . . a com-
> paratively rigorous intellectual life together with ideas on every
> subject under the sun.[31]

The Coventry scheme had several shared features with other new
university proposals. As at York, there was enthusiastic episcopal
backing. The Bishop, Neville Gorton, had made a plea for a local
university in the House of Lords in 1951. From 1958 onwards there
was official support from the town council (although in Coventry
the Conservative Party favoured the upgrading of the local colleges
of art and technology in response to the governmental drive for the
expansion of technical education). The appointment of Lord Rootes
to the chairmanship of the promotion committee was a guarantee
of backing from local industry. As at Norwich, the UGC gave
support in principle before a curriculum was hammered out and
insisted that the local academic planning board should keep before
them national as well as local needs.[32]

Plans for a new university in Lancashire had been devised during
the late 1940s and never entirely subsided. The problem before the
Council for the Promotion of a university in North-West Lancashire
during the late 1950s was to arbitrate between the claims of
Blackpool and Lancaster. Again, 'the antiquity of the city . . . and
a cultural heritage . . . which would benefit a university town'[33]
proved to be the decisive considerations. To the UGC, the need
to do something to reverse the drift to the South (all but one of the
post-war foundations were in the Midlands or the South-East) was
a key consideration:

> It has been suggested to us that there was a need for a further
> university in the work on the grounds that, once students
> moved southwards, they tended to stay in the south. This was
> creating difficulties for industries . . . in the north. We

sympathised and . . . decided to recommend that the seventh new university should be located at Lancaster.[34]

On 23 November, 1961, it was so designated in a parliamentary written reply.

While it was the clear intention of the founders of these new universities that they should offer a panacea to the shortcomings of the existing universities, their novel curricula made it easy for them to be castigated by traditionalists as academically inferior. This factor helps explain why the new universities found it difficult to establish their position within the academic pecking order. The academic snobbery under which they suffered was epitomised by the comments of G.C.L. Bertram, a tutor of St John's College, Cambridge, made in September 1960:

> Nearly all young people of the greatest ability already go to a university. Further expansion of the total university population can do nothing but dilute the abilities already there concentrated. The additional candidates will do little but add to class III in the academic sense . . . With any such dilution, the tendency will continue for degree standards progressively to diverge between universities of present greater and lesser esteem . . . The present debate should be concentrated upon whether further expansion of the universities themselves is really the correct solution. Or should York, Canterbury, Brighton, Norwich and the rest concentrate on something new but necessary — splendid but different?[35]

It is the existence of attitudes such as this within the academic community which help explain some of the problems encountered by these new universities in establishing their credibility, and which suggest too why it was that the new universities were a particular target of the UGC in the economic retrenchment of the early 1980s.

What the expansion of the universities during the post-war era did not achieve was the alleviation of the shortfall of qualified technologists for industry. Indeed, the growing demands of industry for graduate recruits meant that the 1950s saw a significant increase in the number of arts graduates recruited to management positions. By the late 1950s 'arts graduates were being referred to as an elite among managers'.[36]

None the less, the debate which had been initiated by the Percy and Barlow Reports on the nature and scale of technological education both within and outside the universities was pursued during the 1950s. Early in the decade what were to become the main features of future developments were apparent. Proposals for a Royal College of Technologists which might develop as a major award-giving body surfaced in the first report of the National Advisory Council on Education for Industry and Commerce in 1950. This idea was picked up by the 1951 White Paper on *Higher technological education* and reiterated in the 1952 NAC Report. It was a scheme which met with a sympathetic response from industrialists many of whom were anxious to see a reinforcement of the technical colleges if the universities were unable or unwilling to meet their needs. As John Leese, Secretary of the Yorkshire Council for Further Education, observed in the columns of the *TES*:

> The great majority of the representatives of industry, of the local authorities, and the universities, support the proposals of the NAC in favour of a national award-granting College of Technologists, and of higher grants for advanced courses in technical colleges. Nowhere in these discussions — certainly not from the university representatives — does there seem to have been any strong demand for a technical university.[37]

A *Memorandum on higher education* produced in 1954 by a Parliamentary and Scientific Committee showed that there was already a shortfall of 15,000 newly qualified engineers annually in relation to industrial demand and this report too called for a controlling body with powers similar to the UGC.[38] It was only in 1955, when the NACEIC submitted its third plea for a centralised awards system that the government conceded by establishing the NCTA (soon to be known as the Hives Council) to award diplomas in technology, but not degrees.

This hesitancy on the part of the government to accede to what in retrospect appears to have been inevitable stemmed in large part from its determination to ensure that higher technological training remained the preserve of the universities. The 1951 White Paper on *Higher technological education* which called for more applied research within the universities and kept alive the idea first floated in the Barlow Report of one technological university, was welcomed by the educational press and legitimised the new Conservative government's attempts to use the universities as a base for the expansion of training in applied sciences. The *TES* commented in the autumn of 1951 that 'the universities are now well set to maintain their monopoly of higher technological study'.[39] Five months later, introducing the quinquennial Treasury grant to the universities, R.A. Butler suggested that the 20 per cent increase should be used to place greater emphasis on the 'scientific and technical sides'.[40]

A policy of identifying and promoting a small number of the best existing technical colleges was outlined formally by Butler in the summer of 1952: 'The obvious means of immediate advance, as the previous Government realized, is to improve rapidly a few of the major technical colleges.'[41] That this might involve at least one new technological university was made clear by circular 255 in February 1953, which elicited this comment from the *TES*:

> One important thing is to get down in black and white the necessarily limited list of major colleges. Then everyone will know where they are. The rank and file colleges, untroubled by drams of toilsome glory, will once more be able to concentrate on their important task of producing technicians. A few major colleges, on the other hand, will have clearly started on a road which might well end in a technological institution of university rank.[42]

It was a policy which chimed with the thinking of the UGC and which won support from several influential industrialists and scientific researchers. Sir John Cockroft, Director of Research at Harwell, told a meeting of teachers in further education in 1952 that it was important 'to bring a few of the major technical colleges up to unviersity level' and on to UGC funds, as had just happened at Loughborough.[43] Similarly, Sir Fredrick Handley Page told a meeting of the Machine Tool Trades Association later in the same year that the universities should focus far more on those areas of science which related most closely to industry and technology.[44] The outcome was that, in 1952, the Imperial College of Science and Technology was formally identified by the government as the one technological institution to become a fully-fledged constituent of the University of London, and during the next two years the universities of Manchester, Leeds and Birmingham became particular targets for the expansion of technological capacity.

Two quite contradictory factors worked to undermine this policy. The first, most clearly evident during the early 1950s, was the lingering view that it really did not matter how many technologists were produced, since technology could not constitute the basis of a proper education. One *TES* leader in 1952, while welcoming the upgrading of a few existing technical colleges, warned its readers that:

> these technologists, these rulers of factories . . . are inevitably to be the pupils of the teachers of Classics, History, English. It is not the way of this country to let those who will govern go unwashed by the streams that flow from Palestine, Athens and Mediaeval Paris . . . The education of technologists is very much a matter for the humanities.[45]

Objections such as this did have the practical effect of sharpening the debate on the need for and the precise nature of a liberal under-pinning to technological courses, whether they were offered in universities or in technical colleges. The result was that the 1956 White Paper on *Technical education* stressed the need for all training in technical and scientific subjects to be given sufficient breadth to ensure a broad outlook among future leaders of industry. Technology, it argued, must not neglect 'spiritual and human values'.[46] The agency chosen to ensure this breadth was the Hives Committee (the NCTA), which, during the next few years, by insisting upon 'sandwich' elements for the Diploma in Technology and on some element of liberal studies in the courses it validated, steered the Colleges of Technology towards the point at which their awards were seen by the committee of Vice-Chancellors as adequate for entry to a postgraduate course. So a binary system of higher education began to emerge in practice during the late 1950s.

The second major factor which spelt the death of the govern-mental policies of the early 1950s and which led, too, to the develop-ment of the colleges of technology, was a quite sudden widespread realisation that the planned expansion of technological capacity was woefully insufficient. The increasing numbers of qualified school-leavers generated by the trend towards staying on at school beyond the minimum leaving age were augmented by applicants for places in technical colleges from other sources. At first, during the late 1940s it had been demobilised ex-servicemen on FET grants who had swelled the numbers in the colleges. During the 1950s a grow-ing number of overseas students, mostly from Commonwealth coun-tries, anxious to follow 'A' level courses to qualify them for univer-sity entry were joined by adolescents who had had enough of secondary schooling but also sought courses beyond 'O' level GCE. The upturn in the popularity of day-release courses during the early 1950s stemmed directly from the fact that industrialists were grappling with the problems created by a relatively buoyant economy and an under-trained labour force. In sum, these developments created a crisis in the supply of places, and it was inevitable that the technical colleges came to play an increasingly important part in its relief.

During the 1950s an increasing number of observers became persuaded of the value of advanced work in the technical colleges. In 1955, J.A.P. Hall of the Regent Street Polytechnic pointed out, in a letter to the *TES*, that of the University of London degrees in physics awarded that summer, a half of the first class honours degrees were gained by external students working in technical colleges. He went on to argue that, despite the reservations of the Institute of Physics, the time had come for honours degree courses in technical colleges to receive full recognition.[47] Despite the mounting evidence of the merit of the work done in colleges of technology, it was inconceivable that the government would do a complete about-turn in this area of policy. David Eccles explained to a Conference of the Association of Education Committees, shortly after his appointment as Minister for Education, that he would seek to direct expansion through what were identifiably the most successful of the technical colleges, since it would be uneconomical for all LEAs to run advanced courses. He promised: 'I shall use the resources of the law to prevent local authorities putting their prestige above the national interest.'[48] So, the influential 1956 White Paper announced, not only a sharp increase in student numbers and support for sandwich courses, but also the promotion of a small number of technical colleges to become colleges of advanced technology. This was to be the framework within which the governmental conversion to the expansion of the non-university sector of higher education, announced in a Prime Ministerial speech at Bradford in January 1954,[49] was to be implemented. Circular 305 followed to provide the administrative details of this policy, and by the spring of 1957 redesignated Colleges of Advanced Technology were at work in Birmingham, Bradford, Loughborough, Salford and Cardiff, together with three London Polytechnics (Battersea, Chelsea and Northampton) which were now bracketed with them. For these institutions this was a major step towards full recognition as technological universities a decade later. Similarly, the designation of 25 regional colleges, as advocated in Circular 305, provided a template for the polytechnic sector of higher education, which was to wait a further fourteen years for official recognition.

From the Labour side the governmental conversion to the expansion of technological higher education was seen as too half-hearted. Michael Stewart argued in the Commons that what was really needed were technological universities rather than ten colleges of advanced technology, a suggestion which was dismissed by the *TES* as 'ridiculous'.[50] The same journal commended the governmental conversion to the support of technical higher education as showing its awareness 'of the reservoir of talent constituted by the secondary modern schools'.[51] This was a reflection of the not uncommon view that some kind of compensatory higher education was needed to match the expansion of the less prestigious forms of secondary schooling, and helps explain the difficulties experienced by the technical sector in being awarded full recognition within a system of higher education.

During the next few years the continuing governmental commitment to the technical sector and to the promotion of sandwich courses in particular, demonstrated that, as one contemporary put it: 'the great drive . . . opened by the 1956 White Paper was no flash in the pan.'[52] In October 1957 A.A. Part, the Under-Secretary then in charge of the further education section within the Ministry of Education, announced proudly that the number of recognised sandwich courses had doubled since the initiation of the new policy to over 200, that the Hives Council had already recognised 49 courses as leading to a Diploma in Technology, and that the new full-time apprentice training scheme was already catering for over 3000 young people annually in the Southern region alone.[53] The emphasis which the government was now placing upon the technical sector to enable the continuing expansion of higher education was confirmed in December when Edward Boyle, opening the ICI apprentices' school at Billingham, pointed out that three-quarters of the 6500 newly qualified technologists each year were products of the technical colleges, and emphasised that the vast majority had been on part-time courses. This drive was sustained through a pamphlet, *Britain's future and technical education*, which was printed in 1958 and circulated to industrial companies advertising the possibilities of the new Diploma in Technology.

The growing evidence of a high wastage and failure rate among part-time technical college students (a concern which was fuelled by a succession of letters to the journal *Technology* drawing attention to this problem)[54] was an important factor which strengthened the arm of those who saw the sandwich course and block-release arrangements as the most reliable routes to a sustained expansion of the technological sector. Accordingly, both the Crowther Report (1959) and the 1961 White Paper, *Better opportunities in technical education*, emphasised the importance of courses which involved at least an element of full-time work, and this trend is further evidence of the speed at which perceptions of technical education were changing during these years.

The Ministry's commitment was also demonstrated in continuing efforts to 'humanise' curricula in the technological sector. The release of Circular 323, *Liberal education in technical Colleges*, in 1957 ensured that what was seen as a key issue within the universities was not entirely lost sight of within the public-sector institutions. By 1959, the *TES* was reporting that a number of colleges had responded either with significant modifications to course content, or through changes in teaching method which encouraged a more open and heuristic approach to the material being studied. At the Birmingham College of Advanced Technology, in particular, under the guidance of Peter Venables, the 1955 Harvard Report, *General education in a free society*, had influenced the abandonment of formal lectures in favour of seminars, discussions and tutorials.[55] More tangible evidence of governmental support came with the announcement in 1959 that the augmented building programme for technical education (it had trebled in three years to £15 million annually by 1959) was to be maintained until 1964 at least.[56]

These developments in combination meant that the technical sector became an increasingly popular 'overspill' for those who were unable to win a place at university. The late 1950s saw a sudden upturn in the numbers gaining two or more 'A' levels, from 25,000 in the mid 1950s to over 60,000 by 1964. The immediate result was a sudden fall in the percentage of this group who were able to enter university, and consequently 'a spillover of well-qualified young people no longer able to go to university who went instead to colleges of advanced technology'.[57] So, what was fast becoming a transformation of the basic structure of higher education in England, was impelled by social and economic changes which were transforming the lifestyles and aspirations of thousands of young people.

Two developments of the early 1960s confirmed the place of the technical sector within higher education, and both marked the government's increasing recognition of educational expenditure as an important investment which was also of benefit for its own sake. The first was the acceptance in 1962 of the report of the Anderson Committee, which compelled LEAs to fund all full-time students embarked on courses requiring two or more 'A' levels. So the inconsistencies in LEA grant support which had plagued the universities a decade earlier, and which persisted in the treatment of the colleges, were ended: now both private and public sectors were to receive similar treatment. The second important development was the immediate governmental acceptance of the Robbins Report (a White Paper was published within 24 hours of the appearance of the Report). As Layard, King and Moser have observed, this reflected not only the proximity of a general election, but 'more important was the imminence of the bulge and the government's genuine belief in the importance of higher education on both social and economic grounds'.[58]

The major recommendations of the Robbins Committee are well known and need to be restated only briefly. It was foreseen that the number of students in full-time higher education in Great Britain would rise from 216,000 (1962–63) to about 560,000 by 1980–81. This should involve a total of around 60 institutions of university status under the aegis of an enlarged and strengthened UGC. The Colleges of Advanced Technology were to be given full recognition as technological universities, and a number of Special Institutions for Scientific and Technological Education and Research were to be selected for rapid development within the university sector. The NCTA was to be replaced by a Council for National Academic Awards; four-year courses in Colleges of Education were proposed, together with closer links between these colleges and the universities as validating institutions. Perhaps most important, what was to become known as the 'Robbins principle' was the acceptance 'as an axiom that courses of higher education should be available for all those who are qualified by ability and attainment to pursue them and who wish to do so'.[59] These were the terms in which an attempt was made to give shape to an expansion which, in reality, neither planners nor government could do much to control. The emergence of the public sector of higher education was already well under way by 1963, its scope and functions largely determined by decisions taken during the 1940s and 1950s. The Robbins Report could do little more than legitimise what had by then become inevitable.

But this fact did not mean that its recommendations were received universally without controversy. Although during the early 1960s the press had in the main become wildly enthusiastic for the further expansion of higher education, *The Times* and its satellites remained unconvinced of the general trend. One *TES* leader commented guardedly:

The Robbins Committee are among those who would argue that what the people desire the state should give them when possible. Others would reply that public desire is fairly easily controllable and it should not be encouraged to mount so high that the efficiency of institutions is endangered. Further, what do the public really want anyway?[60]

By the end of 1963 the same journal was using its Christmas supplement to present a parody of Robbins, the 'Whythitt Report on Comprehensive Universities' with research 'findings' that 95 per cent of parents thought their children fit for higher education, and postulating a possible two million in higher education by 1980–81![61] Much opinion within the Labour Party was sympathetic to the Robbins Report, and it is difficult to be certain whether R.H.S. Crossman was reflecting his deepest convictions, or merely seeking to score political points, when he argued to the Peterborough Fabian Society that:

> under the Robbins plan in future the failure to pass the 18-plus will have as disastrous a consequence as the failure to pass the 11-plus has had up till now. In the Labour Party, we believe there must be more than one way into higher education. The boy who becomes an apprentice when he leaves school must also have a chance, by combining theory and practice, of graduating with just as good a degree as the boy who gets a scholarship to Oxford.[62]

By the early 1960s Crossman's aspiration was close to realisation in the sense that an increasing number of degree routes were becoming available in applied sciences and technology. But there remained many tokens of the perceived inferiority of these courses. The fact that the UGC had first preferred the new universities, that there was concern to broaden and 'liberalise' technological higher education, and the widespread acceptance that much of the technical provision was an 'overspill' education compensating for that which the universities could not or would not provide; all these factors help to explain why technical education, which had for over a century suffered from an identity crisis within English education, continued to be held in low prestige by many during the 'modernisation' of the years following the Second World War.

Meanwhile, teacher supply continued to be a thorny and

intractable problem. With the upturn in the economy in the early 1950s and the continuing availability of employment opportunities elsewhere, it soon became clear that there would be a growing short-fall in the numbers training to teach. By 1952 the educational press was reporting over a thousand unfilled vacancies in the teacher training colleges annually, three-quarters of them intended for females.[63] Within two years it had been realised that this was to be an enduring problem. The *TES* commented:

> The idea is false that the disappearance of the bulge will also bring in of its own accord the conditions that would make possible nursery schools, county colleges, leaving at 16, three year teacher training, and the rest of the 1944 cornucopia. Merely to reduce primary as well as secondary classes to a maximum of 30, an additional 15,000 teachers would be needed. It is on the recruitment of teachers that all else hinges and here that Ministerial policy has proved most barren.[64]

This journal argued that, in view of the projected one million extra school pupils by the end of the decade, a campaign for the recruit-ment of teachers was necessary 'for the full application of the 1944 Act'.[65]

Briefly, during the mid-1950s it seemed that these fears were illusory, as the Ministry reported: 'buoyant recruitment, later retire-ment and the continued willingness of married women to remain in or return to teaching.'[66] During this lull the NACTST and the ATCDE both pressed the Ministry to introduce three-year training courses for all teachers. H.C. Dent has called it 'one of the larger ironies of educational history' that the underlying reason for this reform was a fear that, by the early 1960s, there might be unemploy-ment among trained teachers.[67] By the time three-year training was introduced in 1960, it was already clear that the opposite was the case, and that the underlying long-term reality was one of teacher shortage. By 1958 the NACTST had reverted to an advocacy of more places for intending teachers, and their fears were confirmed by the deliberations of the Crowther Commission. In May, 1958, a correspondence between Crowther and Geoffrey Lloyd, the then Minister of Education, in which the Ministry was warned that 'further instalments of educational progress might founder for lack of teachers' was made public in an HMSO publica-tion, *The future demand for teachers*.[68]

The initiative was now back with the expansionists, and it

remained there into the early 1960s. In February 1961, as part of a campaign to attract back some of the 50,000 married women teachers who had left the profession in the previous few years, David Eccles launched, with maximum publicity, a leaflet entitled *Come back to teaching*.[69] At the end of the year he conceded in the Commons that some 60 per cent of secondary school pupils were in oversize classes for want of trained teachers, adding that 'we wish it was only an emergency. It is continuing all the time.'[70]

In January 1962 a committee of experts set up by the NUT and chaired by Sir Charles Morris, Vice-Chancellor of the University of Leeds, produced their blueprint for *Investment for national survival*. They drew heavily on the work of John Vaizey and Simon Pratt, whose Research Unit in the Economics and Administration of Education was demanding, as a minimum, 95,000 more teachers by 1970 if existing policies were to be implemented.[71] It was against this background of a growing consensus of informed opinion, that the NACTST report on the training and supply of teachers, which appeared in the spring of 1962, was seized upon by opposition MPs to justify an emergency Commons debate in which they demanded a 'crash programme' to increase the number of teachers in training.[72]

It is hardly surprising, then, that a variety of strategies to meet this crisis were canvassed. One of the more bizarre was Angus Maude's suggestion in 1954 of a resuscitation of the pupil-teacher system:

> A system of apprenticeship for selected girls . . . who should be persuaded . . . to become for three years part-time schoolgirls and part-time assistant teachers under the supervision of qualified teachers in primary schools . . . who would deny that qualities of character are likely to be developed by a period of apprenticeship in a good primary school?[73]

A not dissimilar idea was floated by the *TES* two years later with the suggestion that:

> one small thought suggests itself. . . . How many girls with 2 'A' level subjects should go in for infant teaching? Some certainly. Every infant should have a highly qualified expert in that interesting and fruitful field in charge. But cannot that expert make good use, under her kindly wisdom, of girls who however motherly their ways with small children would not

get within miles of the present training-college entrance test?[74]

The fact that as late as May 1962 David Eccles was still advocating the use of 'auxiliaries' (the employment of unqualified assistants to fully-fledged teachers) as one way of resolving the crisis, shows the residual attractiveness of such schemes within government circles, even though the teachers' unions remained implacably opposed.[75]

Some local initiatives were reported nationally. In 1956, for example, the *TES* publicised attempts by the Saltley Training College to alleviate problems of teacher supply in Birmingham by lengthening the duration of student teaching practices.[76] The teacher shortage impinged particularly on the inner cities and on working-class areas. In 1957, the West Riding authority reported, hardly surprisingly, that it was proving harder to recruit teachers to the mining areas than to spa towns such as Harrogate and announced its own scheme to attract staff to work in less salubrious areas.[77] Several authorities were already tinkering with ideas which anticipated by a decade the EPA allowances introduced in response to the Plowden Report. In 1956 the *TES* attacked 'the proposal that areas short of teachers should be empowered to pay an extra allowance. This is a clumsy expedient.'[78] During the 1950s some local education authorities persisted in attempts to induce young people to 'pledge' to return to their home areas as school-teachers after becoming qualified, even though the Ministry had announced the abolition of similar pledges for entrants to university education departments as early as 1951.[79]

The acute, perennial difficulty in attracting teachers of mathematics and science was an important consideration behind the Burnham Committee's introduction of responsibility allowances for advanced teaching in 1955. Although this eventually became the template for a complete restructuring of teachers' pay scales, it very quickly became apparent that the existing regulations soon resulted in 'wide variations in the allowances paid by different authorities'[80] as this too became a factor differentiating the more affluent parts of the country.

But the response to the problem of teacher supply which had arguably the greatest long-term effect upon the structure of the profession, and which was also perceived at the time as the most controversial, was the introduction of equal pay for women. Proposed by the Burnham Committee in 1955, and implemented in gradations over the following seven years, equal pay for women and men teachers became a reality April 1961.[81] The National Association of Schoolmasters, which had originally broken from the NUT earlier in the century on the issue of equal pay, remained opposed to this development; its President, D.I. Davies, told the annual conference in 1956 that: 'the vast majority of schoolmasters have homes and families to maintain, and the salary which can be adequate for the schoolmistress with only herself to keep is totally inadequate for the schoolmaster with his family commitments.'[82]

A different view was taken by the *TES*, which commented:

> we are presented with the picture of the schoolmaster strug-
> gling to keep a growing family, while the schoolmistress
> disports herself gaily in a car which she will undoubtedly
> engage to have ferried across to France for her holidays. Even
> if the picture were true, it is not necessarily one of injustice.
> It could be maintained that a wife and family were quite as
> much fun as a car and holidays abroad.[83]

It is significant that similar gender stereotypes were used by protagonists on both sides of this argument.

Equal pay was but one of several trends during the late 1950s
and early 1960s which suggested that there might be not only an
expansion of teacher training, but also some breakdown of long-
established hierarchies. Traditionally, the colleges had prepared
students for work in the elementary sector and the university departments had been linked with the secondary schools. The universalisa-
tion of secondary schooling meant that an increasing proportion
of secondary school teachers were inevitably drawn from the training
colleges. At the same time, those colleges began to look more like
fully-fledged members of the higher education system. Three-year
training, introduced in 1960, was quickly followed by proposals from
the NACTST that 'the academic studies of all teachers should
culminate in a degree or equivalent qualification and this should
be distinct from . . . professional training.'[84] This was to be
realised through 'a period of four consecutive years of personal
education and professional training'.[85] Closer affiliation with
universities through the Area Training Organisations was also
recommended. These proposals surfaced just in time to be taken
on board by the Robbins Commission and were to become important policy items during the late 1960s. At the same time the
character of the training colleges was beginning to change. They

became larger in size, a majority were now under LEA rather than voluntary control. Mixed colleges became more common, and in 1963 for the first time the number of male staff exceeded female.[86] The recommendation of the Robbins Commission that these institutions should henceforth be known as Colleges of Education[87] reflected changes that were already under way within them as well as the aspirations which were held for them.

It is clear in retrospect, from the vantage point of the 1980s, that any prospect which these changes seemed at the time to hold out for a lessening of the status hierarchies which have plagued the English teaching profession throughout the twentieth century were illusory. The manner of the implementation of these changes during the late 1960s, with many universities loath to award anything above a general degree to College of Education students,[88] together with the effects of the economic retrenchment of the 1970s, have resulted in the reassertion of familiar patterns; the universities remain to the present day the major providers for the more prestigious secondary schools, and the primary sector is still staffed by a predominantly female and largely non-graduate labour force. As had been the case in the late nineteenth century, a kaleidoscopic rate of change within higher education, linked to a swift expansion, seemed at first to hold out a promise of democratisation: in practice this proved not to be the case.

In the field of adult and further education, too, major changes were under way. Since the early twentieth century the WEA, working in conjunction with university extra-mural departments, had been the main provider of courses targeted at those social groups who had been denied the chance of post-school education. This was often done in conjunction with trades unions through three-year tutorial classes under the aegis of the universities, and much of the work was in one or other of the social sciences.

The 1944 Act forced a major redirection by placing a statutory duty on each Local Education Authority to provide adequately for further education in its area. Quite quickly a wide variety of patterns emerged; evening institutes, short-term residential colleges, adult education centres, village colleges, community colleges and adult wings in secondary schools. There was a small but steady increase in the popularity of dual use of school facilities for such classes, particularly in situations where specialist equipment and buildings (such as gymnasia) were involved. This work was both vocational and non-vocational in character, and proved so attractive to the new middle classes of post-war England that by 1968–69 over 17 million students were enrolled in LEA further and adult education classes of one sort or another.

In this rapidly changing situation it was inconceivable that the pre-existing adult education provision could itself survive without major changes. The well-established links between the universities and the WEA made it possible for the universities to claim the high ground by claiming the more advanced part-time work, at or near university level, for their extra-mural departments. Between 1951 and 1962 the total number of university extra-mural classes being taught at any one time doubled to 5507. The focus of interest shifted markedly away from those social sciences which were of interest to trade unionists, towards literature, local history and the fine arts as these departments increasingly assumed the role of a leisure industry for the comfortably-off middle class. Meanwhile an increasing number of part-time courses, offering professional qualifications on a strong vocational slant, were offered by those 'mainstream' university departments most able to respond to the growing demand for vocationally oriented courses at a high level.

In combination these developments sidelined the WEA. By the late 1960s the universities were educating over 163,000 part-time students; the WEA could attract only 30,000. It may have been the survival of the 'WEA spirit' among some senior members of the Labour Party which strengthened demands for a university of the air during the mid-1960s. Jenny Lee, one of the strongest advocates of what was to become the Open University, maintained strong links with the WEA throughout her political life.

The rhetoric of these years reflected the deep-seated nature of the changes that were taking place. During the 1950s S.G. Raybould, the influential Director of Extra-Mural Studies at the University of Leeds argued consistently for a clearer demarcation between the work of the universities and the WEA, with the WEA catering more for the 'educationally underprivileged' and the universities confining themselves to work 'of a university standard'.[89] Although Raybould was opposed publicly by several other respected university directors, including Robert Peers of Nottingham, it was his view which came increasingly to dominate by the end of the decade. The impact of governmental cuts on the funding of adult education, impinging particularly upon the WEA, led to representations from some trade union MPs and resulted in the establishment of the Ashby Committee in 1953 to advise on funding. The Report's conciliatory tone and its recommendation of no major changes in patterns of financing offered no more than a sop to the WEA.[90] Within a few years it was possible for Roy Shaw, Director of Adult Education at the University of Keele, to put a spectacular end to the silken glove treatment of the WEA by calling for a suspension of 'the tradition in all discussion of adult education whereby the W.E.A. seems to have been accorded the privilege usually reserved for the dead: that in public at least nothing but good shall be said of it.'[91]

In each of the areas of tertiary education there was one underlying similarity during this era of post-war expansion. Whether it was in the field of technical education, teacher training, adult education or the liberal arts the university was paramount. Institutions clambered for university status or at least to ensure that the most prestigious courses either were taught by the universities or received university validation. And in this process, a particular model of university education was the one most commonly aspired to. Universities were perceived as leisured institutions committed to humane studies and a breadth of vision which remained widely admired in post-war Britain. It was to the extent that they were able to realise and sustain this ideal that departments, faculties and quickly developing institutions owed their prestige within a system of higher education which remained acutely conscious of social and academic hierarchies. The 'pecking order' established in this way during the 1950s and 1960s received an ironic recognition in the differential treatment afforded to differing institutions in the economic cutbacks of the late 1970s and 1980s.

It seems likely, too, that there was some informal linkage of the schools and higher education through the stratified nature of the expansion we have observed in both areas. Reid's work on *Social class differences in Britain* has shown clearly that the newer and less prestigious universities attracted disproportionate numbers of students from state schools and from working-class homes. Turning to the new polytechnics which emerged at the end of the 1960s from the technical sector, he found it 'noticeable that the representation of classes 1 and 2 is lower than at universities . . . with considerable variations in the social class compositions of individual polytechnics . . . the proportion of working-class students on non-degree courses was higher than for degree courses.'[92]

In a period of economic expansion, when the educational provision and educational opportunities are expanding to match an upturn in vacancies within the professional sector of the economy, it is easy to find individual examples of educational and careers routes which suggest the openness of the system and its democratisation.

But the evidence so far available suggests that such social mobility may have been achieved within and through an educational system which was becoming increasingly segmented rather than less. The underlying reality may have been that the educational system which emerged after the war was one which imposed tighter definitions of social class on its recipients, which confirmed life-chances for the majority of pupils and which was in many ways a catalyst of social distinctions. If this was the case, then the changes which occurred within the tertiary sector of eduction were an integral part of this process.

References

1. *The British economy: key statistics, 1900–1970* (Times Newspapers 1971), 9.
2. R. Layard, J. King and C. Moser, *The impact of Robbins* (Penguin, London, 1969).
3. *TES*, 28 March 1952.
4. *TES*, 16 January 1953 and 20 March 1953.
5. *TES*, 23 November 1956.
6. Ibid.
7. *TES*, 16 January 1953.
8. H.C. Dent, *Universities in transition* (Cohen & West, London, 1961), 95.
9. *TES*, 2 March 1951.
10. *TES*, 31 October 1952.
11. *TES*, 7 September 1956.
12. *TES*, 14 June 1957.
13. *TES*, 31 January 1958.
14. *TES*, 4 March 1960.
15. *TES*, 5 May 1961.
16. *TES*, 3 March 1960.
17. J. Mulford, 'Schools that lead to Oxford and Cambridge, *Where*, 10 (Autumn 1962), 12–13.
18. G. Boehm, 'Which girls' schools lead to Oxford and Cambridge?', *Where*, 13 (Summer 1963), 4–6.
19. Robbins Report, *Higher education*, Cmnd. 2154 (HMSO, London, 1963), 80.
20. *TES*, 29 March 1963.
21. UGC, *University developments, 1952–1957* (HMSO, London, 1958), 39.
22. Ibid.
23. UGC, *A note on technology in universities* (HMSO, London, 1950), 4.
24. *TES*, 7 September 1956.
25. W.G.V. Balchin, 'Universities in Great Britain: a geographical conspectus' (University College, Swansea, 1958), 14–15.

26. York Academic Trust, Governing Council Minutes, 7 October 1958.

27. York Academic Trust, 'Notes for discussion with Sir Keith Murray at Bishopthorpe Palace at 2.30 p.m. on 24 June 1959', p. 5.

28. UGC, *University development, 1957–62*, p. 75.

29. W.H.G. Armytage, 'A case for Scunthorpe', *New Statesman*, LXI, No. 1564 (3 March 1961), 340–1.

30. Promotion Committee for a University of Essex, Proposal for a University of Essex (May 1960), 6.

31. *The Times*, 16 October 1963.

32. M.B. Campbell, *Nonspecialist study in the undergraduate curricula of the New Universities and Colleges of Advanced Technology in England*, University of Michigan Comparative Education Series, No. 10 (1966), 108.

33. University of Lancaster, *Prospectus, 1964–6* (Lancaster, 1964), 100.

34. UGC, *University development, 1957–62*, 96–101.

35. *TES*, 9 September 1960.

36. M. Sanderson, *The universities and British industry, 1850–1970* (Routledge & Kegan Paul, London, 1972), 355.

37. *TES*, 31 October 1952.

38. M. Argles, *South Kensington to Robbins* (Longman, London, 1964), 90.

39. *TES*, 21 September 1951.

40. *TES*, 29 February 1952.

41. *TES*, 20 June 1952.

42. *TES*, 27 February 1953.

43. *TES*, 9 May 1952.

44. *TES*, 19 September 1952.

45. *TES*, 7 March 1952.

46. *TES*, 18 May 1956.

47. *TES*, 7 October 1955.

48. *TES*, 1 July 1955.

49. *Technical education*, Cmd. 9703 (HMSO, London, 1956), 4.

50. *TES*, 29 June 1956.

51. *TES*, 2 March 1956.

52. *TES*, 17 April 1959.

53. *TES*, 18 October 1957.

54. *TES*, 7 March 1958.

55. *TES*, 6 March 1959.

56. *TES*, 17 April 1959.

57. R. Layard, J. King and C. Moser, *The impact of Robbins* (Penguin, London, 1969), 18–20, 32.

58. Ibid., 22.

59. Robbins Report, *Higher education*, Cmd. 2154 (HMSO, London, 1963), para. 31.

60. *TES*, 25 October 1963.

61. *TES*, 13 December 1963.

62. *TES*, 8 November 1963.

63. *TES*, 15 August 1952.

64. *TES*, 29 January 1954.

65. Ibid.

66. Ministry of Education, *Education in 1955*, Cmd 9785 (HMS, London, 1956), 10.

67. H.C. Dent, *The training of teachers in England and Wales, 1800–1975* (Hodder & Stoughton, London, 1977), 135.

68. *TES*, 30 May 1958.

69. *TES*, 3 February 1961.

70. *TES*, 8 December 1961.

71. *TES*, 19 January 1962.

72. *TES*, 25 May 1962.

73. *TES*, 30 April 1962.

74. *TES*, 14 September 1956.

75. *TES*, 25 May 1962.

76. *TES*, 24 August 1956.

77. *TES*, 24 May 1957.

78. *TES*, 14 September 1956.

79. The author was offered a pledge by one West Midlands LEA in 1958. See also Dent, *The training of teachers*, 131.

80. *TES*, 15 July 1955.

81. Ministry of Education, *Education in 1955*, Cmd 9785 (HMSO, London, 1956), 66; and Ministry of Education, *Education in 1958*, Cmd 777 (HMSO, London, 1959), 90.

82. *TES*, 6 April 1956.

83. *TES*, 11 March 1955.

84. Ministry of Education, *The future pattern of the education and training of teachers* (eighth report of the NACTST) (HMSO, London, 1962), 20.

85. Ibid.

86. J.D. Browne, 'The tranformation of the education of teachers in the 1960s', in E. Fearn and B. Simon (eds), *Education in the sixties*, History of Education Society Conference Papers 1979 (Leicester, 1980), 59–79.

87. Robbins Report, *Higher education*, 119.

88. Dent, *The training of teachers*, 144.

89. For a full treatment of this discussion see: S.G. Raybould, *The WEA: the next phase* (London, 1949); S.G. Raybould, *The English universities and adult education* (London, 1951); S.G. Raybould (ed.), *Trends in English adult education* (London, 1959); R. Peers, 'The future of adult education', *Adult Education*, 25 (1952–3), 87–95.

90. Ministry of Education, *The organisation and finance of adult education in England and Wales* (London, 1954).

91. *Adult Education* (May 1971), quoted by C. Ellwood, *Adult learning today* (London, 1976).

92. I. Reid, *Social class differences in Britain*, 2nd edition (London, 1981), 241.

9

Examinations, 1945–64

During the post-war era the modern system of examinations evolved and took on its social function of sifting large numbers of young people for employment and access to higher education. In 1945 70,000 passes were awarded in the school certificate examination and a further 14,000 at the higher level. The introduction of the GCE in 1951 paved the way for a swift upturn in numbers, since it was now possible for candidates to be presented in a single subject rather than in the range of subjects required by the school certificate. By 1954 the number of passes in individual subjects at ordinary level was 603,000 and at advanced level 88,000. Ten years later the number of 'O' level passes had doubled to 1,264,000 and at 'A' level the figure had almost trebled to 215,000. The addition of CSE examinations in 1965 led to a further increase. These examinations exercised a steadily increasing influence upon English education, impinging on both curriculum and teaching method, even for groups of pupils who were not directly involved. The two key problems during the immediate post-war period for those concerned with the administration of examinations were the logistics of catering for quickly increasing numbers, and the struggle to accommodate recent developments at research level in the subjects being examined. While the second of these factors led to some modifications to subject content, the overall effect was to ensure that there was little time for any serious consideration of revisions to the examining process, or of its impact on the schools. At a time when the schools, higher education and the professions were expanding together there was a need for a device which would mediate transfer from the schools, which would be perceived generally as being fair yet which would preserve the hierarchical nature of the system. The fact that public examinations were able to perform this function goes far to explain their increasing popularity in post-war England.

It is one of the enduring ironies of English education that the remodelling of external examinations after the Second World War originated from growing reservations that the old 'school certificate' examinations were exercising too great an influence upon the school curriculum. Established in 1917 through circulars 996 and 1002, this examination was administered by eight university examination boards. Within a few years of their creation these were seen by many observers as having too great an impact upon the work of the grammar schools, although many schoolteachers welcomed this influence, seeing the examination as a vindication of the excellence of the more successful schools. A Board of Education report in 1932 argued that the original purpose of the school certificate was already lost sight of, and that school curricula were already being dictated by the demands of matriculation. From the mid-1920s onwards several LEAs pressed consistently for some alternative examination geared to the vocational work done in schools (a view which was supported by the NUT), and this led to increasing suspicion by the local authorities that they were under-represented on the SSEC. The Board of Education responded by increasing the number of places on the SSEC held by the LEAs and this was to result after the war in the LEAs playing a much greater role in determining the shape of the new examinations than might otherwise have been the case. So, many of the key issues that were to predominate in the debate on external examinations after 1945 were predetermined by perceptions and power structures which originated before the war.

The Norwood Report was published on 26 July 1943 and was compiled by a subcommittee of the SSEC: its appearance signalled the start of a sustained attempt to reform the structure of secondary school examinations. Its central recommendation in this field was that schools should be released from the tyranny of examinations by ending external examination at 16 + and introducing new forms of assessment for sixth-formers at the point of matriculation. The Report received a fulsome welcome from R.A. Butler, and was used by an influential group within the Board as the starting-point for an initiative to restructure public examinations. Among them were G.G. Williams, the head of the Secondary Branch within the Board, and the newly appointed Senior Chief HMI, Martin Roseveare.[1] In November 1943, Norwood wrote to Williams to warn him of the danger that vested interests threatened any initiatives that were likely to come from the Board, adding: 'both the Oxford and Cambridge locals are doing their best to undermine and belittle the report from pure motives of self-interest.'[2]

Norwood hoped that his report might be kept away from a full meeting of the SSEC, lest the representatives of the examination boards and the LEAs proposed changes which might distort it beyond recognition. Williams, for his part, insisted that the proprieties must be observed, but primed a number of leading committee members to see that the LEAs were 'faithfully put in their place'[3] if there was any attempt to sabotage the Norwood proposals. Within a few months it was Williams in turn who came under suspicion of being too ready to accommodate a range of conflicting views. Martin Roseveare pencilled alongside one draft document prepared by Williams: 'We have had plenty of time to study Norwood. Let us have our policy and preach it boldly . . . We must have a policy, and it must be ours. We must claim it and proclaim it.'[4]

In the event, the examination which was to emerge in 1951 bore little resemblance to the proposals put forward in 1943. The fact that Norwood had also made a great play of the need for a differentiated, tripartite system of secondary schools meant that much of the debate on examinations was posited on the assumption that it was only the small minority of pupils who attended grammar schools who were to be involved. It was in consequence much easier for the pressure groups representing the grammar schools and the universities to force changes upon the Ministry (which by now had replaced the Board), and so to influence the nature of the examination which emerged. So much became apparent as early as 1946, when Circular 103 made it clear that existing grammar schools would automatically be eligible to enter their pupils for external examinations, although any newly designated secondary school must first make a formal application to the Ministry. At the same time, HMIs were instructed to advise the new schools to steer clear of external examinations.[5] In the same year an appeal from the East Midlands Educational Union for permission to use their examinations in secondary modern schools was turned down on the grounds that the examination would 'inevitably limit the development of those schools'. The secondary moderns, HMI advised, were merely 'striving to ape the grammar schools'.[6]

Through Circular 103 the Ministry committed itself to the reform of examinations along the lines suggested by Norwood, and the minimisation of their influence in the secondary modern schools.

In February 1946 the SSEC was reconstituted so that it could become the instrument to achieve this policy. The university examining bodies were excluded, while LEA representation was increased. When it began work in the autumn of 1946, it soon became clear that there was a risk that the universities might set about the development of their own independent examination system unless it was clear that any new examination would serve their purposes for the admission of students. Accordingly, the first SSEC Report, which appeared in July 1947, went some way beyond the Norwood proposals and in fact became the template for a new system of examinations. Norwood's proposal for two examinations to replace the old higher school certificate now gave way to a scheme of three levels of achievement, 'Ordinary', 'Advanced' and 'Scholarship'. While the idea of a scholarship examination kept the universities happy, the acceptance that the ordinary level examination might be attempted by pupils as young as 16 was an acknowledgement that in reality many grammar school pupils left school at that age, and that something must be provided for them if these schools were to go along with the proposals.

Frightened by the prospect of an 'unholy alliance'[7] of the universities and the grammar schools, and sensing a workable compromise solution, Ministry of Education officials rushed out Circular 168 to ensure that the new examination would be introduced in 1951. This emphasised that the new 'O' level examination was intended to be set at the level of a 'credit' in the old school certificate, and reaffirmed that no pupil would be permitted to attempt this below the age of 16. In attempting in this way to retain the spirit of the original Norwood proposals, the Ministry succeeded only in identifying the one contentious issue on which further concessions were necessary if the new examination was to be acceptable to the grammar schools. Predictably, there was a torrent of protests from both the HMC schools and the grammar schools since the proposed arrangement would end their practice of setting up 'express' streams whose pupils were able to spend three years in the sixth form preparing for Oxbridge examinations. Their views were neatly summarised by Dr Terry Thomas, headmaster of Leeds Grammar School and a member of the Norwood Committee, who argued that the age-limit would inflict

> irreparable damage . . . the age bar has no justification on educational grounds and appears merely to be a device to take the examination out of the reach of the new secondary modern

schools. The promising pupil will be kept back and have less time for his sixth-form and scholarship work . . . It looks as if the sixth forms of the future will be mere shadows of the good sixth forms of the past.[8]

During the late 1940s the press (most notably *The Times* and *Times Educational Supplement*) became increasingly convinced of the need to open the new examination to younger pupils, and support for this campaign came in too from Oxford and Cambridge Universities. Increasingly the issue took on an air of partisan contest, since George Tomlinson, as Minister of Education, seemed more disposed to listen to the NUT, which remained a staunch supporter of the age limit. It was not until Labour had left office and the GCE had been at work for a year that the Ministry relented and allowed pupils of less than 16 years of age to attempt the new examination.

The fear that the GCE might become an examination for the grammar schools alone, or that it might have unfortunate effects upon the other schools in a tripartite system, was one which, as we have seen, was already well established during the late 1940s. It was a fear which led to efforts to establish alternative examination routes from the outset. Initially, it was the nascent technical schools which caused concern: within the Ministry, Antony Part observed as early as 1946 that an external examination would become inevitable if sixth-form work developed in the technical schools, and there was widespread concern that the university examination boards made little provision for examinations in practical subjects.[9] The fear that the technical schools might look elsewhere for examination outlets, and that this would lead to considerable overlapping and duplication was clearly articulated at the 1949 meeting of the Northern Counties Technical Examinations Council. Initially, the response of the SSEC was to draw the existing organisations which had experience of examining in technical subjects into discussion on how they might be involved in future developments. Accordingly, the RSA, the Union of Lancashire and Cheshire Institutes, the Northern Counties TEC and the City and Guilds of London Institute were all approached during the late 1940s, and it was agreed in March 1949 that these bodies should all be involved in some way in the new examinations.[10]

Increasingly, though, it was the argument that, unless examinations for the technical schools carried the prestige and privileges commonly associated with the examinations of the major examining boards, these schools could never truly achieve parity of esteem, which won the day. This view was strongly argued by one contributor to *Vocational Aspect* in May 1949, and it led to the emergence a year later of definite proposals for a ninth GCE examining board 'to assume responsibility for examinations in such subjects as were appropriate for students in schools providing secondary technical education . . . and in establishments of further education'.[11]

These suggestions offered a further threat to the view of the Ministry that in a tripartite system secondary schools of different types should be free to develop without the constraints of external examinations. Also, it was made clear by some university representatives that the universities would not take kindly to applicants whose qualifications had been awarded by a technical examining body. Professor H.B. Charlton warned at one meeting that there was no chance of certificates awarded by a ninth board being recognised by Manchester University 'for many years'.[12] Despite these objections, the SSEC was unable to deny the claims of the technical schools, and agreement in principle to the establishment of a ninth examining board in 1951 was given ministerial approval within two years. The new Associated Examining Board set its first examinations in 1955.

But the existence of this new board was no guarantee of the future of the technical schools, which continued to struggle to establish their identity. The demand for passes in 'traditional' subjects meant that, within a few years, the Associated Examining Board was virtually indistinguishable from the other eight. One reason for this was the inflexibility of the universities in responding to applicants from secondary technical schools, as one complaint from the Director of Education for Rotherham made clear in 1957:

This authority established technical high schools for boys and girls in 1952 and 1953, and the time has now come for some of the pupils to seek admission to Universities for courses including technological subjects. Most universities require a student to obtain five passes in the GCE at Ordinary level and, in addition, certain Advanced level passes . . . The five subjects usually include Maths, English and a foreign language and the remaining two must come from an approved list. Unfortunately Technical Drawing, Woodwork and Metalwork are not approved subjects. The pupils attending our Technical High School for boys normally take seven subjects up to Ordinary level of the GCE, including Technical Drawing and a craft, which means they cannot afford to fail in any subject except those which give the school its technical bias.[13]

Once the GCE was established, it became possible for secondary modern schools to encourage their pupils to stay on rather than transfer to neighbouring grammar schools to sit the examination. The Essex authority was one which had encouraged such transfers, but which adopted this new practice immediately. By 1954 there were in total 5600 secondary modern pupils entered for the GCE examination. The revelation that this represented one for every 22 entrants from grammar schools, and that their pass rate of 59 per cent was barely below the figure for grammar school pupils led the *TES* to conclude that 'IQ can be no sure guide.'[14] While this trend was strongly defended by the NUT and its journal the *Schoolmaster*, there were some observers who noticed that its consequence was that the secondary moderns were tending to become pale imitations of the grammar schools in the interests of a minority of their pupils.[15]

Immediately after the war few people had foreseen this upsurge in demand from the secondary moderns for access to external examinations. While a growing number of their pupils aspired to the GCE examination during the 1950s, others were channelled towards private examinations, such as those of the College of Preceptors or the Royal Society of Arts. In some counties, such as Essex and Staffordshire, county leaving examinations were set up by the local authorities. In St Albans seven secondary moderns cooperated to set their own leaving examination; while in south-west Hertfordshire, the leaving certificate was set and marked by the staff of the local grammar schools, and a similar scheme was at work in Ilford.[16] These varying and uncoordinated responses show the extent of the problem faced by the local authorities. It was a crisis which obliged a further drastic rethinking of governmental strategy.

Ministerial opposition to the GCE becoming more widely used was echoed by the Association of Education Committees, whose astute secretary, W.P. Alexander, soon saw the need for some generally recognised qualification which would be within reach of the majority of secondary modern school pupils.[17] Under his influence the EAC began a steady campaign for a second examination which would be more responsive to the needs of the local education authorities. What gave a note of urgency to Alexander's efforts was the knowledge that other organisations were only too willing to fill the gap. In June 1952, Alexander received a letter from J.H.

Simpson, Dean of the College of Preceptors, outlining the plans of the College to develop its own examination for pupils in secondary modern schools.[18] Even more threatening was the initiative of the newly-formed Combined Schools Examinations Board only a month later. This private organisation circulated all chief education officers, announcing what was in effect a resuscitation of the school certificate:

> It has been realized that there are many pupils in our schools and technical colleges who would have been able to take the old School Certificate Examination, but who are quite unable to take the new GCE owing to the standard having been raised so much . . . It is for this 'B' stream in Grammar Schools and 'A' stream in technical and Secondary Modern Schools that this examination has been designed.[19]

In the event the Ministry did not take much persuading to use its influence to convince the training colleges not to recognise these and similar awards; but it was clear that a growing vacuum existed which someone sooner or later would have to fill.

From the early 1950s onwards, Alexander believed that the only way to resolve this problem was by establishing a completely new examination which would be far more susceptible to LEA control. The refusal of the Ministry to countenance too widespread use of the GCE or any major changes to it during its early years played into his hands.[20] By the middle of 1954 a growing number of voices were being raised in support of the EAC position. One correspondent to the *TES* argued for 'the introduction of a new certificate in addition to GCE, designed to embrace all non-GCE types of brain and to capture the interests of all such schoolgoers. Such a certificate would prevent the failure of the comprehensive idea.'[21] The editor of the *TES* concluded gloomily: 'altogether, if they want an examination, it looks as if the modern schools had better start from scratch.'[22]

Meanwhile, the Ministry continued to drag its feet on this issue. Demands from a joint working committee of the AEC and the NUT for a full enquiry met with no response from David Eccles, despite the fact that some of the GCE boards were becoming restive at the way in which their examination was being put to uses for which it had not been planned, and were beginning to lend their weight to demands for a lower level examination. When a ministerial response was made (in Circular 289 on 9 July 1955) it amounted to no more than a grudging acceptance of current trends. The circular acknowledged the increase in the number of secondary modern pupils entering for GCE, but warned that the needs of the majority of pupils in these schools must not be lost sight of. Turning to the question of local experimentation with examinations other than GCE, the circular added:

> the Minister welcomes such experiments, so long as the schools retain their individual freedom and their control over their syllabuses. . . . He does not favour the establishment of any new general examinations of national standing.[23]

It was a stance which was becoming increasingly difficult to justify. Before the end of the year the *TES* reported that Eccles's attempt to dissuade the secondary moderns from too great an involvement in the GCE by refusing to fund examination entries was clearly failing. The Northumberland LEA was defraying the whole cost of secondary modern pupils' examination fees, while in other parts of the country there was clear evidence that parents were willing to find the money from their own pockets. The *TES* concluded that on this issue of secondary modern pupils who were aspiring to external examinations, the Minister 'should pay up with a good grace'.[24]

At the same time, pressure for a new examination below the level of the GCE continued to mount. The observations submitted by the AEC on Circular 289 emphasised that the GCE was already having too great an impact upon the development of the secondary moderns, and that a new examination need not threaten the GCE as the Ministry seemed to fear.[25] This was in line with the thinking of the Association of Municipal Corporations and of the City and Guilds of London Institute, both of which organisations joined in the campaign.[26] In a private note to W.P. Alexander in January 1956, Robert Beloe, the Director of Education for Surrey, added his weight to the call for a committee of enquiry, while expressing his own reservations about the desirability of wholesale changes:

> I myself would not feel at all sure that a new general examination is needed, but I should hope that this question could be examined by the body of enquiry that we recommend to be set up. For myself, believing as I do in the need to allow schools to choose for themselves, I am inclined to favour letting the existing bodies go on trying to find the right form of examinations for pupils of 16 (not 15).[27]

Peter Gosden has shown how the Ministry continued to drag its feet during the late 1950s, attempting to refer the question to the Crowther Committee (which eventually declared against a new national examination).[28] It was only in 1958, after the appointment of Geoffrey Lloyd to the Ministry, that J.F. Lockwood, who was now chairing the SSEC, virtually obliged the setting up of a sub-committee by threatening to go it alone if ministerial sanction was not forthcoming.[29]

Between 1968 and 1970 this new sub-committee, which was chaired by Beloe, went to considerable lengths to gauge the views of educators and industrialists around the country on the value of a new nationally recognised examination at a level below that of the GCE. The responses were very mixed, and many echoed the reservations which Beloe himself had voiced only a few years earlier. A.B. Clegg was a particularly vigorous opponent of any new examination, professing himself

> not convinced that there was a demand from parents. . . .
> He agreed that Principals of technical colleges needed evidence
> that candidates for admission would be able to profit from
> a course of further education, but considered that that prob-
> lem ought to be tackled by means of a closer cooperation
> between Principals and Heads of secondary schools in the
> neighbourhood of the colleges. He would not object if that
> were acheived by a local examination. He did not like regional
> examinations but thought that they were less harmful than
> a lower level national examination would be.[30]

A number of the industrialists who were consulted also had reservations, though for different reasons. A.E. Taylor, who responded on behalf of Stewart and Lloyds, reflected a residual scepticism about academic qualifications with the observation:

> there is a danger of 'too many pieces of paper' to be waved
> under the noses of prospective employers and we would be
> working on a much safer basis if we did face up to the fact
> that most youngsters from Secondary Modern Schools will
> never gain academic qualifications, and the few who do wish
> to continue have a variety of courses and certificates open to
> them.[31]

The arguments which were presented in favour of a new

examination were equally forceful, and it was these which eventually persuaded the sub-committee. J. Wilkinson, the Director of Education for Ealing, wrote to Alexander arguing that 'a lower level could ensure that pupils received a broadly based education without the temptation to concentrate on the two or three subjects they were taking at 'O' level'.[32] Similarly, the IAHM was strongly committed to the idea of a new examination, pressing the view that 'a leaving examination at the end of the Secondary Modern course would give an aim and a purpose which at the moment is lacking'.[33] It was these considerations, together with mounting evidence of a 'qualifications crisis' within the secondary modern schools, which eventually swayed the day.

The Beloe Report was published during the summer of 1960, and its appearance increased the likelihood of a new examination in the foreseeable future. It claimed that the most able 20 per cent were capable of attempting four subjects at GCE, and that a new examination, similarly organised, would enable the next 20 per cent also to attempt at least four subjects. The third 20 per cent of the school population was thought to be capable of making an attempt at a single subject. Since the new examinations should be designed to meet the needs and interests of pupils in the ability range concerned, it was important that they should not be merely a replica of the existing GCE examinations. To this end it was thought important that practising teachers should play a much fuller part in devising syllabuses and in setting the papers. Another ambiguity which had hung over examinations for secondary modern schools throughout the 1950s was clarified by the recommendation that all such examinations should be taken at the age of 16 + .[34]

The reactions to the Beloe Report were as varied as the evidence which had been submitted to it. On the one hand, some authorities made suggestions on how best it might be implemented: H.E. Skerrett, the Chief Education Officer for Northamptonshire, suggested that the new examination could usefully be linked to the GCE by a recognition that its credit level would be the equivalent of the existing pass. While this provision was seen by some as a guarantee of the proposed examination, others were concerned that the examination system was tending more and more to confirm the stratification of English education. Objections to this effect came in from Nottinghamshire, Rutland and Staffordshire, and Percy Lord summarised the response of the Lancashire authority in a strongly worded letter to Alexander in January, 1961:

The system could result in all Secondary Modern Schools taking the 'second level' examination whilst all the Grammar Schools took the GCE. This would undo all the work that has been accomplished in the past ten years to reduce the distinction between these two types of school.[35]

Similar criticisms were made by Alec Clegg in a strongly worded article in the *TES*.

Even stronger criticisms were made by the socialist teachers' organisations, which saw in these developments evidence of the stranglehold which the elite sector had upon English secondary education. The Communist Party Education Advisory Committee warned the SSEC that:

> the proposal for a new examination arises from the failure of the government to grasp the nettle of GCE reform. . . . The GCE as it stands today is undemocratically controlled by the universities, not by the teachers or even the LEAs who run the schools. Its content and standard is adjusted with a view to future university entrants who form only a small percentage of the candidates.[36]

Equally strongly, the National Association of Labour Teachers pointed out that what was being overlooked in these discussions was the very real achievement of the secondary moderns, often working under extreme difficulty:

> The essential feature of a separate, lower standard examination is that it must be lower. It would be intolerable if it were found, in a few years' time, that the standard of the new examination had crept up to, or even passed, the GCE standard. The problem is how to keep the GCE always a step ahead. This can only be solved by manipulation.
>
> Having decided to establish an official lower-level examination, it follows that the higher must be confined to an elite. When the report says (para. 103) that the number of pupils suitable for GCE 'must be regarded as strictly limited' they are speaking the exact truth — and prophesying . . .
>
> The report goes out of its way to repeat that syllabi for pupils below the top 20% must not be replica of GCE syllabi at lower level; they have to be different. We have tried to understand the reason for this, particularly since the committee have

advanced no reason themselves, and have made only the most limited and abortive attempts to devise such syllabi.

The top 20% are the normal grammar intake; this may be the clue to the puzzle. We cannot help suspecting that the report was framed under the baleful influence of the pseudo-psychology of the Norwood Report, and the belief that there are different types of children, who can be sieved into different types of school. This theory always was discreditable, and it is now largely discredited.[37]

In these terms the NALT argued that what was really needed was a reconsideration of the nature of the GCE examination and a widening of its scope.

Confronted by these contrasting views within the teaching profession, the Ministry continued to drag its feet. During the autumn of 1960 David Eccles was reported in the press to have commented on the Beloe Report: 'This is not a very sound proposal . . . though we may be forced by public opinion.'[38] But the SSEC was in no doubt that the time had come for change. In March 1961 it pressed the Ministry to implement the Report, pointing out that events were fast overtaking the administrators, since over 80 per cent of secondary schools were already entering their pupils for one or other of the available examinations: 'If these findings are even approximately accurate, we would submit that the time is already past when it serves a useful purpose to debate *whether* these pupils in their fifth year should be externally examined. The question is *how* they should be examined.'[39]

This view was becoming unanswerable, and on 17 July 1961 David Eccles informed the Commons that he 'reluctantly' accepted the Beloe proposals, but wished to take up the Report's suggestion that there be more research on the most appropriate form of examination before a date was set for implementation.[40]

The SSEC was expanded to allow greater representation of teachers from secondary modern schools, and during the next few years it worked closely with the Ministry's Curriculum Study Group which was set up in March 1962, partly in order to control the growing power of the SSEC. These two bodies now liaised on grading systems, the setting up of new examining boards and, most importantly, on new modes of examination. The outcome was, not that the teachers played a significantly greater role, as had been intended, but that objective testing and multiple-choice questions began to be used at secondary level for the first time. Before the

end of 1961, the mathematics panel of the inspectorate had proposed an experiment in multiple-choice methods of examining
mathematics, and this was taken up by the CSE sub-committee of
the SSEC. The second Examinations Bulletin of the SSEC, which
publicised this work, placed the question of objective testing firmly
on the agenda of those who were involved in implementing the Beloe
Report. By the beginning of 1964 similar projects were under way
in other subject areas. The Southern Board was investigating the
use of similar methods in English, and in various areas work was
being done on the objective testing of science subjects. Later in the
year, an influential submission from P.E. Vernon to the SSEC
argued that 'the projected set up for the CSE appears ideal for the
use of objective examinations'.[41]

It was against this background that a lower-level examination,
the CSE, was introduced in 1965 to complement the GCE. The
new framework of external examinations, hierarchically related to
each other and determining much of the work of the secondary
schools, was to last for over twenty years. This expansion of the
examinaton system after the Second World War is one of the
enduring ironies of English education. From the time of the
Norwood Report onwards the Ministry was overtly, at least, committed to the minimisation of the impact of examinations upon the
schools. Its intention was to leave schools of different types within
a tripartite system to develop along their own lines. Yet within a
few years the interests of the universities and grammar schools were
beginning to dominate the development of examinations to such
a degree that the technical and secondary modern schools were
forced to resemble the grammar schools increasingly closely if they
were to establish themselves at all. Within the teaching profession
it was hard to find any practitioner who had much good to say about
the effects of examinations on the school curriculum or on teaching
methods, yet there was a strong will to ensure that as many pupils
as possible competed for these examinations, and success in preparing pupils for them became increasingly one of the recognised tokens
of successful teaching. The only credible explanation of this
phenomenon is that those concerned with education, both as
teachers and administrators, were responding to deep-seated
changes in the society they served. The professionalisation of society,
an increase in social mobility and the expansion of a highly stratified
system of higher education all strengthened the demand for a widely
recognised system of external validation. Through the GCE and
the CSE, the teaching profession provided it, and in the process

the education system acted as a catalyst of the wider social changes that were taking place.

References

1. P. Underwood, 'External examinations in English secondary schools, 1943–1952', unpublished PhD thesis (University of Birmingham, 1986), 12–22. This is one of two excellent theses on this theme. See also P. Fisher, 'The influence of the Association of Education Committees on the development of secondary school examinations in England, 1943–1964', unpublished PhD thesis (University of Leeds, 1980); and Fisher, *External examinations in secondary schools in England and Wales, 1944–64*, University of Leeds Educational Administration and History Monograph No. 11 (Leeds, 1982).

2. Letter, C. Norwood to G.G. Williams, 10 November 1943, PRO Ed. 12/480.

3. Fisher, *External examinations*, 6.

4. PRO Ed. 147/134.

5. Fisher, *External examinations*, 6.

6. PRO Ed. 147/133. On this point see also Underwood, 'External examinations', 72.

7. PRO Ed. 147/285.

8. *Yorkshire Post and Leeds Mercury*, 18 June 1948.

9. PRO Ed. 136/789. See Underwood, Chapter 6, for a full discussion of the negotiations leading to the setting up of the ninth examining board.

10. P. Gosden, *The education system since 1944* (Martin Robertson, Oxford, 1983), 65.

11. PRO Ed. 147/215. See also Underwood, 237.

12. Underwood, 249.

13. Letter, R. Bloomer to W.P. Alexander, 18 March 1957; file 106b, papers of the Association of Education Committees, Brotherton Library, Leeds.

14. *TES*, 4 November 1955.

15. H. Judge, *A generation of schooling* (OUP, Oxford, 1984), 107.

16. *TES*, 3 February 1956.

17. Gosden, *The education system*, 67.

18. Letter, J.H. Simpson to W.P. Alexander, 13 June 1952; file C56a, papers of the AEC.

19. Letter, E.L. Perkin to Chief Education Officers, 2 July 1952; file C56a, papers of the AEC.

20. See Fisher, 33–7.

21. *TES*, 22 October 1954.

22. *TES*, 17 December 1954.

23. See file C56a, papers of the AEC.

24. *TES*, 25 November 1955.

25. File 106b, papers of the AEC.

26. *TES*, 6 April, 1956 and 13 July 1956.

27. File 106b, papers of the AEC.
28. Gosden, 69.
29. Ibid., 69–70.
30. File B166a, papers of the AEC.
31. Ibid.
32. Ibid.
33. Ibid.
34. Ministry of Education, *Secondary school examinations other than the GCE* (HMSO, London, 1960).
35. Letter, P. Lord to W.P. Alexander, 18 January 1961; file A106a, papers of the AEC.
36. File C57a, papers of the AEC.
37. Ibid.
38. *TES*, 14 October 1960.
39. File C57a, papers of the AEC.
40. Fisher, 65; Gosden, 73.
41. File A107, papers of the AEC.

Conclusion

In this book I have attempted to describe briefly some of the more important characteristics of the unprecedented expansion of the English educational system which occurred during the twenty years following the Second World War. Not only was there an increase in the number of schools and colleges, but they tended to reflect changes in scale which were taking place generally by becoming larger than the institutions of pre-war years. At one level it is difficult to see this expansion as anything other than an unmitigated public good. There can be no doubt that thousands of young people benefited from a schooling which widened their horizons, broadened their personal interests, and which in the process acted as a catalyst of the expansion of industry and the professions. During an historical period when the tertiary sector of the economy was expanding rapidly, education was confirmed as the mechanism which enabled those lucky enough to feel its full benefits to aspire to career routes which, in many cases, had been beyond the wildest dreams of their parents and grandparents.

The result was that the widely-held view of schooling which saw it as essentially egalitarian and democratic was strengthened. The emerging examination system was the universally accepted guarantor of standards, and it was generally thought to be fair in its impact. The efforts of the schools were submitted to objective public scrutiny in this way, and the attention of the disadvantaged was directed to their own shortcomings rather than to the contributory factors which might have accounted, in part at least, to their failure to compete with their more successful peers. It is hardly surprising, then, that the post-war era was the high point for popular belief in the state system of education and that the policies of both major political parties were directed to the furtherance of popular education.

What also emerges from the evidence collected in this book is that the nature of that educational expansion was determined by a number of factors. Perhaps paramount was what I have called the educational inheritance. The model of what was perceived to be a good education had been forged in the elite institutions of the late nineteenth and early twentieth centuries. As English society moved rather tardily towards universal schooling, that was the model which predominated. So, while governmental policy was clearly directed towards the promotion of a differentiated system of schools, universities and colleges, the prestige of a humane, liberal education percolated throughout the system and ensured that the new accretions (the secondary modern schools, the new universities and later the technological universities) were judged by the extent to which they conformed to the existing model. This dynamic, which ensured that attempts at curricular differentiation would at best meet with limited success, also meant that the less well-funded new institutions were doomed from the outset to be little more than pale shadows of the pre-existing schools and colleges. Another aspect of the educational inheritance was that the English had come to place great store by the pastoral functions of their educators, and this consideration made it easier to take a condescending view of new foundations such as comprehensive schools which by their size suggested that this traditional function might be difficult, if not impossible, to maintain. Within the field of higher education it led to a determination to maintain numerous small universities rather than a few large ones on a scale similar to those in North America, and this strategy, too, had major repercussions during the retrenchment of the 1980s.

Another significant determinant was the suburbanisation of society, which, as we have seen, necessitated an uneven distribution of educational resources, and resulted in the creation of an educational system which reflected social distinctions more precisely than ever before. It was inevitable that the bulk of new schools should be located in the new overspill areas and that in consequence the inner cities were forced to make do, in the main, with the existing building stock. We will need many detailed studies of precisely how the catchment areas of schools evolved at local level before we shall be able to understand fully the nature of this process (and there remains the interesting and important exception of those prestigious grammar schools situated in late Victorian suburbs which felt the effects of urban blight in the mid-twentieth century), but there is already enough evidence to allow us to conclude that, after the war, the school became the reflection of its suburb to a greater degree than ever before. In the long run, too, it became inevitable that the drift to the south, which as we have seen was well under way during the 1950s, had implications for the education system.

These differentiations were echoed in the educational rhetoric of the period, as educational institutions were repeatedly judged with reference to perceptions of their place within a social hierarchy. What seems to have been happening is that the stratification of society as a whole was changing subtly at mid-century, and the education system responded by becoming the service industry to these new stratifications. Power, prestige and wealth remained unevenly distributed: if anything, although much poverty was eliminated, inequalities deepened during the post-war era. Structural changes wthin the economy signalled the rise of a new middle class, the owner-occupiers who peopled the fast-growing suburbs. These were the people towards whom both Harold Macmillan and Harold Wilson targeted their popular appeal. By the 1980s this group had come to monopolise the rhetoric of education. Immediately after the war, an education system was devised which precipitated the creation of this social class. Its emergence ensured that, for the foreseeable future, England was to be a society which gave only a limited role to women, to the new ethnic minorities and to the working classes.

During the immediate post-war years, so long as it was serving an expanding economy, the educational expansion may have seemed to be truly democratic in its effects. The reality was otherwise. Between 1945 and 1964 the English education system developed in ways which were to confirm the deep social cleavages which only became fully apparent during the 1980s. In these pages I have tried to give a glimpse of that process as it happened. It is appropriate to end by returning to the prospect held out by R.A. Butler, that education should become 'accessible to all'. We are forced to conclude that it did, but in ways and with consequences which could hardly have been foreseen by any listener in the House of Commons in 1944.

Select Bibliography

Governmental reports, policy statements and circulars have been omitted from this list in the interest of brevity, although full references are available in the text to those cited. See M. Argles and J.E. Vaughan, *British government publications concerning education during the twentieth century*, History of Education Society Guide to Sources No. 7 (Leicester, 1982) for a full listing.

Allsopp, E. and Grugeon, D. (1966) *Direct grant grammar schools*, Fabian Society, London.

Argles, M. (1964) *South Kensington to Robbins*, Longman, London.

Armytage, W.H.G. (1955) *Civic universities*, Benn, London.

—— (1970) *Four hundred years of English education*, Cambridge University Press, Cambridge.

Association of Assistant Mistresses (1950) *Curriculum eleven to eighteen*, AAM, London.

Atkinson, M. (1949) *Junior school community*, Longman, London.

Banks, O. (1955) *Parity and prestige in English secondary education*, Routledge & Kegan Paul, London.

Barker, R. (1972) *Education and politics*, Clarendon Press, Oxford.

Bell, C. (1963) *Middle class families: social and geographical mobility*, Routledge & Kegan Paul, London.

Benn, C. and Simon, B. (1972) *Halfway there*, 2nd edn, Penguin, London.

Berdahl, R.O. (1959) *British universities and the state*, Cambridge University Press, London.

Biddiss, M. (1977) *The age of the masses*, Penguin, London.

Blyth, J.A. (1983) *English university adult education*, University Press, Manchester.

Blyth, W.A.L. (1965) *English primary education: a sociological description*, 2 vols, Routledge & Kegan Paul, London.

Bogdanor, V. and Skidelsky, R. (eds) (1970) *The age of affluence*, Macmillan, London.

Boyle, E. and Crosland A. with Kogan M. (1971) *The politics of education*, Penguin, London.

Briggs, A. (1979) *The history of broadcasting in the United Kingdom*, 4 vols, Oxford University Press, Oxford.

Burn, D. (1958) *The structure of British industry*, 2 vols, National Institute of Economic and Social Research; Economic and Social Studies, No. 15, Cambridge.

Butler, R.A. (1971) *The art of the possible*, Penguin, London.

Campbell, F. (1956) *Eleven-plus and all that*, Watts, London.

Campbell, M.B. (1966) *Nonspecialist study in the undergraduate curricula of the new universities and colleges of advanced technology in England*, University of Michigan Comparative Series, No. 10, Michigan.

Catty, N. (1941) *Learning and teaching in the junior school*, Methuen, London.

Central Advisory Council (1947) *School and life*, HMSO, London.

Centre for Contemporary Cultural Studies (1981) *Unpopular education: schooling and social democracy in England since 1944*, Hutchinson, London.

Cole, G.D.H. (1956) *The post-war condition of Britain*, Routledge & Kegan Paul, London.

Conservative Party Political Centre (1950) *One nation*, National Union of Conservative and Constitutional Associations, London.

Cotgrove, S.F. (1958) *Technical education and social change*, Allen and Unwin, London.

Council for Curriculum reform (1945) *The content of education*, University Press, London.

Cruickshank, M. (1963) *Church and state in English education*, Macmillan, London.

Dale, R. *et al.* (1976) *Schooling and capitalism*, Routledge & Kegan Paul, London.

Dancy, J.C. (1963) *The public schools and the future*, Faber, London.

Daniel, M.V. (1947) *Activity in the primary school*, Basil Blackwell, Oxford.

Deakin, N. *et al.* (1970) *Colour, citizenship and British society*, Panther, London.

Dent, H.C. (1944) *The Education Act, 1944*, University Press, London.

—— (1961) *Universities in transition*, Cohen and West, London.

—— (1970) *1870-1970: a century of growth in English education*, Longman, London.

—— (1977) *The training of teachers in England and Wales, 1800-1975*, Hodder and Stoughton, London.

Douglas, J.W.B. (1964) *The home and the school*, Macgibbon and Kee, London.

Dunleavy, P. (1981) *The politics of mass housing in Britain, 1945-75*, Clarendon, Oxford.

Durgnat, R. (1970) *The mirror for England: British movies from austerity to affluence*, Faber, London.

Edwards, R. (1960) *The secondary technical school*, University Press, London.

Fabian Society (1972) *Labour and inequality*, David Neil, Dorking.

Federation of British Industry (1949) *The education and training of technologists*, FBI, London.

Fenwick, I.G.K. (1976) *The comprehensive school, 1944-1970*, Methuen, London.

Field, F. and Haikin, P. (1971) *Twentieth century state education*, Oxford University Press, Oxford.

Fisher, P. (1982) *External examinations in secondary schools in England and Wales, 1944-64*, University of Leeds Educational Monograph No. 11, Leeds.

Flexner, A. (1930) *Universities: American, English and German*, Oxford University Press, New York.

Floud, J., Halsey, A.H. and Martin, E.M. (1957) *Social class and educational opportunity*, Heinemann, London.

Gagg, J.C. (1951) *Common sense in the primary school*, Evans, London.

Gardner, D.E.M. (1942) *Testing results in the infant school*, Methuen, London.

Giles, G.C.T. (1946) *The new school tie*, Pilot Press, London.

Glass, D.V. (1954) *Social mobility in Britain*, Routledge & Kegan Paul, London.

Glennerster, H. and Pryke, R. (1964) *The public schools*, Young Fabian pamphlet No. 7, Fabian Society, London.

Goldthorpe, J.H. (1980) *Social mobility and class structure in modern Britain*, Clarendon, Oxford.

Gordon, P. (1980) *Selection for secondary education*, Woburn Press, London.

Gordon, P. and Lawton, D. (1978) *Curriculum change in the nineteenth and twentieth centuries*, Hodder and Stoughton, London.

Gosden, P.H.J.H. (1976) *Education in the Second World War*, Methuen, London.

—— (1983) *The education system since 1944*, Martin Robertson, Oxford.

Gregg, P. (1967) *The Welfare State*, Harrap, London.

Gross R.E. (ed.) (1965) *British secondary education*, Oxford University Press, Oxford.

Halsey A.H. (ed.) (1972) *Trends in British society since 1900*, Macmillan, London.

Halsey, A.H. *et al.* (1980) *Origins and destinations: family, class and education in modern Britain*, Clarendon, Oxford.

Havighurst, A.F. (1962) *Twentieth Century Britain*, Row, Peterson and Co., Evanston, Elmsford.

Himmelweit H.T. *et al.* (1958) *Television and the child*, Oxford University Press, Oxford.

History of Education Society (1979) *Post-war curriculum development: an historical appraisal*, December 1978 Conference Papers, HES, Leicester.

—— (1980) *Education in the sixties*, December 1979 Conference Papers, HES, Leicester.

Hunt, J.M (1961) *Intelligence and experience*, Ronald, New York.

Incorporated Association of Assistant Masters (1946) *The nation's secondary schools*, IAAM, London.

Institute of Physics (1948) *Education and the training of technologists*, IOP, London.

Jackson, B. and Marsden, D. (1962) *Education and the working class*, Routledge & Kegan Paul, London.

James, E. (1949) *The content of education*, LSE, London.

Jarausch, K.H. (ed.) (1983) *The transformation of higher learning, 1860–1930*, University of Chicago Press, Chicago.

Jenkins, R. (1959) *The Labour case*, Penguin, London.

Judge, H. (1984) *A generation of schooling: English secondary schools since 1944*, Oxford University Press, Oxford.

Katznelson, I. (1973) *Black men, white cities*, Oxford University Press, Oxford.

Kelsall, R.K. (1979) *The social structure of Britain: population*, 4th edn, Longman, London.

Kogan, M. (1978) *The politics of educational change*, Manchester University Press, Manchester.

Kotschnig, W.M. (1932) *The university in a changing world*, Oxford University Press, Oxford.

Labour Party (1945) *Let us face the future*, LP, London.

—— (1950) *Labour and the new society*, LP, London.

—— (1951) *A policy for secondary education*, LP, London.

Lawson, J. and Silver, H. (1973) *A social history of education in England*, Methuen, London.

Layard, R., King, J. and Moser, C. (1969) *The impact of Robbins*, Penguin, London.

London County Council (1947) *Replanning London schools*, LCC, London.

—— (1950) *Trends in primary education*, LCC, London.

—— (1961) *London comprehensive schools*, LCC, London.

Maclure, S. (1984) *Educational development and school building: aspects of public policy, 1945-73*, Longman, London.

Manchester Education Committee (1947) *Trends in junior school education*, MEC, Manchester.

Marwick, A. (1970) *Britain in the century of total war*, Penguin, London.

—— (1971) *The explosion of British society, 1914-1970*, Macmillan, London.

—— (1982) *British society since 1945*, Penguin, London.

McCallum, R.B. and Readman, A.V. (1947) *The British general election of 1945*, Oxford University Press, Oxford.

Middlesex Education Committee (1965) *Primary and secondary education in Middlesex, 1900-1965*, MEC, London.

Middleton, N. and Weitzman, S. (1976) *A place for everyone: a history of state eduction from the eighteenth century to the 1970s*, Gollancz, London.

Mountford, J. (1972) *Keele: an historical critique*, Routledge & Kegan Paul, London.

Murphy, J. (1971) *Church, state and schools in Britain*, Routledge & Kegan Paul, London.

Musgrave, P.W. (1967) *Technical change the labour force and education: a study of the British and German iron and steel industries, 1860-1964*, Pergamon, Oxford.

National Foundation for Educational Research (1950) *The allocation of primary school leavers to courses of secondary education*, NFER, Slough.

National Society for the Study of Education (1943) *Forty-second year book*, University of Chicago Press, Chicago.

National Union of Teachers (1949) *Nursery-infant education*, NUT, London.

Noble, T. (1975) *Modern Britain: structure and change*, Batsford, London.

North-Eastern Junior Schools Association (1949) *Basic requirements of the junior school*, University Press, London.

Nursery School Association of Great Britain (1945) *Planning the new nursery schools*, University Press, London.

Oates, D.W. (1946) *The new secondary schools and the selection of their pupils*, Harrap, London.

Parkinson, M. (1970) *The Labour Party and the organisation of secondary education, 1918-65*, Routledge & Kegan Paul, London.

Perkin, H.J. (1969) *New universities in the United Kingdom*, OECD, Paris.

Pollard, S. (1969) *The development of the British economy, 1914-67*, Edward Arnold, London.

Raymont, T. (1946) *Seven to eleven*, Longmans Green, London.

Richmond, W.K. (1949) *Purpose in the junior school*, Redman, London.

Robinson, E. (1968) *The new polytechnics*, Penguin, London.

Rubinstein, D. and Simon, B. (1973) *The evolution of the comprehensive school, 1926-72*, Routledge & Kegan Paul, London.

Runnymede Trust (1980) *Britain's black population*, RT, London.

Ryder, J. and Silver, H. (1970) *Modern English society*, Methuen, London.

Sampson, A. (1962) *Anatomy of Britain*, Hodder and Stoughton, London.

Sanderson, M. (1972) *The universities and British industry, 1850-1970*, Routledge & Kegan Paul, London.

Seaborne, M. and Lowe, R. (1977) *The English school: its architecture and organisation. Vol. 2, 1870-1970*, Routledge & Kegan Paul, London.

Selleck, R.J.W. (1972) *English primary education and the progressives, 1914-1939*,

Routledge & Kegan Paul, London.

Silver, H. (1973) *Equal opportunity in education*, Methuen, London.

Simon, B. (1971) *Intelligence, psychology and education*, Lawrence and Wishart, London.

—— (1974) *The politics of educational reform*, Lawrence and Wishart, London.

Simon, S. (1948) *Three schools or one?*, Frederick Muller, London.

Sissons, M. and French, P. (eds), (1963) *The age of austerity*, Hodder and Stoughton, London.

Sked, A. and Cook, C. (1979) *Post-war Britain: a political history*, Harvester Press, Brighton.

Smith, A. (ed.) (1974) *British broadcasting*, David and Charles, Newton Abbot.

Smith, A.H.C. (1975) *Paper voices: the popular press and social change, 1935-1965*, Thames and Hudson, London.

Spinks, G.S. (1952) *Religion in Britain since 1900*, Andrew Dakers, London.

Stewart, W.A.C. (1972) *Progressives and radicals in English education, 1750-1970*, Macmillan, London.

Tawney, R.H. (1922) *Secondary education for all: a policy for Labour*, Labour Party, London.

Taylor, W. (1963) *Secondary modern school*, Faber, London.

Thompson, D. (1965) *England in the twentieth century*, Penguin, London.

Times Newspapers (1971) *The British economy: key statistics, 1900-1970*, Times Newspapers, London.

Truscot, B. (1951) *Redbrick university*, Penguin, London.

Tunstall, J. (1983) *The media in Britain*, Constable, London.

Vaizey, J. (1958) *The costs of education*, George Allen and Unwin, London.

Vaizey, J. & Sheehan, J. (1968) *Resources for education*, Unwin, London.

van der Eyken, W. (1973) *Education, the child and society*, Penguin, London.

Venables, P. (1978) *Higher education developments: the technological universities, 1956-1976*, Faber, London.

Vernon, P.E. (1957) *Secondary school selection*, Methuen, London.

Weinberg, I. (1967) *The English public schools*, Atherton Press, New York.

Whitehead, A.N. (1932) *The aims of education*, Williams and Norgate, London.

Williams, R. (1961) *The long revolution*, Penguin, London.

Workers Educational Association Advisory Committee (1950) *Secondary education*, WEA, London.

Worswick, G.D.N. and Ady P.H. (1952) *The British economy, 1945-50*, Clarendon, Oxford.

Yates, A. and Pidgeon, D.A. (1957) *Admission to grammar schools*, NFER, Slough.

y Gasset, O. (1946) *Mission of the university*, Routledge & Kegan Paul, London.

Youngson, A.J. (1960) *The British economy, 1920-57*, George Allen and Unwin, London

Index

Abrams, M. 119
Abse, L. 105
Acts of Parliament *see under* topic (e.g. Education)
Albemarle Report 91
Alexander, W.P. 89, 92, 141, 190–6
Allen, Lady 30
Allen, R.G.D. 160
Amory, H. 76, 161
Archbishop of Canterbury 5, 6
Armytage, W.H.G. 163
Astor, Viscountess 17
Atkinson, M. 23
Attlee, C. 3-12 *passim* 29, 38, 73-4, 77

Bacon, A. 137
Baker, T.E.G. 164
Balchin, W.G.B. 161
Bantock, G.H. 25
Barlow Report 59, 64-5, 165-6
Beloe Report 119, 192-6
Benn, C. 146
Bernstein, B. 146
Bertram, G.C.L. 165
Bevan, A. 78
Beveridge Report 6
Black Papers 25
Boyle, E. 73-88 *passim* 106, 139, 140, 170
Briggs, A. 18
Burt, C. 37-8
Butler, R.A. Introduction, 7, 73-9 *passim* 89-90, 104, 131, 167

Campbell, F. 147-8
Cartwright, E.S. 66
Catty, N. 24
Charlton, H.B. 189
Chilvers, B. 160
Churchill, W. 4, 73, 77
Clark Report 63
Clay, H. 7
Clegg, A. 18, 105, 108, 193, 195

Cockroft, J. 167
Cole, G.D.H. 7
Cove, G. 39, 46
Crosland, A. 78, 121, 138
Crossman, R.H.S. 173
Crowther, G. 79, 174
Crowther Report 139, 171, 174

Daniel, M.V. 24
Daniels, J.C. 105
Davies, D.I. 177
de Lissa, L. 21, 23, 24
Dent, H.C. 118, 174
Dobree, B. 66
Douglas, J.W.B. 111, 146
Douglas Home, A. 74
Drakeley, T.J. 59

Eccles, D. 88-90, 105-8, 112-22 *passim* 130-45 *passim* 169, 175-6, 191-6
Eden, A. 75, 133-4
Education Acts
    1902 17
    1944 6-9, 16-27 *passim* 34, 38-9, 111-16
Edwards, J. 30

Fairgreave, J. 28
Faith, A. 83
Fenwick, K. 130, 136, 146
Flecker, H.L.O. 51
Fleming, G. 132
Fleming Report 32-3, 49-51, 121-2
Flexner, A. 65
Floud, J. 109, 111, 146

Gagarin, Y. 139
Gagg, J.C. 24
Gaitskell, H. 78, 137-8
Gardner, D.E.M. 23
gender issues *see* women
Giles, G.T.C. 27, 39
Glass, D.V. 147
Gorton, N. 164

208

Index